GREED AND GLORY ON WALL STREET

THE FALL OF THE HOUSE OF LEHMAN

KEN AULETTA

WARNER BOOKS

A Warner Communications Company

This Warner Books edition is published by arrangement with Random House, Inc.
201 East 50th Street, New York, New York

Cover design by Harold Nolan

Warner Books, Inc., 666 Fifth Avenue, New York, NY 10103

w A Warner Communications Company

Printed in the United States of America
First Warner Books Printing: March 1987
10 9 8 7 6 5 4 3 2 1

Library of Congress Cataloging in Publication Data

Auletta, Ken.
    Greed and glory on Wall Street.

    Reprint. Originally published: New York : Random House,
1986.
    Includes index.
    1. Lehman Brothers.   2. Wall Street.   3. Brokers—
United States. I. Title.
HG5129.N5A8   1987   332.66'09747'1   86-23416
ISBN 0-446-38406-2 (pbk.) (U.S.A.)
    0-446-38407-0 (pbk.) (Canada)

THE CRITICS APPLAUD
GREED AND GLORY ON WALL STREET

"RIVETING...masterfully documents how greed—greed for power, greed for money—came to fracture the foundations of a firm whose roots in American finance stretched back to 1850. Auletta brings an admirable degree of richness and realism to this story."
—*Washington Post Book World*

□

"IT'S A BLOCKBUSTER YOU CAN'T PUT DOWN."
—Studs Terkel

□

"FASCINATING READING...ably told...recounted with estimable reportorial skill....One is riveted by their story."
—Christopher Lehmann-Haupt, *New York Times*

□

"A REFRESHING BUSINESS BOOK....WE GET WHAT IS USUALLY IMPOSSIBLE TO INCLUDE IN FINANCIAL REPORTING—THE PASSIONS, EGOTISM AND GREED, THE PRIVATE MOTIVES THAT REALLY SHAPE THIS WORLD....It says what really happened, and that is quite new to business reporting."
—*Boston Globe*

□

"A WOW OF A BOOK...DON'T MISS IT."
Liz Smith, *New York Daily News*

□

"A BESTSELLER IN INVESTMENT CIRCLES...crammed with the kind of dramatic confrontations—between personalities and corporations—that you expect to find in a good novel."
—*Business Week*

□

"SETS A NEW STANDARD FOR BUSINESS JOURNALISM."
—*Washington Monthly*

more...

About the author
KEN AULETTA is a writer for the *The New Yorker,* a columnist for New York's *Daily News,* and political commentator on WCBS-TV. He is the author of *The Streets Were Paved With Gold, Hard Feelings, The Underclass,* and *The Art of Corporate Success: The Story of Schlumberger.* For his articles in *The New York Times* that formed the basis of this book, Ken Auletta won two of the most distinguished business awards: Dartmouth's Champion-Tuck Award, first place, for "outstanding reporting that improves the public's understanding of business and economic issues," and UCLA's Loeb Award, also first place, for "distinguished business and financial journalism."

TO MY PARENTS,
AND RICHARD AND BONNIE

INTRODUCTION

A FEW DAYS AFTER LEHMAN BROTHERS KUHN LOEB WAS sold to Shearson/American Express in April 1984, Peter G. Peterson was holding court at the Candy Kitchen in Bridgehampton, Long Island, a coffee shop–ice cream parlor that is a magnet for the writers, producers, publicists and businessmen who spend their weekends in or near that fashionable resort. The former chairman of Wall Street's oldest continuing partnership shared his booth with journalist William Broyles, who had taken his son and daughter there for waffles. Broyles tried to juggle Peterson's obvious appetite for an audience with the incessant demands of his children —for maple syrup, milk, a fork, a napkin. I happened by in search of the morning papers, and Bill invited me to join them. Oblivious to the children, Peterson went on with riveting tales of what really happened to the partnership launched by the Lehman family one hundred and thirty-four years before.

Peterson's account seemed worthy of a Theodore Dreiser novel, and Broyles, a talented writer, expressed interest in pursuing the story. Peterson said that Ed Klein, editor of the *New York Times Magazine,* had called him that Friday to say that he had not yet settled on a writer, but wanted to know whether Peterson would cooperate on a story about the death of Lehman Brothers. Peterson said he would.

He seemed almost buoyed by news of the sale of the company he had once guided, as if the humiliation of the firm were a personal vindication, which, in a sense, it seemed to be. For just nine months before, in July 1983, Peterson had been ousted as chairman by his longtime colleague, Lewis L. Glucksman. His tale told, Peterson wandered from our table to another, where he repeated his tale. Broyles and I were left buzzing about what a hell of a story this might make. For Lew Glucksman, who had won the power struggle with Peterson, sounded like a fascinating cross between a paranoid Captain Queeg and a pathetic soul like Dreiser's Charles Drouet, the traveling salesman with pretensions of grandeur in *Sister Carrie.*

Because I intruded on his conversation with Peterson, Bill Broyles had first crack at the story. But after thinking about it overnight, Broyles decided that a book on Vietnam had first claim on his time. Without a green light from Broyles, I would not have chased this story. I thank him.

The first thing I did was make a couple of calls to people I knew at Lehman. They confirmed the bare outlines of much of what Peterson said, cautioning that this was not a simple morality play with cardboard heroes and villains. It sounded like a terrific story, one that might expand my limited knowledge of Wall Street and its blizzard of new jargon—greenmail, leveraged buyouts, "Pac-Man" defenses, the two-tier, front-end loaded, boot-strap, bust-up, junk-bond takeover. Perhaps, I thought, what happened at Lehman might provide a vehicle to explore a larger story about how Wall Street and capitalism were changing.

But first I had to decide where to tell this story. I already knew the *Times Magazine* was committed to publishing an account.

As luck would have it, the *Times* telephoned early that week. The conference call came from Executive Editor Abe Rosenthal and Deputy Managing Editor Arthur Gelb. They asked if I would undertake a magazine assignment for them, but the subject they proposed, while important, just didn't arouse me. I said no. There was a pause. Then I said, "You know what I'd love to do is a long piece on the fall of Lehman Brothers." They liked the idea.

Ed Klein and I met for breakfast and agreed that I would spend the better part of a year reporting and writing a two-part, 25,000-word article for the *Times Magazine.* Throughout the reporting, writing and editing process the *Times* editors were extraordinarily supportive. In addition to Rosenthal, Gelb, Klein and Deputy Magazine Editor Martin Arnold, I wish especially to thank Michaela Williams, who edited the pieces with great care and was a pleasure to work with. Andrew Yarrow and Phyllis Shapiro performed fact-checking feats. Mary Marsh, a friend, slaved to help organize cartons of research material.

The idea for this book arose after I was well into the reporting for the pieces. I went to Jason Epstein at Random House, who has published and edited three of my four previous books, and said I thought the full story of what happened at Lehman and what was happening on Wall Street could not be contained in a 25,000-word article. He worried that two articles in the *Times* might dull interest in a book. I tried to reassure him that there was no way to cram this melodrama into a few magazine pieces. He took a chance on this book, which turns out to be almost five times the length of the pieces the *Times* published.

Jason took one other chance on this book. Joan Ganz Cooney is one of his closest friends; of the twenty people invited to her wedding to Pete Peterson, Jason was one. He likes and admires Pete Peterson, whom I had met a few times at Jason's Sag Harbor home. When the book was nearly complete I cautioned Jason that Peterson, and perhaps Joan, would be displeased by parts of the manuscript and suggested he might want someone else at Random House to edit it. Jason declined, saying that publishing books was what he did for a living. He was confident that his friends Joan and Pete understood that this was my book, not his. Jason is special.

I might have written a very different book had I failed to win the cooperation of the two main participants—Pete Peterson and Lew Glucksman—each the son of immigrants, each an American success story, each destined to clash. Peterson sacrificed all but a few Sunday mornings in the summer of 1984 to meet me at seven in the morning at a diner in Southampton. In all, I spent about fifty hours interviewing him. Lew Glucksman at first was harder to pin down; feeling burned by the media, he wasn't eager to talk. But in time he relented and in the end spent about thirty-five hours with me. Neither man emerges quite as he expected to, but I wish to thank each for his time and patience.

Time was a great ally. At first many of the participants refused to cooperate. Eventually, I did interview each member of Lehman's board of directors, each member of the executive and operating committees, more than half of the seventy-seven partners, numerous associates, secretaries, former partners and people on and about Wall Street. I had access to Lehman's financial records and many internal documents. While reporting, I went back to the participants many times to confirm dialogue, to check facts, to prod their memories. Whether they are pleased or not by the outcome, I thank the partners and employees at Lehman for their assistance, particularly those whose special help it is probably wiser not to acknowledge. I also thank Peter Cohen and the executives at Shearson/American Express for cooperating and encouraging others to make themselves available.

A word about my method: I have tried to put the pieces of the Lehman puzzle together without resorting to journalistic shortcuts and the air of omniscience that infects much of the new journalism. At the risk of "slowing the narrative"—a phrase too freely uttered by editors eager to blur the line between fiction and nonfiction—I have used only the words actually given to me directly in interviews and have tried to attribute these words and thoughts to people. I have invented no dialogue. I do not enter the mind of someone unless he or she invites me. I have tried, wherever possible, not to accept a single version of a dialogue or incident, but instead have checked details and dialogue with the main participants, including adversaries. Where there was disagreement about what happened in a meeting, about who said what to whom, rather than rely on a solitary source or version, I have tried to let the reader know who is speaking; where recollections differ as to what was said, I have indicated as much. When I have asserted, without attribution, that something was said or done, I have based these assertions on the testimony of adversaries who agree.

A few caveats: No reporter can with 100 percent accuracy re-create events that occurred some time before. Memories play tricks on participants, the more so when the outcome has become clear. A reporter tries to guard against inaccuracies by checking with a variety of sources, but it is useful for a reader—and an author—to be humbled by this journalistic limitation.

Although I talked to more than forty Lehman partners and to numerous Lehman employees, my narrative relies heavily on the recollections of the fifteen or so members of the Lehman board and operating committee. In the critical last year of Lehman's life as a private partnership, these were the decision makers. It is also worth noting that this is not intended to be a book about how typical investment bankers go about their business, though I trust the book will shed some light on investment banking. The story I tell here focuses on a tumultuous period at Lehman Brothers, one in which scheming and jockeying for power was as commonplace as it is in

politics. Unavoidably, some readers may draw the unwarranted conclusion that Lehman partners did little else but hatch political plots.
The extraordinary profitability of the firm through 1983 suggests
another conclusion.

This book has been a labor of love. Intellectually, it took me places
I had not been before. It opened doors to a financial world whose
dominion over our lives continues to spread. It both taught and
depressed me.

It also left me grateful to the many others who had a hand in this
book, including: the people at Random House, especially: Peter
Osnos, who offered some valuable journalistic advice, Becky Saletan,
Jason Epstein's senior editorial assistant, Sallye Leventhal, his editorial assistant, and copy editor Sandy Schoenfein; Nora Ephron and
Richard Reeves, friends who read parts of the manuscript and helped
save me from myself; my editors at the New York *Daily News,* who
kindly granted me a leave of absence from my weekly column; my
agent, Esther Newberg, who, like the best agents, is one part business
representative, one part critic and one part mother; and Amanda
Urban, who is equal parts critic, friend and loving wife.

GREED AND
GLORY ON
WALL STREET

FOR YEARS THE RESENTMENTS HAD BEEN BUILDING. AND now, at a luncheon at the Equitable Life Assurance Society on July 12, 1983, they began to erupt within Lewis L. Glucksman, the co-chief executive officer of Lehman Brothers Kuhn Loeb. That a short, rumpled man with the face of a Russian general, whose shirt pocket often bristled with pens, who wore garish ties and short socks that slipped to his ankles, who was disparaged by Wall Street bluebloods as a lowly "trader"—that he would try to oust Peter G. Peterson, his imperious co-chief executive officer and the chairman of the venerable investment banking house, astonished his partners at Lehman and all of Wall Street.

In contrast to the unpolished Glucksman, Pete Peterson possessed an imposing résumé: summa cum laude graduate from Northwestern University, president of Bell & Howell at thirty-four, Secretary of Commerce in the Nixon Administration, and the man credited with rescuing Lehman Brothers from collapse in 1973 when he assumed command and with having helped steer it to five consecutive profit-breaking years. Just eight weeks earlier, in what Peterson considered a magnanimous act, he had elevated the relatively unknown Glucksman to co-chief executive officer. Lehman partners applauded.

The fallout from the explosion triggered by this July luncheon lifted this story from the business pages to the front pages. Thirteen days later, Peterson would be forced out of Lehman. Within nine

months, Wall Street's oldest continuing investment banking partnership, a firm that had survived for one hundred and thirty-four years,
would collapse under Lewis Glucksman's stewardship and would be
sold to Shearson/American Express.

At the time of the Equitable lunch, Lehman Brothers was more
profitable than it had ever been in its long history, averaging $15
million a month in pre-tax and pre-bonus profits over the preceding
twelve months. With capital of almost $250 million and equity of
$175 million,* Lehman ranked as one of Wall Street's powerhouse
investment banking houses. Unlike dozens of old-line firms that had
already succumbed to the pressures of consolidation that have been
reshaping Wall Street—Blyth, Eastman, Dillon; Loeb Rhoades;
Hayden Stone; Hornblower & Weeks; White, Weld; Kuhn Loeb, for
example—Lehman had rebounded strongly from its travails of the
early seventies. Business was so brisk that projections for fiscal 1983,
which would end on September 30, once again promised to shatter
all previous records.

The modern melodrama that resulted from this lunch is a many-
sided tale. It is a story about the life and the death of Lehman
Brothers, and one of irreconcilable conflict between two men. It is
a story of a poisoned partnership; of cowardice, intrigue and deceit.
It is a story of greed for money, power and glory. It is a reminder
that human folly and foibles—not the bottom line of profits, not
business acumen, not "scientific" management or the perfect marketing plans or execution—often determine the success or failure of an
organization. In its broader implications, the fall of the House of
Lehman opens a window onto the forces that are reshaping Wall
Street and the American economic system.

---

*Capital is a larger number because it includes the firm's subordinated debts, including debts
to departed partners, who will be paid over a period of time.

T HE STORY BEGINS ON JULY 12, 1983. JOHN B. CARTER, PRESI-
dent and chief executive officer of the Equitable Life Assurance Society of the United States, the nation's third-largest
life insurer, had invited Pete Peterson to lunch in the private Hyde
Room at Equitable's corporate headquarters thirty-eight floors
above the Avenue of the Americas and West 51st Street. Peterson
invited Glucksman to join him. This was not done grudgingly. On
a professional level Peterson knew he needed Glucksman. For three
years, Glucksman had managed the day-to-day business of the firm;
all of the departments reported to him, and his knowledge of Lehman's affairs was vast. Moreover, Peterson had an agenda for the
lunch and he wanted Glucksman's cooperation to carry it out. And
on a personal level Peterson enjoyed taking credit for producing
what he called a "new," a tamer Lew Glucksman. It was undeniably
true that after almost twenty-one years at Lehman, Glucksman had
become a calmer, less volcanic executive; he had shed about seventy
pounds and improved a wardrobe once dominated by light suits and
wide ties.

Peterson knew that Equitable and Lehman had engaged in a modest amount of business together. Lehman Brothers, like other investment bankers, served as an intermediary, matching wealth with
ideas, those who needed capital with those who accumulated it. The
choices the firm offered clients were broad: Lehman could midwife
companies wanting to merge, proffer financial advice to avert or spur
takeovers, advise local governments and countries, assist managers
wishing to take their companies private by arranging so-called leveraged buyouts or by divesting unwanted divisions, help underwrite
and sell corporate and government bonds, manage pension and
money funds, trade various securities, gamble their own monies on
stock hunches, speculate in the rise or fall of interest rates. For an
investment banker, the fees and profits from these transactions were
immense. In a private partnership like Lehman, the wealth of the
firm was owned by the partners, who variously claimed from 500 to
4,500 shares of common stock apiece. Together with the preferred
stock, the average partner's equity totaled $2.3 million in the fall of
1983. Partners were paid salaries ranging from $100,000 to $150,000,*
bonuses ranging from $200,000 to $1.6 million, and a 3 percent

---

*Peterson and Glucksman were paid $225,000, and members of the board of directors
received $175,000.

dividend on the value of their preferred stock, of which the senior partners owned the majority. In a good year, a fairly senior partner who owned 2,000 shares—a fifth of the partners owned this sum—made pre-tax income equal to a salary of about $2 million.*

Peterson drove his executives hard before each business meeting, demanding detailed information about the companies they wished to do business with and the key executives who would be involved. He insisted on strategy sessions, detailed memoranda, marketing plans. The Equitable luncheon was no different. Even this "casual" luncheon demanded a series of parleys. Lehman strategists became conversant with that piece of Equitable's $53 billion worth of assets then under management by various investment banks, including Lehman, and Equitable's $30 billion in pension assets, of which Lehman also handled a share. They war-gamed new ideas to broach with Equitable. For years Peterson had been pressing his partners to go beyond their normal advisory role, a role in which Lehman's income was derived mostly from fees, to go beyond their underwriting and other trading functions, where profits were often hostage to an uncertain market or to fluctuating interest rates and to shrinking profit margins in a deregulated environment where customers shopped for the cheapest fees. Instead of serving simply as an intermediary or risking its capital to accommodate important clients, Peterson was pushing his partners to risk more of their own capital on new business ventures, on leveraged buyouts, in real estate ventures where there might be no ceiling on earnings. This was the kind of merchant banking practiced by Lehman Brothers for much of its then one-hundred-and-thirty-three-year-old history, the kind of risk-taking that once financed the railroads that linked the new American nation or gave birth to the airlines that shrank the globe. If Lehman could advise an average of seventy-five large corporations a year on mergers and acquisitions, why couldn't it tap its own capital to purchase a major interest in a company? The risks were greater but so were the rewards, as Equitable and Allen & Company and Odyssey Partners and several of Lehman's major competitors, including First Boston, had already demonstrated.

*To realize the equivalent of $2 million pre-tax, assume that a Lehman partner received a $125,000 salary, a relatively modest $350,000 bonus and that his stock appreciated by $500 per share or by $1 million—for net pre-tax earnings of $1,475,000. Assuming a 57 percent tax rate on ordinary income and 25 percent on capital gains (including state and local taxes in both cases), the partner's after-tax income would be about $1 million. One would have to earn $2,200,000 of ordinary pre-tax income to equal this compensation.

From Lehman's standpoint, the luncheon was designed to educate Lehman and, Peterson hoped, point toward a joint business venture of some kind with Equitable.

The tension between Glucksman and Peterson was hinted at by the fact that they were chauffeured uptown separately. Peterson rode to the lunch with J. Tomilson Hill III, a young Lehman banking partner he had helped to recruit; Glucksman rode with a member of his own team, Sheldon S. Gordon, head of equity trading and sales at Lehman, one of four major divisions at Lehman (the others being banking, fixed-income trading and investment management). "If I could avoid being with Peterson, I'd avoid being with Peterson," explained Glucksman. "I couldn't stand the monologues."

During cocktails, Glucksman and Peterson exchanged perfunctory greetings and mingled with the other seven guests at opposite ends of a bar area just outside the executive dining room. Glucksman began to seethe almost as soon as they entered the Hyde Room, a snug, cream-colored corner room dominated by a long, white-linen-covered dining table. It did not please Glucksman to notice that his co-CEO was invited to sit beside John B. Carter, at one of two places at the head of the rectangular table, while Glucksman was seated toward the far end of the table, to the right but not alongside chairman Robert F. Froehlke, who sat alone facing Carter and Peterson. Across from Glucksman, and to his right, sat two Equitable vice presidents. Glucksman later said he felt as if he were confined to the bleachers.

Then came "the speech," as Glucksman derisively described a typical Peterson presentation. *Oh, how he had come to detest that speech!* He knew it was coming when Peterson began to drop names. The *A* list usually included "Henry" (Kissinger), whom he worked beside in the Nixon Administration and in preparing the Nixon-Brezhnev Summit meeting; "Paul" (Volcker, chairman of the Federal Reserve Board), whom he consulted on the international debt crisis; "the Prime Minister" (Nakasone of Japan), with whom he had hosted a lunch just weeks before; "Art" (Buchwald), with whom he played tennis.

Glucksman's pale blue eyes narrowed as he listened to Peterson talk about his tenure as president of the Economic Club of New York, about how he had helped forge the Bi-Partisan Budget Appeal to build public support to reduce the alarming federal deficits, about how the American political system dispensed too much pleasure and not enough pain, about how, if we were to compete with Japan, consumers needed to save and invest more, and spend less. *Too much pleasure and not enough pain*—Glucksman had heard "the speech" so often he could recite it.

While Glucksman stewed, Peterson launched another pet speech, this one about how he was pushing merchant banking at Lehman. He remembers Peterson proclaiming, "Leveraged buyouts"—which require huge infusions of borrowed capital and thus often divert precious savings from other perhaps more productive investments— "are the way to go." Peterson invoked the name of former Treasury Secretary William E. Simon. In 1982, Simon's Wesray Corporation put up a few million dollars to purchase Gibson Greeting Cards from RCA in a leveraged buyout. The bulk of the purchase price—$80 million—was paid when Gibson borrowed money against its own assets to pay RCA. A year later, in May 1983, Gibson made a public stock offering in which Simon pocketed over $80 million in profit on the Gibson stock he sold and retained stock valued at about $50 million. In all, over a four-year period Simon and six partners had bought nineteen companies with total revenues of $8 billion.

"Pete at this particular time was obsessed with the amount of money William Simon made selling Gibson," says Glucksman. "And he couldn't stop talking about it." Since Peterson was a member of the RCA board that approved the sale to Simon, since Lehman Brothers represented RCA, and since Simon then went on to embarrass RCA by making such colossal profits, Glucksman was humiliated that Peterson would even mention Simon to Equitable. Nor did Glucksman understand why Peterson droned on rather than sitting back and listening to those more expert in merchant banking. "We had never done a leveraged deal," says Glucksman, "and the problem was that we looked like amateurs."

As soon as Peterson began talking, Glucksman lowered his head and glared at his shrimp cocktail, noisily fidgeted with the silverware and banged his heavy chrome chair closer to the table. He glanced across at his partner Sheldon Gordon, rolled his eyes and stared up at the stern portrait of the Equitable founder, Henry B. Hyde. Glucksman couldn't understand why Peterson didn't shut up!

Peterson could not help but notice the din from Glucksman's end of the room. Pausing to peer down the table, he saw Glucksman perched on the edge of his chair, his shoulders now hunched over his broiled tenderloin, which he was only picking at. "I was clearly aware of some tension, such as Lew's interrupting discussions at our end of the table," Peterson recalls.

Belatedly, Peterson tried to include Glucksman in the conversation. Several times he asked, "Lew, what do you think?" Glucksman seized on the questions as opportunities to silence Peterson and plunged into embarrassing monologues on how investment banking had changed or how Lehman recruited young associates. "It was almost like a canned speech," recalls one participant. "He really shut Peterson down. His speech really made no more sense than Pete's speech in the context of why Lehman was there...Lew was trying to demonstrate that he was in charge."

The tension between the two was palpable among the nine men gathered in the room. "John Carter and I both remarked after the luncheon that Lew strove to have the concluding comment on every subject," says Equitable's executive vice president Robert M. Hendrickson, who arranged the luncheon with Peterson. "By the end of the lunch it seemed apparent there was a fair amount of tension between Glucksman and Peterson."

This was remarked upon by the two other Lehman partners who had attended the lunch. When he returned to Lehman later that afternoon, Sheldon Gordon, who had shared Glucksman's limousine, told Glucksman he was "embarrassed"* by Peterson's half-hour speech and by the way Peterson "hogged" the limelight. When J. Tomilson Hill returned to his office he told partners of the "crazy scene" he had witnessed. Those he told wondered how long the eight-week-old co-CEO marriage between Peterson and Glucksman would last. But their doubts were stilled by the firm's bountiful profits—$123 million pre-tax in 1982, up from $117 million in 1981. Besides, partners remembered that when the co-CEO announcement was made eight weeks before, Glucksman had smiled for his partners and the press and proclaimed that he was gratified. What many partners didn't know was that blunt-talking Lew Glucksman was acting. The resentments of an adult lifetime were percolating within him. The "emotional volcano," as François de Saint Phalle, one of his partners, referred to him, was about to erupt.

*Gordon reluctantly confirms this.

L EW GLUCKSMAN HAD SPENT A LIFETIME ACCUMULATING resentments. The son of middle-class Hungarian Jews, he constantly inveighed against the "Our Crowd" Jews in banking— symbolized in his mind by the Lehman family. He thought of them as WASP's, not as fellow Jews. "All my life I resented it," Glucksman says, referring to the bigotry that he felt kept a heel to the throat of East European Jews and other minorities on Wall Street. Vividly he remembers how one senior partner, decades earlier, advised him not to apply to join the Century Country Club in Westchester, an "Our Crowd" bastion. He can still recite the exact number of blackballs—seventeen—he once received when he tried to join the New York Athletic Club. "I didn't know seventeen people there," says Glucksman. The club historically discouraged Jewish membership, but Glucksman thought it would be a convenient place to swim each morning on his way downtown. Intent on reversing the rejection, Glucksman went to see then partner George Ball. The former Under Secretary of State in the Kennedy and Johnson Administrations and Ambassador to the United Nations in the Johnson Administration contacted his friend William Bernbach, a partner in the ad agency, Doyle Dane Bernbach, who knew the club's membership chairman. Bernbach, who was not a member, tried to do a favor for Ball by looking into the matter. He reported back to Ball that Glucksman collected more blackballs than anyone else in the history of the club. Ball relayed this to Glucksman, who exploded. That night Glucksman telephoned Bernbach, whom he did not know, and screamed, "You were the kind of Jew who should have gone to the gas chambers!"* Why Glucksman should have blamed Bernbach, who was only an intermediary, suggests Glucksman's mercurial temperament. Bernbach, a gentle, fragile man who passed away a few years ago, told Ball he had never had a more unpleasant conversation in his life.

In his mind, Glucksman linked those who blackballed him to those who tried to fire him from Lehman in 1973 when his trading department lost $7 million. When he was angry he sometimes compared these partners to Germans who looked away while Jews were deported in cattle cars. Although Peterson was the son of Greek immigrants and was raised in unpretentious Kearney, Nebraska, his ties to the establishment and his patronizing manner made him one of *them* in Glucksman's eyes. He thought Peterson was too much the

*Glucksman confirms the conversation.

Washington "insider," cultivating clients during expensive meals, networking relationships, dropping names, worrying about his own press notices and behaving as if investment banking still hinged on old-school relationships rather than market-responsive transactions. Peterson, in Glucksman's view, still acted as if the SEC had not liberalized the rules under which corporations were financed and as if corporations had not hired their own skilled financial vice presidents, who nowadays often coolly selected investment banks on a deal-by-deal basis.

More and more, Glucksman knew, investment banking earnings depended on whether your firm, in competition with other firms, was selected to perform a specific function or transaction rather than carrying on a long-term relationship with a stable group of clients. Peterson called this "de-clienting the business." The traditional banking business, which concentrated on advising corporations and underwriting, was being shoved aside by a host of "new products." The institutional clients Glucksman had cultivated—the pension and mutual funds, insurance companies, powerhouses such as Citicorp, Bankers Trust, American Express, and the investment banks that traded huge blocks of stock—now dominated the stock market. Among them, they accounted for 90 percent of all trading volume on the Big Board.

Unavoidably, tensions arose between "traders" and "bankers," two groups of people performing different functions. Essentially, a trader buys or sells securities—bonds, stocks, options, financial futures, commercial paper, certificates of deposit, Treasury bills, Eurobonds—either for clients, for which they collect a fee, or by gambling directly with the firm's own money. The trader must make quick, firm decisions, often by consulting a jumble of numbers on a cathode-ray tube during and after hurried phone calls.

Bankers, on the other hand, usually have a longer horizon. A banker often invests several years in cultivating a relationship before it turns into a client. They earn fees for serving as financial consultants to corporations, for putting together new issues, for merging or divesting companies.

Glucksman knew Wall Street had changed. He knew that the giant firms and money managers who served as custodians of other people's money now strove to prove that they could maximize the return on their investments. To do this they constantly shifted their funds, hedged their bets, sought immediate winners. Few invested in the long-term profitability of companies they believed in. In an atmosphere of uncertainty, of roaring inflation or fickle interest rates, hunches became king. Volatility, not stability, became the normal market environment—in 1983 alone, thirty billion shares or 60 percent of all outstanding stock changed hands. Among the traders who dominated the market, Lew Glucksman was one of the best.

To the traders he hired Glucksman often handed out free copies of Charles Mackay's *Extraordinary Popular Delusions and the Madness of Crowds,* the classic study of mob psychology and the irrationality of markets.*

It gnawed at Glucksman that despite this rise of trading activity on the Street and at Lehman, despite the new importance of commercial paper and equities—trading and sales functions for which he had long been responsible at Lehman—he felt traders were still being treated shabbily. The old-line banking division at Lehman was producing a declining share of profits—only about a third of the firm's profits in 1982 and 1983—yet bankers still held 60 percent of Lehman stock, still allowed the trading departments only thirty-five of the firm's seventy-seven partnerships. And bankers still had their own man, Peter G. Peterson, on top.

Glucksman was not like *them.* He arrived at his desk before six, his wide tie already yanked down and to the side, like a noose, his jacket flung on a chair. Soon his pants would be sprinkled with cigar ash, his hands blackened by newsprint from ripping articles out of the *Wall Street Journal,* the New York *Times* and the New York *Daily News* to review with "my team," as he liked to refer to his staff. He proudly wore an inexpensive Seiko watch with a shiny steel band, almost always ate lunch at his desk on the trading floor instead of in Lehman's elegant forty-third-floor partners' dining room. On his office walls were hung portraits of clipper ships, fish and a bright-red —"Chief Glucksman"—fireman's hat. His office etiquette was democratic—he conversed with secretaries and clerks, and employees were free to drop in and see him. Instead of a windowed suite of offices overlooking the tip of Manhattan and New York harbor, as Peterson enjoyed, his private quarters off the trading floor were windowless and cramped, with seats for five people to squeeze around his fake green-leather-top desk. It was dubbed "the chart room" because Glucksman, who loves boating and fishing, had hung navigational charts of the Florida Keys on the walls.

On the trading floor, Glucksman was in the process of covering

*Published in 1932 by Farrar, Straus.

all the windows, so that the entire focus of the vast room would be turned inward, so that the hundreds of analysts and clerks huddled before their Telerate and Quotron screens would have nothing to distract them. Glucksman usually worked in a glass-walled office toward the center of the room known as "the fishbowl," where his people could see him, feel his presence, watch him propel his five-foot, nine-inch body out of his glass office and around the trading floor, head down, shoulders slightly stooped, hear him bellow profanities—"Fucking-A-Well!" "Dipshit!"—watch his round face redden with rage, see him burst the buttons on his shirt or heave something in frustration, watch him suddenly hug or kiss employees to express appreciation.

"He's a very mercurial, highly emotional man," observes former Lehman board member George A. Wiegers, who left in the spring of 1983 to become a partner at Dillon, Read. While praising Glucksman's talents, Wiegers also remembers how excitable he was: "Glucksman was a guy who once ripped the shirt off his back in a rage." He sometimes rewarded or terminated employees whimsically. Another partner, who had been an ally, calls Lew "a slob. We always used to joke about whether Lew would get through a meal without spilling food on his suit."

That is one dimension of Lew Glucksman. Another is offered by Florence Worrel, his former secretary, who recalls how he worried about the children of employees, and how he helped them get into private schools, offered personal loans, and once dispatched his driver to take her daughter to Harvard. Employees fondly remember how he would pause and laughingly instruct them how to use words like *gelt* or *shmuck*.

"There are so many facets to him," says partner James S. Boshart III, who began as his clerk and became his administrative right arm. "He was a very tough man, a very emotional man, a very smart man, a very caring man. A lot of this talk of him being tough was an act. Once he was very upset because we had the trading floor built at 55 Water Street and someone put curtains in his office. In a rage, he pulled down the curtains rather than wait for the workers to come. He did it for a reason. He felt that the man who ran the trading floor should be feared. Lots of places have trading floors where people have a sense that the managers don't know or don't care what's going on. They never felt that way about Lew Glucksman. His legendary temper was carefully cultivated. He did it because he wanted people

to know there was someone to answer to. The real Lew Glucksman
had difficulty telling people difficult things."

The two dimensions of Lew Glucksman are put together by vice
president Ralph L. Schlosstein, a capital-markets-group banker who
worked on the trading floor and respected Glucksman: "Lew
managed people the way Lyndon B. Johnson did—through a combination of fear and love."

This combination, along with Glucksman's shrewdness in anticipating the future flow of stocks and interest rates, forged a trading
operation much envied on Wall Street. Of Glucksman, Peterson says,
"Lew built commercial paper into an $18 to $20 billion business.
Even his more ardent critics will tell you that he was one of the best
in the business at credit analysis."

In style or personality, Glucksman and Peterson were opposites.
Peterson, with his thatch of jet-black hair, his clear-framed eye-
glasses, deliberate manner, trim figure and deep voice, conveys authority. He is an earnest man, whose tie is rarely loosened. Although
Peterson can display a dry, self-deprecating wit, particularly before
an audience, he usually appears solemn. "Pete is a strange man,"
observes a prominent businessman whom Peterson considers a
friend. "We always see each other at various events. Yesterday we
went to a cocktail party at Henry Grunwald's [editor-in-chief of
Time Inc.]. I saw Shirley MacLaine and walked over and con-
gratulated her on her cover story in Time. We were chatting, and
Pete walked over and started talking about the federal budget!"

Unlike Glucksman, Peterson immerses himself in public issues
and the world outside. He is a leading catalyst behind efforts to slash
the federal deficit, to spur greater savings and productivity, to cope
with mounting Third World debt. He sits on the boards of six blue-
chip corporations, is treasurer of the Council on Foreign Relations
and serves as a trustee of the Japan Society and the Museum of
Modern Art. On his office wall hung original paintings by Jasper
Johns and Robert Motherwell, autographed pictures of former Soviet Premier Brezhnev, framed photographs of Peterson with former
Presidents Nixon and Ford, with former Secretary of State Kissinger, with Nixon's entire Cabinet, with Japanese Prime Minister
Nakasone.

At the firm, Peterson was Mr. Outside; Glucksman was Mr. Inside. Peterson cared more about the public weal and status, Glucksman about power. Peterson accepted and enjoyed an ambassadorial
role—with clients, with competitors, with government, with the

press and public. And he had an extensive social life outside of Lehman. He enjoyed attending an art or theater opening, an elaborate East Side dinner party. His talented third wife, Joan Ganz Cooney, president and founder of the Children's Television Workshop, which produces *Sesame Street*, had ushered him into New York's literary world, where Peterson dined with writers, wrote articles for the *New York Review of Books* and was recruited to write a book about the roots of the federal deficit.

For all Peterson's stature and worldly experience, there is an innocence about him. His view of New York, for instance, is still that of an impressionable, awestruck arrival from Nebraska for whom the city is a Liz Smith column crammed with the names of movers and shakers. When *New York Magazine,* in its year-end 1984 issue, asked a group of New Yorkers to describe what the city meant to them, Peterson replied, in full:

> Living in New York is like living out a tale of many cities. Where else at breakfast can you run into the foreign policy elite like Henry Kissinger and Winston Lord having coffee with the minister of Pakistan, and where else at lunch can you, in one room, see the newscasters and book-makers like Tom Brokaw, Dan Rather, Bill Moyers, Jason Epstein, Bob Bernstein, and Mort Janklow, and—best of all and of increasing relevance to me—in a city that is not youth-adoring, where else in the evening are the brightest stars in the room such people as Brooke Astor, Bill Paley, Irene Selznick, Jacob Javits, and Mollie Parnis?

Glucksman's life, on the other hand, rotated around Lehman. Those Glucksman considered his closest personal friends were usually those he did business with. Rarely did he see them outside the business day. He counts among "my closest friends" Terry M. Cone of Cleary, Gottlieb, Steen & Hamilton, one of two law firms that did the bulk of Lehman's legal work. Yet Cone says he has never visited Glucksman's apartment. They had numerous business dinners— "which constitutes social life for him," Cone says. Unlike Pete and Joan Peterson, Lew and Inez Glucksman rarely entertained. In fact, they were no longer close to each other. She was a part-time editor for a publishing company and had been a full-time mother of two grown daughters. At the end of a long day, Lew Glucksman would often scoop up some memos or a tool catalogue so he could contemplate furniture to build or repair, and he would have his driver wait outside as he dined alone in a Chinatown restaurant. When he got away, it was usually for lonely pursuits—skippering one of his boats, fishing, cabinetry. He sits on only one corporate board—Revlon— and served on the New York University board and, until 1984, as a board member of the Port Authority of New York and New Jersey.

If Peterson is the prototype of a smooth corporate titan, the earthy, volatile Glucksman was the opposite—a "jungle fighter." A fellow board member observes: "Glucksman's flaw was that there was an angry pig inside the man. He wasn't after money. He was after power, complete control." But Glucksman didn't perceive himself this way. What he dreamed of doing for Lehman was what Gustave Levy had done for Goldman, Sachs, or John Gutfreund had done for Salomon Brothers—build a muscular, modern investment bank.

Glucksman's urge for power was fueled by resentments. He came to resent Peterson's preference for memos rather than meetings; he often complained about the way Peterson kept people waiting while he juggled telephone calls, about the wall of secretaries guarding access to him, about his condescending manner. "Ride out to the airport with me, Lew," he would command. Peterson, who always worried about his own weight, would say, "Meet my fat friend Lew."

Peterson's appeal owes more to his stature, his contacts, his considerable intelligence and the aggressive homework he does rather than to his charm or magnetism. His ability to recruit new business staggered even his detractors, like Lehman partner Henry R. Breck: "The leavings from Pete's table were enough to run a good little investment bank." But the attention Peterson lavished on clients was rarely turned toward his partners, much less to those who worked in the trenches. One of his Lehman admirers, partner Stephen Bershad, says, "He would set his mind on something and see nothing else. He would walk down the hall with a stack of letters and read the mail while going out to a meeting and write replies and just throw them over his shoulder, assuming someone would be there to pick it up." He would call partners at odd hours, ask them to ride uptown in his chauffeured Oldsmobile, and then ignore them as he talked on the telephone or scanned a memorandum. "He can be described as 'frank' or as 'cruel,' depending on your point of view," observes partner Robert S. Rubin, who thought him "cruel."

Glucksman thought Peterson was self-centered, haughty, uncaring. "I knew the man ten years but I never had a personal conversation with him," says Glucksman. In fact, the Equitable lunch reminded him of another incident. As if the bone were still stuck in his throat, Glucksman becomes livid when he recalls how Peterson treated him "like a flunky" at a mid-seventies meeting with client David Rockefeller at the Chase Manhattan Bank. Glucksman's version of this meeting is that he and Lehman had just successfully completed a major financing for Chase and that he and Peterson walked alone to the meeting, Glucksman briefing him on the details along the way. They rode up the elevator together, stopping at the seventeenth floor. When they got to Rockefeller's office, Peterson told him, "I want to go in alone." Peterson's version is that they both went in to Rockefeller's office, conducted their meeting, and as they were leaving, the Chase chairman asked to have a private word with his friend, the chairman of Lehman. Peterson says he could hardly have refused.*

Whether Glucksman's or Peterson's version is correct is almost irrelevant. What is relevant is that this and other wounds still pained Lew Glucksman. It irritated him when Peterson said, as he still does, that "I didn't have a detailed grasp of that part of our business that was increasingly important—trading, futures, brokerage, commodities." This angered Glucksman because these trading functions were then generating two-thirds of Lehman's profits. And now that trading was getting its day in the sun, he feared that Peterson was angling within a few years to sell the firm for a substantial premium over the current share price. Rumors to that effect circulated freely throughout Lehman, fueled by the open desire of many partners to sell and become instant millionaires, and by one pregnant fact: partners were required to begin selling back their stock when they reached age sixty. Since Peterson was then fifty-seven,† Glucksman believed the chairman secretly plotted to sell the firm before reaching that milestone. Glucksman, also fifty-seven, says he picked up hints to this effect, but never anything concrete.

Glucksman knew, and the partners knew, that for several years now he, not Pete Peterson, had been managing the day-to-day business, had chaired the operations committee, which Peterson did not even serve on. Meanwhile, Peterson focused on a core group of clients, on bringing in new business, on strategic planning and marketing. Ever since Glucksman was made chief operating officer in 1980, Peterson had been delegating more and more responsibility to him; by 1983, the chairman worked directly only with a handful of Lehman partners—Roger Altman on new business development,

---

*David Rockefeller declined to be interviewed.
†All ages in the book are given for the time the events transpired.

Stephen Schwarzman on corporate mergers, David Offensend* on corporate finance clients, Robert Brown on public finance, and vice president James W. Hood on all marketing and public relations. Despite his growing isolation from the board as well as the rank and file at Lehman, Peterson rightly believed it was he who set the strategic framework for the firm's success and who acted as a rudder for Glucksman, an opinion shared by many partners, though not by Lew Glucksman. "Over the last five years, Peterson didn't play an active role in the management of the business," says Glucksman. "I brought him up to date. We played a charade with him"—pretending he was in charge. It annoyed Glucksman that to the outside world Peterson got all the credit for successes Glucksman came to feel were his. "I got sick and tired of Pete always saying the same thing," says Glucksman. "Pete was a guy totally obsessed with the world hearing the name Pete Peterson."

TO GLUCKSMAN, THE WAY HE WAS TREATED AT THE EQUITABLE lunch was the final indignity. He returned to Lehman Brothers that afternoon in a rage. One of those he turned to was partner Jim Boshart, then thirty-eight, a native of suburban Rockville Centre, Long Island. The blond six foot five New Yorker had landed a basketball scholarship to Wake Forest University, where he starred as forward, averaging 14 points a game in his senior year. Upon graduation, Boshart was drafted into the Army, served two years, and was then hired by Glucksman in 1970, partly because Glucksman liked to recruit athletes and those with a military background, men who appreciated his "team" concept, and partly to improve the Lehman basketball team. The team went from zero wins and four losses when Boshart joined, to twelve wins and four losses at the end of the season. And in thirteen years, Boshart rose from clerk in the money market division to chief administrative officer of Lehman. In his various jobs at the firm, the lean, boyish-looking Boshart always worked directly with Lew Glucksman.

Jim Boshart was a staff man, and unlike his more aggressive partners, was a superb listener, an idealist—a "Boy Scout," as one partner, with a mixture of disdain and admiration, referred to him. Over the years, Jim Boshart had become the surrogate son Glucks-

*Offensend was a vice president, not a partner.

man never had. He also became a bridge between Glucksman and Peterson. Glucksman may have been exasperated by Peterson, but he was often guarded in expressing his true feelings to the chairman. To Peterson, Boshart was an informal channel, someone who could decipher and interpret how Glucksman actually felt, which was sometimes unclear. Peterson felt comfortable with this arrangement because he felt comfortable with Boshart's modest, Jimmy Stewart wholesomeness, his decency. By Peterson's count they met at least three times daily, usually to discuss anything from personnel, recruitment or administrative matters to Lew Glucksman's mercurial moods. Sometimes Boshart would listen to monologues for hours. It did not appear to trouble the chairman that his main set of eyes and ears within Lehman belonged to a man more devoted to Glucksman than to him.

Boshart recalls what Glucksman said to him after the Equitable lunch: "He described the meeting and said he really felt he hadn't been viewed with respect commensurate with his role in the organization."

Glucksman was even blunter with fellow board member Robert S. Rubin, then fifty-one, his closest friend at Lehman from the time both had become partners in 1967; the man he called "my *consigliere.*" Rubin, like Glucksman, was reared in a middle-class Jewish household, and went to public schools in Brookline, Massachusetts. Although at Lehman he was a brooding loner, at Brookline High School he had captained the basketball team and was active in an assortment of extracurricular endeavors. In his senior year he was voted "Most Versatile" by his classmates. Rubin joined Lehman in 1958, after graduating with "highest distinction" from Yale, being selected a Baker Scholar while studying for an M.B.A. from the Harvard Graduate School of Business Administration, and serving three years in the Army. As a member of the banking department, Rubin had been singled out as a comer, a man who could one day preside over Lehman. He was elevated to the board of directors in 1972 and placed in charge of the banking division in the mid-seventies. "I thought Bob should have been president of the firm," says former partner Michael Thomas. "I thought he had the character and the decisiveness. He certainly knew technically as much as anyone. He was really relaxed. Bob could take it or leave it. He didn't have an iota of personal ambition."

But things soured for Rubin at Lehman sometime during Peterson's reign. Although he still served on the Lehman board and on the commitments committee, which decided which clients Lehman would do business with, and was co-chairman of the pricing committee, which determined the firm's position in pricing securities before they were sold, his star had dimmed. Peterson had removed Rubin as head of banking in 1977, after Lehman merged with Kuhn Loeb. It was no secret that Rubin and Peterson detested each other. In 1977, Rubin moved from the banking division offices to a tiny office off the trading floor, where, aside from shepherding the important RCA account, his responsibilities were vague. He had no staff except for a secretary. His somewhat disheveled appearance—long black sideburns, a prominent, indented nose, and a high, domed forehead —may have contributed to the impression that he was a little odd. Nevertheless, partners—including Peterson—freely consulted Rubin on a range of issues, for his financial acumen was legendary. Around Lehman he was known as "the senior partner for judgment." Like Glucksman, he was revered by some partners, hated by others. And he may have been drawn to Glucksman by a common feeling that they were outsiders.

So when Glucksman told "Ruby," as he also called him, of the Equitable lunch, Rubin was sympathetic. He recalls Glucksman saying, "I couldn't believe his performance at lunch. I'm not going to the next lunch . . . I'm going to talk to Pete. This can't go on like this. Something's got to change." From Glucksman's point of view, the timing for a confrontation was certainly propitious. With trading profits skyrocketing, he was at the apex of his power at Lehman. It was the moment to strike.

THE PHONE IN PETERSON'S FORTY-THIRD-FLOOR CORNER office rang early the next morning, July 13, 1983. "Has Mr. Peterson come in yet?" Glucksman asked Melba J. Duncan, Peterson's Jamaica-born executive assistant. She explained that Peterson was attending a breakfast meeting outside the office. Miss Duncan remembers "lots of urgent" calls from Glucksman that morning. When Peterson arrived about ten, she told him of Glucksman's calls. Peterson jotted a few "operational" items, as he recalls them, on a yellow legal pad and, wanting to appear solicitous, walked down the two flights to see Glucksman.

Peterson entered what was called "the living room," a spare office with no desk, a single couch and a couple of chairs. This office, one of three Glucksman used, was located just off the trading floor at the end of an executive corridor. Glucksman preferred this site for operations meetings and formal interviews. Usually, he kept the light-brown venetian blinds open, so he could peek through the clear glass window onto the trading floor. Today the blinds were closed.

"I just thought it would be one of our weekly meetings," says Peterson. He barely got into the first item on his agenda when he noticed that Lew "seemed a bit tense, as if he were psyching himself up." Peterson put down his pad and, like a doctor facing a patient, peered at his co-CEO.

"What do you want out of life, Lew?" asked Peterson.*

"I've been giving a lot of thought to my life," answered Glucksman. "You know how important boats and cruising and ships are to me. Kind of in the same way I have satisfaction when I'm in charge of a boat, I'm beginning to get the same feeling about Lehman. I'd like to do the same thing at Lehman Brothers." Glucksman spoke of how the full range of his abilities was not used at Lehman and how, if given the chance, he could do at least as well as John C. Whitehead, co-CEO of Goldman, Sachs, or John Gutfreund, who managed Salomon Brothers.

Peterson was astonished. He remembered how happy and honored Glucksman had said he was when Peterson had volunteered to make him co-CEO eight weeks before. Surely Lew Glucksman, a trader, an inside man who displayed little fondness for the client side of the business, who was hardly known to the outside world, surely he didn't think he could run Lehman Brothers? Hadn't Glucksman admitted to him in May that he needed Peterson's firm guiding hand as chairman?

Peterson is a man of many talents, but sensitivity to people is not counted among his virtues. Often he seemed oblivious to the feelings of many of his partners, including those of some he felt close to. He

*Both men agree on the exchange that followed.

talked about himself—his deals, his issues—rarely about them. While many respected Peterson and credited him with saving the firm, few felt close to him. They had tired of his one-sided conversations, of being summoned to the chairman's office without notice and expected to appear, sit and wait while Peterson's battery of secretaries raced through a pile of telephone slips; it bothered partners that Peterson would forget their wives' names or brusquely telephone their homes when he awoke at five-thirty; that he got his name in the papers, and they rarely did.

Peterson was unaware that Glucksman felt humiliated or that he believed that Peterson was serving out his time at Lehman while robbing Glucksman of the credit to go along with the responsibility he already enjoyed. Peterson believed his outside activities—his work on the Brandt Commission that focused on the problems of the Third World, his successful effort to recruit 250 top corporate executives to join the Bi-Partisan Budget Appeal, which was dedicated to achieving a balanced federal budget—lured business to the firm, much as Felix Rohatyn's high-profile chairmanship of New York's Municipal Assistance Corporation attracted business to banking rival Lazard Frères. While many partners were pleased with the luster these activities brought Lehman, Peterson had no idea that his public role rankled Glucksman and his allies.

As Peterson sat listening to Glucksman's "rambling soliloquy," he was perplexed. And for good reason. Had Glucksman expressed a desire to run Lehman himself in April or early May, before Peterson promoted him, he could have understood. Instead, Glucksman had showered him with gratitude. He even organized a tenth anniversary luncheon for Peterson on June 6, and allowed the firm to spend $25,000 on a Henry Moore sketch to present to the chairman. Glucksman had even offered an effusive toast, in which he recalled what "a great honor it has been to work with Pete Peterson, and how I look forward to working with him for many years in the future."*

Peterson asked his co-CEO to explain what he meant by ships and Lehman Brothers.

"This is my whole life," said Glucksman. "I really don't have alternatives. It seems to me that with all of your talents and associations, you have options. You've talked of other things you can do. Are you at the point in your life where you're ready to do other stuff?"

---

*Glucksman does not deny the toast.

Peterson remembers thinking: Sixty days ago we agreed to share power. We announced it to the world. We committed the full partnership, not just him and me, to a course of action. Lew said he was thrilled and grateful. I initiated it. I was sympathetic about bringing Lew in, inviting him to meet with the press. I talked with him about an eventual transition and lining up younger partners under him who could fill key roles—Sheldon Gordon, François de Saint Phalle, Roger Altman. Now this?

"Lew, let me see if I understand what you're saying," said Peterson. "Are you saying you want to run the business alone? I don't understand what you're saying."

"Well, there are things I want to do differently," said Glucksman. "It's time to heal the wounds at Lehman Brothers."

"What wounds? Heal wounds with whom, Lew?"

"You've had this problem with Bob Rubin."

"Yes, I've had problems with Bob Rubin."

It was no secret that the chairman considered Rubin a brilliant but negative man, a "passive" banker who rarely left the office, who resisted the infusion of outside capital in 1974, who resisted the merger with Kuhn Loeb in 1977, who resisted Peterson's efforts to set up a new business and product development office, who resisted his marketing efforts and who even resisted when Peterson solicited his advice about making Glucksman president in 1981. It was Peterson who removed Rubin as head of the banking department in 1977. The chairman was not alone in his view of Rubin. Many partners found him negative and uncommunicative—a sphinx. He was a loner, a tense, taciturn man who, in the words of one partner who respected him, "believed that in the privacy of his own office he would make the right decision and people should just follow him." Peterson thought he was a nitpicker who seemed to believe in "civilized anarchy" and thus frustrated his desire to run Lehman Brothers like a corporation. Glucksman, however, made it clear that he thought Rubin performed a consistent and valuable function as the house skeptic, the firm's institutional memory.

"Who else?" asked Peterson.

"Bill Morris," replied Glucksman.

"Yes," responded Peterson, who removed Morris as head of the investment banking division in 1982. He reminded Glucksman that Glucksman had agreed with the transfer. To the chairman's way of thinking, Bill Morris—like his close friend Bob Rubin, but without Rubin's redeeming brilliance—was a capable banker but a type: a traditional, passive banker who waited for the telephone to ring; Morris did not develop marketing plans to recruit clients, would not go along with efforts to terminate weak partners, mocked Peterson's countless memos about cutting costs or pushing "new products," and resisted the chairman's appointment of Roger Altman as head of the new-business-development group. Morris, Peterson thought, focused too narrowly on a few important clients in the energy business—the Kerr-McGee Corporation and Daniel Industries, on whose boards he served.

Glucksman reminded Peterson that Morris was an important member of the firm, a member of the board of directors. He knew, but did not say, that Morris thought the chairman was neglecting the firm and was, in Morris's words, a callous man "not terribly interested in the nitty-gritty of administering things; he was very interested in the appearance of things."

"Who else?" asked Peterson, impatiently.

"Eric Gleacher."

"Yes," said Peterson. Eric was a talented mergers and acquisitions partner, but he didn't think the former Marine lieutenant had the management interest or people skills to run the M. & A. department. That is why Peterson had removed him from this position in 1982. He knew that Eric Gleacher was one of the few people in banking who felt close to Lew and that he was a real asset to the firm; but Peterson was a corporate man, someone who says he believed in team play and a chain of command. Eric, he said, was not a team player, he sneered at the thought of filling out daily telephone call reports.

"Who else?" Peterson asked.

"Henry Breck."

"Yes," said Peterson, who remarked that the head of the Lehman Management Company (Lemco), Lehman's investment management subsidiary, was "not a guy who builds managers and thinks about marketing." Breck may have attended all the right schools—Buckley, Groton, Harvard, Oxford—but Peterson, like some other partners, was wary of Breck. Perhaps it was the seven mysterious years Breck had spent in the C.I.A. Perhaps it was his ties to Rubin and Morris, his closest friends at the firm. Perhaps it was the disdain Breck communicated to Peterson and others.

"Those are only four people out of seventy-seven partners that there have been some problems with," said Peterson. "That's not a great piece of news that I have problems with those four partners."

"I think I can heal the wounds," said Glucksman.

"You mean you think I can't heal them."

"That's right."

"What do you want, Lew?"

"I'm talking about running the business *now*, Pete."

"What do you mean *now?*"

"September 30," said Glucksman, picking the last day of their fiscal year, a day just over two months off. "I don't want to wait three years for you to retire because I know now that I'm fresh and eager to do the job. Who knows how I'll feel in three years." Glucksman says he then pressed Peterson for a timetable of when he might leave. Although the two men were the same age, Glucksman was confident that Peterson would leave Lehman before he did. "The question was," he says, "would it be at his convenience or mine?"

Peterson was dumbfounded. He listened, sympathetically he thought, to a man who he now worried might have plotted to corner him in this conversation, perhaps while boating and fishing alone, perhaps in conversations with Bob Rubin, whom Peterson saw as a schemer. He wondered whether Glucksman had quietly polled the twelve-member board and lined up votes. He couldn't believe that board members like Peter Solomon, Harvey Krueger, Yves-André Istel or Edmund Hajim would have remained silent had they been polled. Peterson had assumed that his financial success at Lehman and his access to corporate boardrooms would assure him support from the board of directors in any showdown. But the remote Peterson had not said more than a perfunctory hello to some board members for months.

Peterson was not an impulsive man. He liked to sift options. He knew that at age sixty, just three years hence, he would be required, like all Lehman partners, to begin cashing in his stock. But, though he had written a memorandum to Rubin and Glucksman on November 26, 1980, which spoke of "my own transition plans" and mentioned his interest in participating in a handful of investments with venture capitalist Eli Jacobs, a friend and business associate over the years, Peterson had no thoughts of leaving immediately. He now thought of a two- or three-year transition period, as he had mentioned in a July 23, 1981, memo to Rubin and Glucksman, which they signed: "I of course have every intention of making LBKL my principal base for *at least* [his italics] five years." Peterson was careful in their conversation in Glucksman's office not to mention any possible transition dates to his co-CEO.

"Obviously, Lew, you and I have to have many more discussions on this. I want to be sure I understand your problem."

The meeting dragged on for five hours, ending just after three o'clock. At one point, fruit salads arrived from the Lehman kitchen, delivered by tuxedoed waiters who had no idea of the momentous colloquy they were interrupting. Nor did partners who wanted to see Glucksman or Peterson; they paced back and forth in the corridor, wondering what was going on in there. Jim Boshart remembers needing to see Glucksman, and loping down the corridor every half hour or so. Always the door was closed. "What the hell are they talking about for five hours?" he remembers thinking.

The meeting ended inconclusively. The two men agreed to confer again. Peterson wasn't alarmed. He thought of Glucksman as an electric personality, one capable of irrational behavior. He looked on the session, he recalls, as "a first discussion." The firm was then earning pre-tax and pre-bonus profits of $15 million a month; Glucksman might cool off and retreat. Peterson had been in therapy since his second marriage dissolved in 1978; now happily married to Joan Ganz Cooney, he thought he was in touch with his own feelings while he believed Glucksman was "a stranger to his inner feelings," his unconscious. He hoped that once Glucksman realized what a rash thing he had done, perhaps he would repent.

But Glucksman did not repent. He was a gambler used to quick, firm decisions. *Make a market* (set a price on a stock or bond). *Buy. Sell. Hedge. Don't hesitate.* "What makes a good trader more than anything," says Glucksman, "is the willingness to take losses." To take risks. After the meeting, Glucksman hurried to Bob Rubin's office down the hall and told him and Boshart what had happened. Glucksman said he had been explicit with Peterson and wanted him out now. But he told his two colleagues he was concerned that Peterson would hear what he wanted to hear. "So he suggested I talk to Pete," recalls Boshart. Although Glucksman says the confrontation in his office with Peterson was unplanned, based on impulse, now his determination hardened. Like Machiavelli's Prince, Glucksman knew he had to move fast, had to kill, not merely wound Peterson.

He was surprisingly confident that Peterson would leave. He realized that Peterson had not said no, had not threatened a donnybrook. He sensed that Peterson did not have the stomach for a fight. Peterson had been through his share of soul-wrenching experiences in recent years—the 1973–1974 struggle to save Lehman Brothers from collapse, surgery in 1977 for a brain tumor that turned out to be benign, a painful and much-discussed divorce, a happy remarriage that was clouded by several cancer scares his wife had had. Glucksman calculated that Peterson would not want to get into a messy public brawl that might leave nothing but carnage at Lehman and tarnish Peterson's public image. Even if Peterson prevailed, he would have to assume that Glucksman and at least part of his trading team would move to another firm, as he came close to doing in the mid-seventies. If this happened, it would leave Peterson once again to manage Lehman on a day to day basis, something Glucksman knew Peterson dreaded.

Glucksman smelled weakness. He had quickly sized up the transaction and told Rubin and Boshart he believed that with a generous golden handshake, Peterson would leave. When he did, Lew Glucksman would be at the helm of his own ship.

T O MOST IMMIGRANTS IN THE MID-NINETEENTH CENTURY, New York was the gateway to the New World. But when Henry, Emanuel and Mayer Lehman decided to leave the family cattle business in Bavaria, they chose by instinct or luck to settle in Montgomery, Alabama, a hub of the cotton trade. The first of the brothers to leave their home in search of fortune was Henry, then twenty-three and the oldest. Henry settled in this city of 4,000 citizens and 2,000 slaves. His two brothers soon followed, and in 1850 they established a trading and dry-goods business called Lehman Brothers.

Cotton trading burgeoned—until the War between the States intruded. The Lehman brothers became partisans of the Confederacy, whose original capital was Montgomery. On March 16, 1854, Lehman Brothers purchased a slave. The deed, signed by Hugh R. Segars of Montgomery, reads:

Received of H. Lehman & Bro. nine hundred dollars in full payment for a negro girl named Martha about fourteen years old. The said girl I warrant sound in body and mind, and a slave for life. I also warrant the title free from all encumbrances.

Mayer Lehman, the youngest brother, was, according to the official Lehman family centennial published in 1950, "sufficiently active in war work to earn the accolade of 'one of the best Southern patriots' bestowed upon him in the final year of the Confederacy." He counted among his close friends the leading political figures of the Confederacy, including Hilary A. Herbert, after whom he would name his youngest son, Herbert, who later became a Lehman partner and then an illustrious governor and United States senator from New York.

With the end of the war, however, New York beckoned. By 1868 the brothers had shifted their headquarters to lower Manhattan, where they were instrumental in founding the New York Cotton Exchange. Soon they branched out to trade sugar, grains, coffee and petroleum. The expansion of Lehman Brothers coincided with the post-Civil War expansion of trading in stocks and bonds.

The traditional investment banks with their old-school elders—J. P. Morgan, Brown Brothers, the Harrimans—were offering conservative financing to established companies. It fell to the Lehmans and a remarkable group of German-Jewish merchants to invent more speculative means of financing upstart companies. "Let the Jews have that one," was a familiar refrain on staid Wall Street.

Two years after Appomattox, Lehman Brothers undertook to raise funds (by selling bonds) for the state of Alabama, which was desperately in need of investment capital. The brothers supported a multitude of new Southern ventures, from textile mills to railroads. Later they pierced the financial establishment to help form two major banks—the Mercantile National Bank, which later merged with the Irving Trust Company, and the Mutual Alliance Trust Company, which later became Manufacturers Trust Company.

The Lehmans were not alone. Marcus Goldman in 1869 launched what would become Goldman, Sachs & Company and pioneered the use of what is known today as commercial paper. In return for lending a merchant, say, $900, Goldman would receive a written promise from the merchant to pay back $1,000. That paper could then be traded like a security. Jacob Schiff, like his partner-to-be, Solomon Loeb, walked to work on lower Manhattan daily, collecting IOU's and stuffing them into his stovepipe hat.

On Wall Street, where the reputations of these and other German-Jewish investment bankers grew, they were accepted, even honored. But they were not accepted by the Astors and Morgans and other representatives of America's reigning social families. So the Lehmans and Loebs and Schiffs and Goldmans and Sachs and Seligmans and Warburgs and Kuhns and Guggenheims and Strauses formed their own aristocracy, their own German-Jewish private club (the Harmonie), their own Temple Emanu-El, their own private schools.

As time wore on, these new millionaires strove to assimilate. By the 1870's, writes Stephen Birmingham in *Our Crowd*, many German Jews who arrived around 1848 began to separate themselves from new East European immigrants: "A careful distinction was drawn between . . . 'the better class of Jews' and 'vulgar Jews,' between 'Sephardic' and 'German,' and, finally, between 'refined Hebrew ladies and gentlemen' and 'Jews.' "

Dorothy Schiff, who once owned and served as publisher and editor-in-chief of the New York *Post,* and whose grandfather, Jacob Schiff, became a principal at Kuhn Loeb, recalls her mother's experience: "My mother was Jewish but had fallen in love late in her teens with "Billie" Thaw, the younger brother of Harry Thaw.* His mother in Pittsburgh was horrified because she was Jewish. I think that affected her her whole life. Although she married my father, I don't think she was in love with him. She wanted to get out of that whole Jewish thing, which is why I suppose we moved to Oyster Bay."

By the turn of the century, America was bursting with energy. A second generation of Lehman relatives, who had joined the firm in the 1870's and 1880's, now chose to downplay commodity trading and to concentrate on investment banking. The prospering companies were those that emphasized not just production but distribution of products—department stores, food chains, new technology. Lehman Brothers helped raise the money to launch Studebaker, to produce the first pneumatic tire, to spur the giant utility companies. Joining with Goldman, Sachs, in 1906, Lehman initiated one of the first major underwritings to raise funds for an American corporation, the General Cigar Company. Soon Lehman and Goldman joined forces again to underwrite Sears, Roebuck & Company.

Early in the new century, leadership of the firm came to rest on the shoulders of Emanuel Lehman's son, Philip, who earned $20 a

---

*Who killed Stanford White.

week when he joined the firm in 1882. At the age of twenty-four, in 1885, Philip was made a partner. For the next sixty-two years, until his death in 1947, he helped guide Lehman Brothers.

By the end of World War I, the primary focus of Lehman Brothers had shifted still further from commodities to investment banking, which then consisted mostly of raising capital and proferring financial advice. By this time the firm had five partners, all Lehmans—the second generation sons: Philip, Arthur and Herbert; and the third generation: Allan and Harold. But the crush of business had become too much for five partners, and in 1924 Lehman began to accept nonfamily partners—the first being John M. Hancock, a former naval officer who worked under Bernard M. Baruch at the War Industries Board. By 1950 there would be seventeen partners, only two of whom were Lehmans.

By the mid-twenties, Philip's son, Robert, began to assume principal responsibility for the partnership. He was a small, trim man, about five feet seven inches, with well-tanned, smooth skin and a dapper appearance. Unfailingly polite, Robert nevertheless knew what he wanted. First he wanted to move the firm. And in 1928 the headquarters of the partnership was transferred from a cramped space in the Farmers Loan & Trust Company building at 16 William Street to Lehman's very own eleven-story triangular Italian Renaissance-style building at One William Street, in the heart of the financial district.* For the next fifty-two years this would be the home of Lehman Brothers.

THE BANKING ACT OF 1933 SEVERED THE INTIMATE RELATIONSHIP that existed between investment and commercial banking. To shore up a weakened banking system, a protective wall was erected between the two. Lehman shed its ties to commercial banking and concentrated even more on investment banking. As World War II approached, Lehman Brothers had either raised or invested its own capital to nurture such giant corporations as Gimbel Brothers, R. H. Macy, Continental Can, RCA, American, National, Trans World Airlines and Pan American World Airways, the Jewel Tea Company, B. F. Goodrich, and the Campbell Soup Company. After

---

*This building's historical significance pre-dated Lehman, for it was the original home of J. & W. Seligman & Company, an early Wall Street firm.

meeting visionaries who came to him with ideas about tubes that would transmit pictures and airplanes that would circle the planet like birds, Robert Lehman—who often told his partners, "I bet on people"—made Lehman the driving financial force behind RCA and the birth of television, TWA, Pan Am, Hertz, several Hollywood studios, and various department store and oil and rubber giants. Lehman Brothers was at the epicenter of those business forces that have shaped not just the American economy but the American culture as well. By 1967 the House of Lehman was responsible for $3.5 billion in underwriting. In volume, Lehman was among the top four investment banks.

Over a period of more than four decades, Bobbie, as he was called, presided from a nine-by-fifteen-foot office that was shaped, it was once said, "like a badly cut slice of pie." Some partners had offices four times the size. Yet there was no doubt who decided—alone— the size of a partner's annual share of the firm's earnings. "Bobbie did not like organization," says former Lehman President Warren Hellman, who joined Lehman in 1959, and whose family was linked to the Seligmans. "If he was an administrator, it was not the standard textbook type. Since it was unclear who would run the firm when he was gone, he decided to put the top seven to eight executives on an executive committee and rotate the chairman each month. Each month the chairman would try valiantly to impress him . . . Partners fought like hell. A lot of them disliked each other personally. But the common thread was tremendous respect and admiration for Bobbie Lehman—and a desire to make money."

"He was a dozen different men," says Lew Glucksman. "Bobbie seemed to be the mildest of men, but he was like a Mafia don who could be nice because he could send people out to do his dirty work. Bobbie's specialty was keeping people at each other's throats."

A more inspired impression of Bobbie Lehman is conveyed by investment banker Felix Rohatyn. He remembers coming back to New York after the Korean War and going to work for the legendary banker Andre Meyer of Lazard Frères: "I used to go over to Lehman with Andre Meyer. If Andre aspired for Lazard to be viewed as any other firm, it would be Lehman Brothers. And if he aspired to be viewed as any other individual, it would be Bobbie Lehman. The partners at Lehman were all men of stature. They were principals. You dealt with them as owners of a great house. You felt that if there was any such thing as a business aristocracy, and at the same time a highly profitable venture, that was it."

A FTER A LONG ILLNESS, BOBBIE LEHMAN DIED IN 1969. HIS death left a void, for he had been the firm's guiding spirit for forty-four years. For all those years Bobbie enjoyed watching competition among his partners almost as much as he enjoyed watching his stable of beloved horses race. There were tales of fistfights among partners at the Polo Lounge at the Beverly Hills Hotel; for nineteen years senior partners Frederick Ehrman and John Hertz did not speak, although their desks were five feet apart in the partners' room on the third floor. Squabbling was normal among the vain and talented partners—over bonuses, over credit for bringing in a piece of business. The squabbling, the aggressive internal competition, the entrepreneurial spirit—all became part of the Lehman culture. As did the sense that partners belonged to an exclusive men's club, to a firm that attracted men of intellect and breeding and offered them a decorous dining room to equal the finest restaurants, the choicest Bordeaux wines, the freshest Havana cigars, a gymnasium, a masseur, stimulating company and a sense that you were doing God's work.

As long as Bobbie was present, there was someone to cork the venom, to police the warring factions. "Bobbie was not much of an investment banker," says Andrew G. C. Sage II, who joined the firm in 1948 and is still there. "He wouldn't know a preferred stock from livestock. But he was a hell of a psychologist." There was no doubt that he was everyone's benefactor. The walls at One William Street were graced with Botticellis, Goyas, El Grecos, Rembrandts, Renoirs, Matisses, Picassos, Cézannes—all on loan from Bobbie's private art collection worth an estimated $100 million. In the morning, black waiters in beige linen jackets brought coffee, tea or pastries from "our kitchen," as partners referred to the culinary castle managed by the former chef of Pavillon. Bobbie's patrician calm, his absolute, unquestioned rule, his friendships with the Whitneys and the Harrimans, his golden touch in spotting embryonic enterprises, gave security and structure to a group of partners better known for their individual accomplishments rather than their team skills. Inevitably, Bobbie's death in 1969 ushered in a period of chaos.

The partner chosen to succeed Bobbie as chairman was Joseph A. Thomas, who had been with Lehman since 1930. Among Thomas's numerous exploits was that he almost single-handedly raised the money to launch Litton Industries. Yet within months Thomas became enfeebled by emphysema and alcohol. The firm's counsel, Edwin Weisl, Sr., of Simpson Thatcher, on whom Bobbie, and later

Thomas, leaned, also became ill. Those senior partners who might have filled the void—former General Lucius D. Clay, who won fame as the American who frustrated the Soviet blockade of West Berlin; Paul Davies, a former corporate executive and, along with Clay, a national Republican Party luminary; Paul Mazur, the retail expert who organized Federated Department Stores; Monroe Gutman, who managed the Lehman Corporation, the firm's investment arm; Harold J. Szold, who ran the banking division; Edwin Kennedy, who helped build several oil giants; Herman Kahn, who developed private placements; banker John Hertz, who shared Bobbie's love of horses and owned such winners as Count Fleet and Reigh Count—all were gone or too advanced in years. Partners were alarmed, and consequently several withdrew their capital. Over a two-year period, ten partners—more than one-fifth of the firm's managing directors—left. And in those days a withdrawal of capital was especially injurious because partners collected their cash almost at once, not over two-and-a-half to five years, as was later the case. "It was like the War of the Roses—continuous warfare," says former partner Kenneth Lipper, who later became a partner at Salomon Brothers and then served as Deputy Mayor of New York City. After a reign of confusion, Frederick L. Ehrman, a talented but gruff and aloof "Our Crowd" banker, was installed as chairman.

With business slipping, partners debated, as they would a decade later, whether to shrink the firm and concentrate on investment banking or to continue to try to expand into a full-service firm. Their fears were amplified by their dislike of Ehrman, who had joined the firm in 1941. In large meetings, recalls partner Andrew Sage, Ehrman would cut off colleagues, declaring, " 'That's the stupidest idea I ever heard of!' He had no manners. Someone would say good morning to him in the elevator and he wouldn't answer." Behind his back, partners called him "Friendly Fred." When Lew Glucksman was made a partner in 1967, recalls James Glanville, a former Lehman partner, "Fred Ehrman told him, 'We made you a partner but you'll never be a member of the Century Country Club.' "

Ehrman compounded his difficulties by setting out to restore "discipline" at Lehman following four years of drift. This violated Lehman's peculiar culture, which stressed individual accomplishment; Lehman partners thought of themselves as entrepreneurs who managed their own profit centers. They did not wish to feel "managed." Even in Bobbie Lehman's heyday, they felt free because he never raised his courtly voice, always soothed them with praise, rarely displayed the clenched fist.

Bobbie Lehman was their benefactor, as he was a benefactor of the arts, of sleek horses, of Pan American or Hertz. "Everyone wanted Bobbie's applause," says Herman Kahn, who joined Lehman as a $15-a-week office boy in 1928, filling the vacancy left by Billy Rose, who went on to become a fabled Broadway producer. "Bobbie was the golden bull on the top of the hill for whom we were all panting."

Fred Ehrman tried to rule by fear. When business plunged in 1973, partners mutinied. "I organized a palace revolution," says former senior partner George Ball, still savoring the memory. From his years in Washington as Under Secretary of State in the Kennedy and Johnson Administrations, and as Ambassador to the United Nations, Ball had learned something of palace intrigue, and he shrewdly waited for a weekend when two of the firm's senior partners and Ehrman allies—Lucius Clay and Paul Davies—were out of town. The logical successor to Ehrman was Ball, who, like Clay and Davies and other Washington notables, had been recruited by Bobbie. Ball, however, was not interested.

Unlike the 1983 Lehman coup, the 1973 version included many more co-conspirators, including Lew Glucksman, Bob Rubin, Pete Peterson, Ball and most of the board. They gathered in August at Ball's United Nations Plaza apartment. The circumstances then were different. After strong profit years in 1971 and 1972, Lehman experienced what former partner Kenneth Lipper, in a top-secret August 20, 1973, memorandum, called "a severe decline in its business to a degree which has probably never before been experienced." By July 1973 the firm was losing money at an unprecedented annual rate of $9 million. Costs had spiraled out of control. The partnership was imperiled. These losses followed another humiliation: just a few years before, the firm was censured by the New York Stock Exchange for sloppy record-keeping. Panic gripped Lehman partners.

The day after the board members agreed at Ball's apartment that Ehrman would be ousted, Ball and Ehrman's nephew, Warren Hellman, who was president of the firm and whose great-grandfather, grandfather and uncle once headed the Wells Fargo Bank, were delegated the task of telling Ehrman. To this day Hellman cannot remember the expression on his uncle's dour face, but he does remember the color socks he wore—gray, and how the elastic was worn, leaving the socks to fall to his ankles. Throughout their brief conversation Hellman's eyes remained fixed on his uncle's feet.

Peterson also remembers visiting Ehrman to suggest, as he would to Lew Glucksman a decade later, an orderly transition period. "The gracious thing to do is to finish out the year and let you announce your successor," he remembers suggesting.

"No way," Ehrman snarled at him.

The board also was not receptive to an orderly transition. They wanted Ehrman out—now. Aware that the days ahead would be stormy, that benevolent Lehman had to excise employees, tighten cost controls and locate fresh capital, the board turned to the partner with the most administrative experience, the former Secretary of Commerce who had joined Lehman less than two months earlier—the vice chairman, Peter G. Peterson.

GENEALOGICALLY, PETE PETERSON'S BACKGROUND WAS MUCH different from that of those well-bred West European Jews—like the Lehmans, the Schiffs, the Loebs, the Warburgs—described in Stephen Birmingham's *Our Crowd.* Nor was he steeped in the lore and spirit of investment banking, coming as he did from a corporate career, first in marketing and then at Bell & Howell. Nor did his lineage betray prominent ancestry, as did that of former Lehman partners or associates such as ten-goal polo star Tommy Hitchcock, Jr., who died in World War II and was married to a Mellon, or Jamie Niven, son of actor David Niven, or Jeffrey Byers, the late son-in-law of William Paley, or Count Andreis von Bismarck.

The Petropouloses (the name was first changed to Peterson—son of Peter—by his father's older brother) followed the Union Pacific Railroad to Kearney, Nebraska. George Petropoulos, Pete's father, came to America at age seventeen and went to work in the caboose of a freight train as a dishwasher. George Petropoulos skimped and saved and asked relatives to arrange a marriage to a fellow immigrant whom he had never met, Venetia Paul. Eventually, they had hoarded enough to open the Central Café, a twenty-four-hour-a-day restaurant that served everything but Greek dishes. To this day Peterson, who along with his younger brother John mopped floors and scrubbed dishes and served food, can recite from memory the daily specials—"hot beef sandwich, mashed potatoes, white bread, apple pie and all the coffee you can drink for twenty-five cents." He also remembers the Ku Klux Klan parading in front of the Central Café with signs protesting "the Greeks."

Pete participated in a statewide competition and came in first, winning a Regents scholarship to Kearney State Teachers College. He stayed one year, excelling in math. In 1944 he volunteered for the Navy, but with 20/450 vision, he flunked the physical examination. Wanting the best for their son, his parents dipped into their savings and sent him to M.I.T. Boston was his first exposure to big-city life, to culture and to great wealth. His almost two years at M.I.T. were also the occasion of his first visits to New York. Nostalgically, he still recalls the train from Boston to New York. He would take the train with a college friend, Generoso Pope, who would invite him to stay with his family at their sumptuous 1040 Fifth Avenue apartment. The Pope family, which owned a cement company and *Il Progresso*, unofficially adopted the boy from Nebraska, taking him to Radio City Music Hall for the first time, to the opera, to Sulka's, where he marveled at the silk ties and shirts. Since Peterson was too poor to travel back to Nebraska, the Popes invited him to stay for Christmas and gave him gifts as if he were part of the family. The bond between Peterson and Pope was strengthened by their common immigrant past. "We used to joke about being immigrants," says Peterson.

Although Peterson transferred to Northwestern after a year and a half because he wished to attend a business school and study retailing, to this day he and Generoso Pope, who is the publisher of the sensational tabloid, the *National Enquirer,* among other ventures, remain friends. A special bond was formed, Peterson says, because both men are parents of a retarded child. And soon after Peterson left Washington in 1973, Pope retained Lehman to serve as his investment banker. He also asked Peterson to serve as his personal financial adviser and the co-executor of his estate, tasks for which he paid him about $75,000 annually through mid-1984.*

After graduating summa cum laude from Northwestern in 1947, Peterson worked in Chicago, earning $12,000 a year at Market Facts, Inc., a market research company; at night he studied marketing at the University of Chicago, graduating with an M.B.A. in five quarters. He married Dorothy Krengel and joined the University of Chicago faculty as a $5,600-a-year associate professor, teaching

*Peterson abrogated this financial arrangement in September 1984, soon after I asked him about his ties to Pope. He remains an executor of the Pope estate, although he says he now refuses to accept a fee for this. Concerned about appearances, he insists that he has never had anything to do with the *Enquirer* itself. That is not quite the case. As an investment banker, he has represented the *Enquirer* in business negotiations. And Peterson concedes that when Pope was searching for an attorney who knew publishing, he recommended his own attorney, Morton Janklow, to serve as counsel to the newspaper, a position Janklow's firm still holds.

nights while continuing to work days for Market Facts. A few years later he moved to McCann-Erickson in Chicago as a market researcher. Within a brief span, after pitching and luring such new accounts as Peter Pan Peanut Butter, Swift, and Rival Dog Food, Peterson was managing McCann's Chicago office.

By the age of twenty-seven, Peterson was divorced from his first wife and had married Sally Hornbogen, a small, vivacious woman who would eventually bear him five children. They moved to a fashionable house in Kenilworth, a Chicago suburb, where they became tennis partners of neighbors Loraine and Charles Percy, then president of Bell & Howell, one of Peterson's advertising accounts. In those days, before television came to dominate our lives, before German and Japanese cameras crowded the market, Bell & Howell was a more visible company than it is now. Its movie cameras were a household name. Spurred by Peterson, Bell & Howell sponsored Edward R. Morrow's *CBS Reports.*

Peterson enjoyed advertising, but he was becoming restive. He and Percy talked often of the future. Percy dreamed of running for public office, Peterson of running a corporation. "I saw in him qualities that went far beyond advertising," says Percy, who urged him to become Bell & Howell's executive vice president for marketing. One day Peterson accepted. In 1961, at the age of thirty-four, Peterson ascended to the presidency of this corporation of 13,000 employees. After Percy decided to enter politics, running unsuccessfully for governor of Illinois in 1964, and then successfully for the United States Senate in 1966, Peterson succeeded him as CEO. "He got into a lot of details at the company," recalls Percy. "Pete particularly liked working with the engineering department. He liked to think in terms of a product that didn't exist. He brought a great deal of thought to the simplification of photography." As the head of one of Chicago's major employers, a friend of the governor's and both senators, a trustee of the University of Chicago, a lover and patron of modern art, Pete and his wife Sally became a socially prominent couple in the Windy City.

In December 1970, George Shultz, a former colleague and former Dean at the University of Chicago, who was then serving as Director of the Office of Management and Budget, telephoned from the White House to say that President Nixon wished to see him. When they met, in early 1971, Nixon offered Peterson a position as Assistant to the President for International Economic Affairs. Peterson accepted. "The challenge there," says Peterson, "was that there wasn't even a definition of the problem." The dollar was overvalued. Productivity was declining. Energy costs were soaring. The NATO alliance was riven with disagreements. United States economic supremacy was being challenged. Trade agreements with the East beckoned. The State Department was not focused on international finance, and National Security Adviser Henry Kissinger was preoccupied with other matters, including a miserable war in Vietnam.

Peterson supervised the principal staff work leading to the replacement of the international gold standard with a floating exchange rate. Working with Kissinger, he helped prepare for the Nixon-Brezhnev Summit of 1972, and chaired important trade negotiations with the Soviet Union, Poland and Japan. In the first volume of his memoirs, *White House Years,* Henry Kissinger says of Peterson's appointment:

> I agreed enthusiastically when, at OMB Director George Shultz's urging, the new post of Assistant to the President for International Economic Affairs was created at the White House—though it technically represented a diminution of my power. Peter Peterson, its first incumbent, and I established a close working relationship reinforced by personal friendship. Peterson, equipped with a subtle and wide-ranging mind, taught me a great deal about international economics; I respected him enormously, and this was another reason why I intervened rarely and only when an overwhelming foreign policy interest seemed involved. The arrangement worked well until the frontal assault on the White House staff system by the new Secretary of Treasury, John Connally . . . He refused to send memoranda through or receive instructions from him; if he needed White House guidance, he simply crossed the street from the Treasury and went to the Oval Office . . . He had reduced Peterson to the role of a spectator even before Nixon ended Peterson's agony by appointing him Secretary of Commerce, a position he filled with great distinction.

Peterson may have had difficulties within the government, but in status-conscious Washington he was in orbit. Sally and Pete Peterson became, along with Kissinger, among the few Nixon Administration luminaries who accepted invitations to Georgetown parties and who dared dine at the home of Washington *Post* publisher Katharine Graham. Peterson counted among his friends columnists and senators who opposed Nixon, he played tennis with Art Buchwald and Robert McNamara, he was usually available to the media, including those Nixon considered "enemies." The flatness of the terrain made Peterson stand even taller.

Peterson was immeasurably aided by Sally's lively personality. The Petersons often gave dinners and "movie parties," courtesy of their Bell & Howell cameras, dispensing popcorn to guests. To this day, people in Washington can remember the irreverent statements the irrepressible Sally would make about Nixon during Watergate, the way she would puncture with a joke a pompous statement from Pete. When they speak of Peterson it is usually of "Sally and Pete." What is often remembered about Pete is that he was the rare Nixon Cabinet member who would deign to come to their homes and talk freely. Ever the rationalist, he believed one tried to reason with adversaries. Besides, the power structure of the Washington colony would persist long after the stone-faced Republicans in the White House were gone.

Six months into the second Nixon Administration, Peterson was looking for work. His turf battles with Connally had persisted, as the Secretary of the Treasury, often with success, fought to cut the Secretary of Commerce out of the economic decision-making process. In addition, Peterson's social friends irritated the White House. "Pete was canned because he was a leaker," says one member of Nixon's Cabinet who remains a friend of his. Peterson offered this explanation to friends: "My calves were so fat I couldn't even click my heels." He remembers once playing tennis at the home of Katharine Graham, whose husband Phil had been a fellow trustee at the University of Chicago. The phone rang; it was Nixon calling for his Secretary of Commerce. Soon thereafter, Peterson recalls: "I remember meeting the President one day and he said to me, 'That's an interesting idea. I suspect it's an idea your friends of the Georgetown cocktail set like.' " Peterson says he would tell Nixon's aides, "By being with those people, Henry and I can debate them." To no avail. The Nixon Administration, wanting to remove him from Washington, proffered a major post in Europe. Peterson declined, deciding that he'd like to come to New York and explore investment banking, where he might amass the fortune that had so far eluded him.

"Ehrman was the guy who had the idea to bring Pete in," recalls Andrew Sage. Ehrman, who was then sixty-seven, visited with Peterson and arranged for him to meet with key partners, including George Ball, Lucius Clay, Paul Davies, Warren Hellman and Lew Glucksman. Glucksman recalls: "Fred Ehrman sprang on Warren Hellman and me the fact that he was recruiting Pete Peterson as vice chairman. Warren and I both went through the roof. It certainly wasn't a promotion for Warren or me. Fred was doing a lousy job. Pete had no particular qualifications to be brought in as vice chairman."

Glucksman and Peterson first met for dinner at Warren Hellman's home. Hellman, who remains a friend of Peterson's, has a different recollection. "Pete had a good reputation. Everyone was enthusiastic about his coming to the firm."

Before agreeing to the Lehman offer, Peterson seriously considered becoming a senior partner at Salomon Brothers. For this surging Wall Street partnership, whose reputation and expertise were concentrated in trading, the acquisition of Peterson was seen as a way to strengthen the banking, or corporate, side of their business. "He would have been number three in the pecking order," says Salomon managing partner John Gutfreund, who interviewed Peterson. The firm made it clear that Peterson would stand behind Billie Salomon and then Gutfreund and that Peterson would not be permitted to sit on any corporate boards, a Salomon Brothers policy. Since corporate boards are a source of clients and outside compensation, and since he would rank below a shrewd, powerful trader like Gutfreund at a firm dominated by trading, Peterson chose Lehman.

Peterson joined Lehman on June 6, 1973. Two months later he was chairman. "Lehman at that time was a mess," says Felix Rohatyn, who had administered Peterson's blind trust during his federal service and whose banking firm, Lazard Frères, worked for Bell & Howell. "They wanted Pete to help settle the place down and at the same time establish corporate relationships. He took over the firm and in a short time he did an absolutely brilliant job."

When he took over, Peterson was stunned to discover that Lehman was run like a candy store and appalled that partners spoke of "my clients," as if they would remain so forever. The firm did not have departmental budgets; even while they were losing money, partners were spending lavishly on the best hotels, the most expensive restaurants, and justifying it by quoting Bobbie Lehman: "At Lehman we go first class." The pace was leisurely, reflecting the firm's very own Italian Renaissance-style building, Bobbie Lehman's splendid art collection, which graced the walls, the mahogany desks and crackling fireplaces, the private gym and masseur, the elegant eighth-floor dining room supervised by Mathum Allanos, the former Pavillon chef. Lehman functioned as if corporate titans were still dependent on "my banker."

Peterson remembers arriving at Lehman in June and being advised to meet with Joe Thomas. Although by this time Thomas had stepped down as chairman, he remained an influential figure at the firm. On this day president Warren Hellman told Peterson that Thomas was up in the eleventh-floor health club. Peterson had heard the legends of Thomas's swashbuckling exploits, of how he raised the first capital that breathed life into Litton Industries, of how he fathered American Export Lines, Halliburton Industries, served on the board of Black & Decker, Getty Oil, Litton and other major companies, collected more substantial bonuses than most of his partners, and now owned more Lehman stock than any other partner. He had heard that Thomas was a rugged individualist who thought the New York *Times* was a left-wing newspaper and only read the New York *Daily News* and the *Daily Racing Form*, who invested in thoroughbred horses and Caribbean property.

"I didn't even know where the health club was," says Peterson, who went upstairs in search of Thomas. Entering the gym that morning he saw only a man stretched out naked on a massage table, clear plastic tubes connecting his nostrils to an oxygen tank. In one hand the naked man held a lit cigar and in the other a glass of vodka. A *Daily Racing Form* rested on his ample stomach. A television set was blaring. And Don Cannon, the masseur, was on the phone with a bookie placing the man's bets. Warren Hellman remembers that Peterson wandered back downstairs and said, "I didn't see anyone up there except a guy with two oxygen tubes, a cigar and a martini." Peterson remembers that he and Thomas had a nice chat, although he also remembers nervously glancing at the lit cigar and the combustible oxygen tank.

Within a year, Peterson slashed expenses—paring, for example, the number of employees by a third, from 955 on September 30, 1973, to 663 the following September. The new chairman had his eye on the competition, and at that time Lehman counted ten firms as its chief banking rivals—Kidder, Peabody; Salomon Brothers; First Boston Corporation; Lazard Frères; A. G. Becker; Merrill Lynch; Morgan Stanley; Goldman, Sachs; Dillon, Read; and Halsey, Stuart.

Peterson also had his eye on Lehman's internal weaknesses, which were delineated for the new chairman in a confidential hundred-and-one-page report that the board commissioned from two partners, Kenneth Lipper and Joseph J. Gal. Completed in December 1973, and stamped "Most Confidential," the report highlighted these "significant weaknesses": (1) "the lack of a carefully defined business strategy"; (2) "a fragmented and undisciplined approach to running its business"; (3) "a portion of the partnership whose ability, training, and/or work habits are inconsistent with the competitive demands of the marketplace and with Lehman's present business"; (4) "too small a professional staff relative to the number of clients to be serviced and transactions to be processed"; (5) "a bond distribution system which is in chaos and an equity distribution system which is experiencing declining market share"; (6) "recent management changes throughout the organization"; (7) "high overhead relative to current revenue levels"; (8) "comparatively limited capital." The authors warned that "in our judgment the long-term future of this firm is uncertain."

"The Firm must face up to the fact that the ability, training, and/or work habits of a substantial number of partners (totaling perhaps 10 to 15 throughout the Firm) are inconsistent with the competitive demands of the marketplace and with that expected of Lehman partners," the authors concluded. "These individuals should be phased out according to some specific plan. *The single most important conclusion of this study is that the quality of the partnership is the key to our present problems and to our ability to be successful in the future* [their italics]."

Peterson was determined to phase out some partners and to reinvigorate the forty-four-man partnership with new blood. But he was sensitive to how fragile the partnership was, and he moved slowly. It wasn't until September 1976 that he replaced seven senior members of the board, reducing the average age of the board from fifty-six to forty-seven years. After his friend Warren Hellman left in 1977 to start his own venture capital firm, Peterson left the presidency vacant.

To address the composition of the partnership required Peterson to confront a strategic question: What kind of investment bank did Lehman wish to be? With remarkable prescience, the internal report had sketched how investment banking had changed, and was likely to change further: "As the nation industrialized, financing was the most important element of corporate life, since shortages of goods created demand which eliminated marketing as the key feature. Few of the inventor-entrepreneur class understood how to raise capital; they had limited contacts with financial institutions and knew of only the handful of investment banking firms whom they could solicit to assist them in the critical function of raising capital . . . Personal contacts, imaginations, salesmanship and an entrepreneurial orientation were important characteristics of successful investment bankers.

"The maturation of American industry, professionalism among the new management class and the development of broad capital markets reversed some of the above factors, at least on a superficial basis. The major corporate names which Lehman Brothers desires as clients are now solicited, not soliciting, parties. Marketing and high-technology operations have replaced finance as the elements of major concern to chief executives and much of the latter has been delegated to skilled financial vice presidents. These professionals often design their own issues and view the investment banker simply as a distributor. Therefore, many of Lehman's traditionally high-margin products have been reduced to commodities, where price and distribution are more important in selecting a banker than historic and social relationships."

What was called for, Lipper and Gal suggested, was a less passive Lehman strategy, one that recognized that Lehman could not remain a carriage-trade banking house. To prosper, the firm had to broaden the financial services it offered. This strategic view perfectly coincided with that of the new chairman, who quickly saw that Lehman had been resting on its laurels. While others questioned whether this stranger to Wall Street knew enough about banking, Pete Peterson believed that his corporate background prepared him for the task ahead. He had been trained to think strategically, to prepare organization charts and marketing plans, to devise and sell "new products." The challenge excited him.

But first he had to address the capital question, from which all else flowed. In 1974, with the assistance of George Ball, and despite internal resistance from Bob Rubin and a few others who believed Peterson's plan would alter the private nature of the Lehman partnership, Peterson persuaded the world's thirty-fifth largest bank, Banca Commerciale Italiana (BCI) of Milan, to invest $7 million in Lehman Brothers in exchange for 15 percent of the firm's stock. As part of this package, Peterson presented a dramatic cost-cutting plan, including a slashed payroll and reduced partners' salaries. In subsequent years, in addition to luring BCI to invest further capital, Peterson would also engineer two significant mergers, first with Abraham & Company, a brokerage firm, and then the more momentous 1977 merger with prestigious Kuhn Loeb and its blue chip clients. In the decade of Peterson's stewardship, Lehman's capital multiplied ten times.

Besides the capital, strategic and overhead crises, another crisis confronting Peterson in these early days involved Lew Glucksman. Investment banking had been changing, from a business based in large measure on personal relationships and advice to a business based on a variety of transactions and an instinct for gambling on interest rates and stock market shifts and the invention of new financial instruments. Clients began to explore a variety of financial tools; they shopped for the firm with the broadest sales distribution network, the most experience, the cheapest price. One of those new financing tools was commercial paper, a "product" pioneered a hundred years before, but not widely used until it was popularized in the United States by Gustave Levy at Goldman, Sachs, which today handles about 30 percent of the $220 billion or so of dealer commercial paper outstanding.

Commercial paper works the same way it did when Goldman invented it: Instead of borrowing from a bank or the bond market, a company issues an unsecured IOU, usually repayable in thirty days, sometimes longer. (The company can also "roll over," or renew, the loan on different terms.) Investment firms like Goldman, Sachs and Lehman typically act as agent, collecting a fee for placing these IOU's with large investors. They can also serve an underwriting function, taking some of the paper into their own accounts to help provide the funds sought by a client.

Commercial paper was one of several "new products," as Wall Street calls them, which had been gaining wide popularity since the early sixties, along with money market accounts, tax exempt bonds, bankers acceptances, among others. To serve their clients and to tap into huge brokerage fees, traditional investment banking houses had begun to diversify and offer these "new products." Lehman was no exception. And thus it was that Bobbie Lehman hired Lew Glucksman to take charge of these operations. When Peterson became chairman of Lehman, Lew Glucksman had already been there for more than a decade.

L EWIS GLUCKSMAN WAS RAISED ON MANHATTAN'S UPPER West Side, in more comfortable surroundings than Pete Peterson enjoyed in Kearney, Nebraska. His parents, unlike Peterson's, were both born in America, the children of Hungarian Jews.* His mother, Zipporah, cared for a series of West End Avenue apartments (they moved frequently) as well as the three children, of whom Lewis was the second. His father, Jack Glucksman, owned a factory that assembled table lamps, and though he lacked a college education the senior Glucksman was well traveled in search of marble for his lamps. The family was not rich, but had enough money to own an automobile in 1939, a considerable luxury at the time. Lewis graduated with about a ninety average from DeWitt Clinton high school in 1941 at the age of fifteen, though he failed one course: analytic geometry. His father knew a Congressman from Indiana who urged him to send Lewis to Indiana University. After a brief visit Jack Glucksman agreed. Lewis stayed a year, but because transportation from New York to Indiana was difficult during the war, Glucksman transferred to the College of William and Mary, a school that now claims him as a loyal member of its board of visitors. He also serves on the board of sponsors of its business school.

On his seventeenth birthday, Glucksman lied about his age and enlisted in the Navy, where he served on a submarine chaser in the Atlantic. The Navy, he says, taught him that loyalty begets loyalty, up and down the line. It also aroused a lifelong interest in both naval warfare and marine life. Glucksman was released from the Navy a lieutenant in June 1946 and returned to William and Mary that fall, where he changed his major from pre-med to accounting.

With a liberal arts and accounting degree, in 1947 Glucksman migrated to Wall Street, where he first went to work as a credit reporter with Dun & Bradstreet. He then held a series of other unsatisfactory jobs. Restless, he enrolled nights at New York University's Business School, receiving an M.B.A. in finance in 1951. He credits the years at N.Y.U. with opening his "intellectual horizons"; his gratitude is evident through his service as an N.Y.U. trustee and his sponsorship of the L. Glucksman Institute for Research in Securities Markets at the N.Y.U. Graduate School of Business Administration.

In 1952, Glucksman became a securities analyst at A. G. Becker,

---

*Initially, Glucksman suggested that his family lived more modestly than was the case. After the *Times* pieces appeared, I asked him if there were any inaccuracies. He said his father actually owned the factory I had been led to believe he merely worked in.

a Wall Street investment bank. He left to become an arbitrageur—purchasing securities, commodities or currency in one market and selling them at a better price in another market—for L. F. Rothschild in 1954. During his four years at Rothschild, Glucksman met and married Inez Salinger, who worked as an editor at a book publishing company. He returned to Becker in 1958, as co-manager of its new commercial paper business. At that time, he recalls, only Goldman, Sachs was in this business, and Becker was so determined to catch up that they offered Glucksman a percentage of the profits. Within five years he says he built a $1 billion-plus business, pioneered new commercial paper products, and was earning up to $2 million annually.

Bobbie Lehman was jealous of Becker's commercial paper operation and of Gus Levy's successes at Goldman. It bothered him that his clients went to Goldman or Becker to issue and trade paper. Although there was resistance to forming a trading facility at Lehman, resistance to hiring the "pushy" Glucksman, as some referred to him, and reluctance to raid another firm—it was then considered ungentlemanly—Bobbie hired Lew Glucksman and much of his Becker team in 1962 to launch Lehman Commercial Paper, Inc. Glucksman says Lehman offered him 10 percent ownership of the subsidiary in return for an investment of $35,000.

Glucksman felt he had arrived. "From my kind of background," he says, "Lehman epitomized a level of success in banking that was not generally available. They were the pillars. You looked upon Lehman as the furthest you could go."

Glucksman's rise at Lehman was swift. He became a partner in 1967, one of only a handful of nonbanking partners. He was placed in charge of all money market and trading activities in 1969, elevated to the board in 1971, and to the executive committee in 1972; by 1981 he was president and chief operating officer, and most Lehman managers reported to him. Glucksman's rise coincided with the ascendancy of trading at Lehman and on Wall Street in general. In 1975 the fixed income and securities divisions at Lehman provided $18.5 million of Lehman's pre-tax and pre-bonus profits; by 1983 this number had soared to $127.4 million. And by 1983, Lehman's securities trading and distribution functions employed 1,863 people. Begun as an appendage to banking, by 1983 trading and distribution accounted for more than two-thirds of Lehman's profits.

The firm Glucksman joined included many talented individuals who liked to celebrate their "entrepreneurial spirit," their ability to "get tough deals done." However, even then some partners complained, as partners would later, that Lehman was too entrepreneurial, too loosely managed, too narrowly preoccupied with individual rather than team success. "Lehman Brothers was a culture of the virtuoso," observes Joseph Thomas's son, Michael, who left Lehman in 1971 and went on to become a successful author. "Lehman Brothers was like the New York Philharmonic: great musicians who are impossible to conduct."

At Lehman, in the ten years Peterson presided, bonuses hinged largely on seniority and on profits that they as *individuals* claimed or were given credit for, rather than on a fixed percentage of the *firm's* overall profits for a two-year period, as is the practice among the seventy-three partners at Goldman, Sachs. At Morgan Stanley all seventy-six partners are on the board of directors, and meet monthly. Lehman, with its looser structure, placed a premium on the individual rather than on the team. For years there was no central filing system. Partners tended to hoard their clients. Lehman board deliberations were cloaked in secrecy, and for the last year of its life as a private partnership no minutes were kept of board meetings. Even as late as 1982, when Glucksman and Peterson wanted to get rid of the executive committee, they did not have an open dialogue or even make an announcement; they simply abrogated it by no longer inviting members to meet. Lehman's corporate culture, many say, was poisoned by an every-man-for-himself ethos. Personal ambition and greed are essential to the success of a banking firm, but other qualities contribute to success, including teamwork, leadership, strong management, luck, a common tradition or culture. The knock on Lehman Brothers was that it placed too much emphasis on individual greed—"blood money," former partner Eric Gleacher calls it —and too little emphasis on common purpose. As long as profits expanded, partners worked together, were willing to suffer the cruelest indignities. In bad times, as Fred Ehrman learned, authority dissolved because it was not bound by anything but individual greed.

Few Lehman partners disagree that the highly individualistic Lehman culture attracted great talent and also great problems. But by common consent, the one Lehman division that had enjoyed a corporate sense of teamwork was Glucksman's commercial paper division. Yves-André Istel, who was a senior international banker at Lehman, had his share of run-ins with Glucksman, and ultimately left for First Boston in the fall of 1983. Nevertheless, Istel described Glucksman's operations this way: "Commercial paper—which was Glucksman—

was the best managed, had the best esprit de corps, and was the best run—almost a separate company. That may have been the best part of Lehman in terms of the way it was managed, the way it thought of itself, and in terms of quality of operation."

IN 1973, THE YEAR PETERSON JOINED THE FIRM, GLUCKSMAN HAD built the commercial paper division to a hundred and nineteen employees, but that year the bond market collapsed. The commercial paper division sustained stunning losses. A Lehman internal audit found that by the summer of 1973 the "aggregate dollar amount positioned for speculation" by Lehman Commercial Paper had reached $496 million; Glucksman was investing Lehman's own capital in certificates of deposit and other commercial paper, rather than just selling this paper to investors. The memo also said Glucksman's operation "had an unrealized market loss at July 31, 1973, of about $6.7 million." Glucksman, like other traders, had been playing his hunches, betting that interest rates would drop. If they did, Lehman would realize massive gains from its commercial paper holdings and from New York State Housing Finance Agency notes Lehman had also invested in. Instead, rates rose, cutting sharply into the value of Lehman's bulging portfolio. Nor was Lehman the only firm to suffer trading losses at this time. Even such a premier trading house as Salomon Brothers turned in a $6.6 million loss for the year ending September 30, 1973.

This did not still the cry for Glucksman's scalp among the forty-four partners, most of whom were in the banking department (by late 1973, the commercial paper division included only three partners). Fred Ehrman was determined, says George Ball, "to kick Glucksman out of the firm because of the losses." Several of the senior partners—including Paul Davies, Lucius Clay and Herman Kahn—thought the overweight trader with the stains on his tie was "crude." Herman Kahn couldn't shake the memory of how Glucksman had spoken in the presence of "the golden bull," as he called Bobbie Lehman: "He was obscene to the point that one time I went to him and said, 'You don't say, "*I don't give a rat's ass!*" in front of Bobbie Lehman.'" Glucksman could feel the pressure building, but few partners spoke to him about their unhappiness. The Lehman way was to whisper, to form cabals. "Glucksman told me we had to sever our relationship because Ehrman was after him and he didn't want it to hurt me," recalls banker Eric Gleacher, one of Glucksman's few friends on the banking side. Gleacher ignored the advice, as did senior banking partner James Glanville, a member of the board who enjoyed challenging the powers-that-be at Lehman.

The partner who saved Glucksman's scalp was Pete Peterson. By August, Peterson had taken Ehrman's place and championed Glucksman, saying that the person who had the ability to dig them out of the hole they were in was the very person who had helped get them in it. Peterson dispatched Bob Rubin, a banking partner whom everyone conceded was brilliant, "to watch Lew and work with him," remembers Peterson.

Rubin, who became a partner the same year as Glucksman, came to believe that Glucksman had been used as a "scapegoat" by bankers. He says Glucksman had sent regular memos to Ehrman and others, informing them of his decisions, and they were not challenged. Peterson has a different recollection, saying that Ehrman and Warren Hellman, the president, were "shocked by the losses" and that his own file contained no such memoranda from Glucksman. Hellman agrees with Peterson that he received no warning memos. But he also affirms Rubin's position: "I don't remember any memoranda from Lew. On the other hand, if you read the monthly gray book carefully, you could have picked up that Lehman's government bond inventory was going up and up. The information was available."

Glucksman's feeling that he had been victimized was confirmed by Rubin, and Rubin would become Glucksman's best friend at the firm, the financial whiz who could digest and poke holes in Glucksman's brilliant financing schemes, the cautious adviser who slowed him down, who tempered his intuitive judgments with a cold eye, the fiercely private man who shared Glucksman's view of *them*. To this day Glucksman remembers Rubin's role in saving his neck, not Peterson's. To Glucksman, Rubin was unlike many bankers in that he did not automatically hate all traders. Rubin was a loyal friend.

Under Peterson, Glucksman made a comeback. With Peterson concentrating on cost cutting, raising new capital, recruiting new business, crafting a full-service corporate plan and a marketing strategy, and selling Lehman to the outside world, Glucksman concentrated on rebuilding and expanding the firm's trading capacities. By 1975, Lehman was in the black again, earning $24 million, pre-tax and pre-bonuses; and only one-quarter of these profits were generated by the banking department. "Glucksman was this mad genius type," says former Lehman partner Kenneth Lipper. "He built this entire department in defiance of his environment. Of all the people at Lehman Brothers, Glucksman is the only one you could describe as a hero. He was a one-dimensional person. But his one dimension was so unique that he stood out. That was his greatness, and his destruction. He was a tormented person. He believed he was as good as anyone around him. And because he thought *they* wouldn't accept him, he was going to beat them down."

By November 1975, Pete Peterson appeared alone on the cover of *Business Week,* looking off into the distance. The cover story was entitled: "Back from the Brink Comes Lehman Bros."

D URING THE TEN YEARS IN WHICH THEIR LIVES CROSSED AT Lehman, the relationship between Peterson and Glucksman was an odd one. On a personal level they were never intimates. Except for a drink they had together at Oscar's Delmonico in 1973, when Peterson was deciding whether to join Lehman—Glucksman can recite the time and the place—for the next ten years they never dined or shared a drink alone. When Peterson married Joan Ganz Cooney in 1980, a few Lehman friends were invited to the small ceremony presided over by the Greek Archbishop, including part-time advisory directors George Ball and James Schlesinger, a former Cabinet colleague; Lew Glucksman and the other members of the executive committee were invited only to the Cosmopolitan Club reception.

Their galaxies were distinct. Peterson was a prominent Republican whose friends included Henry Kissinger, William Paley, Katharine Graham, Barbara Walters, Brooke Astor, the Rockefellers; he sat on six prestigious corporate boards; he owned a ten-room apartment overlooking the East River in Manhattan's exclusive River House, its walls covered with his extensive modern art collection, which includes works by De Kooning, Henry Moore, Rothko and Richard Hunt. Art books cover the coffee tables, and in the den the bookshelves are crammed with works on current affairs. Peterson, like Glucksman, rises at dawn, not to meet with his team but to dictate into a machine in his office; when he arrives in the office after a business breakfast, he expects that teams of secretaries will have his dictation transcribed. Now Peterson is chauffeured about in a dark, four-door Oldsmobile,* and keeps a $45,000 slate-blue two-seat Porsche 928 with a sunroof in the driveway of an expansive home overlooking Georgica Pond in East Hampton.

Lew Glucksman, on the other hand, boasts of being a Harry Truman Democrat (who nevertheless voted for Reagan) and of owning the American car of a client (Chrysler). At Lehman he rose early and mingled with members of "my team," as he called them; he sat on just one corporate board (Revlon), devoting his outside energies to serving as a principal fundraiser for New York Hospital, to helping New York University, William and Mary College, and to fulfilling his obligations as chairman of the finance committee and director, until December 1984, of the Port Authority of New York and New Jersey. His walls are covered with pictures of clipper ships, navigational charts of the Florida Keys, and paintings of fish; his bookshelves are dominated by histories of maritime battles, studies of marine life, and tool catalogues, although he can surprise associates by suddenly bringing up the work of Joyce Carol Oates and other contemporary novelists. Unlike Peterson, whose East Hampton home is shielded from the road by tall pine trees and tasteful landscaping, Glucksman's former home in nearby Three Mile Harbor had a flag out front for all to see: DON'T TREAD ON ME.

When Glucksman reveals his true feelings, he can be remarkably blunt. When Fred Ehrman died not long after he was booted out as Lehman's chairman, and partners huddled to express sorrow and offer tributes, Glucksman would have none of it. "Let's not be hypocrites, gentlemen!" he snapped.

Although Peterson saved Glucksman's job at Lehman in 1973, tensions between the two men rose over the next five years. Peterson thought of Glucksman as a ferociously "volatile," sometimes brutish man. Tales came back to him of Glucksman throwing a telephone at partner Allan Kaplan (Kaplan and Glucksman deny it, though other partners remember him throwing a telephone and once shoving

---

*At Lehman, Peterson also had an Oldsmobile.

Kaplan against an elevator wall), of Glucksman heaving a plate of
underdone fried eggs at a glass wall in his office or ripping the shirt
off his own back in a rage (Glucksman also denies all of this).
Peterson heard that Glucksman would meet with junior partners or
associates, close the door to his office, and ask them, "Will you join
my team?" There was a gulf between the two in their approach to
cost controls. "Lew, by temperament, did not really believe in building profits by reducing costs," says Peterson. Throughout his years
at Lehman, Peterson would send a stream of memos to his managers,
including Glucksman, demanding cost containment, urging "a firm-
wide review on where we can cut expenses," asking for reports on
"break-even levels of the firm by division," proposing to determine
"measurements of output per man." Glucksman, on the other hand,
believed profits were best generated by expanding business, which
meant confronting every opportunity and having ample staff to do
this. In other words, by taking risks. Peterson also wanted to expand
and branch out, but more cautiously. To Glucksman this telegraphed: "Pete wanted to cut back. I didn't think we could remain
a nine-hundred-man firm. I was willing to put more money back into
the business." Glucksman envisioned pulling even with, if not over-
taking, Goldman, Sachs and Salomon Brothers in trading.

It bothered the chairman that Glucksman joined bankers like
Robert Rubin in criticizing the merger he engineered with Kuhn
Loeb in 1977. "I was not that enthusiastic about it," admits Glucksman. "As a student of mergers, my belief is that this merger was not
a good one." Lehman, he felt, paid too much for too little: "You got
no additional foreign business, which we needed." The negotiations,
conducted by Harvey Krueger, president of Kuhn Loeb, and Rubin,
head of Lehman's banking division, were protracted and often bitter.
Each time they broke down, Peterson stepped in to rescue them. He
came to feel that Rubin, perhaps aided by Glucksman, was trying to
kill the merger. "For reasons totally unclear to me," says Peterson,
"Rubin and a few others were trying to sabotage the acquisition."
When the negotiations concluded, Peterson replaced Rubin with
Kuhn Loeb's Krueger as chief of the banking department, which
displeased Glucksman.

Added to these business disagreements between Peterson and
Glucksman was the bad chemistry at Lehman and throughout Wall
Street between bankers and traders. Ten or twenty years ago sales
and trading supported banking, offering supplemental services to
banking clients; in recent years, as interest rates have fluctuated

wildly and new financial products have blossomed, sales and trading have become a profit center in their own right, accounting for hefty portions of the profits of most major investment banking firms. The new volatile environment has pushed bankers and traders to work more closely together, forming hybrid functions—like capital markets groups, teams of bankers who work on the trading floor and provide companies with the latest menu of financing possibilities.

This transactional environment has transformed banking as well as expanded the importance of trading functions. The spotlight, for example, now shines on a new group of bankers, the merger and acquisition, or M. & A., specialists, who have more in common with traders than with traditional bankers. Like commandos dropped behind enemy lines, they have become celebrated warriors. "These were different guys," observes Martin Lipton, a lawyer prominent in the takeover game. "They were more aggressive, much more transactional-oriented. They were dealing with a different commodity. They were dealing in war. Up until 1974 and the International Nickel Company's offer to buy the Electric Storage Battery Company, none of these firms were involved in hostile takeovers." Although International Nickel won an extended bidding war, the deal turned out to be a financial disappointment. The legacy of the deal is that it became a landmark. Prior to this date, blue chip companies did not become raiders, and top investment banks did not get involved in initiating hostile takeovers. Investment bankers and most corporations considered hostile takeovers unethical.

The banking world has changed. Nevertheless, the war of stereotypes between bankers and traders persists. "It's like cowmen and farmers in the West," observes Andrew Sage, Lehman's most senior partner in terms of service. Traders are often caricatured as poorly educated drones with digital minds, robots hunched over their Quotron and Telerate screens, crudely barking orders, thinking for the moment, not the longer term. Bankers, in turn, are often cartooned as elitists, as Ivy League preppies in suspenders who rise late, take long lunches and, like salesmen, massage contacts but do not produce a product.

This polarization was particularly acute at the House of Lehman, where—unlike Goldman, Sachs or Salomon Brothers—there was no history of significant trading prior to Glucksman's arrival in the early sixties. "It was evident in the way Lehman set up its commercial paper division," observes Robert Rubin. "It was set up as a corporation, even though we were a partnership. People were afraid of it. They tried to isolate themselves from risk. They set up Lehman Commercial Paper, Inc., with only $350,000 of capital." In 1971, to protect partners from personal liability in case of lawsuits or bankruptcy, the firm was officially incorporated in the state of Maryland. The partners, of course, still owned the business, but risked no personal exposure.

At Lehman, trading and banking functions were kept physically distinct. Until 1980, when the Lehman offices were finally consolidated at 55 Water Street, the trading operation was actually located in a different building from the House of Lehman at One William Street. Glucksman, who was then working out of 55 Water Street, pushed hard for the firm to consolidate into one modern headquarters, where there would be room to expand. "Pete and I almost came to blows because he didn't want to move to 55 Water Street," recalls Glucksman. Peterson awards himself more credit: "The toughest decision I had to make was the move to Water Street in 1980. The investment bankers hated that. They didn't want anything to do with that group. They found them a lower form of species. They were the elite. Those guys over there were referred to as 'animals,' as 'crude,' as 'short-term.' " The decision to move was finally made in 1977, and when it was made Peterson left little doubt as to who deserved the credit. He gave Glucksman a pen and pencil set, inscribed: TO LEW GLUCKSMAN, "FATHER" OF 55 WATER STREET.

Though Peterson strove to appear evenhanded, Lew Glucksman could not have been pleased to read the July 31, 1974, issue of *Financial World,* in which Peterson said: "My understanding of the great successes of this company and its creative contribution to banking is that the essence of this firm has been in creative entrepreneurial work and not in other areas such as trading, etc. There are plenty of very good people who do that job very well." Peterson's attitude was not lost on Glucksman, who noticed that the chairman rarely ventured onto the trading floor, didn't mingle with trading or distribution people, had lunched only once with a key trader and fellow board member, Richard S. Fuld, Jr.; the chairman volunteered to people that he also knew little about trading, an attitude that Glucksman felt communicated disdain. So vexed was Glucksman that he began to visit headhunters to explore leaving Lehman.

Peterson had his own vexations. He was troubled that Glucksman was a friend and ally of board and executive committee member James Glanville, a Texan who headed Lehman's energy business and who openly disparaged Peterson. Glanville, who had become a partner in 1961, led the opposition within Lehman to Peterson's new marketing plans and "new product" memos and to his vision of transforming Lehman into a full-service firm. When Peterson began to accept Glucksman's position about consolidating the firm under one larger roof, which would mean abandoning their eleven-story building on William Street, Glanville led the resistance, blaming Peterson, not his friend Glucksman. To the board he stormed, "You get more space and you'll get more people. Size will be the death of the company." Glanville, whom Peterson detested, says the real reason for the push to move was that "Pete wasn't happy with the size of his office. He felt in Bobbie's shadow there. I can't emphasize enough what an ego the man has." Peterson tried to turn the other cheek, but it was difficult. In March 1977, Peterson announced that Lehman would move to 55 Water Street.

Glanville, Glucksman and Bob Rubin huddled often, sometimes mocking their solemn chairman. At meetings of the eight-member executive committee, they were often arrayed in opposition to Peterson. On the surface, the Glanville-Glucksman alliance made no sense, since Glanville was opposed to growing those parts of the business managed by Glucksman; if Glanville had his way, Lehman would remain a traditional investment banking firm. This suggests that the cement for the alliance was a common hatred of Peterson. To Peterson, no matter how much oil business Glanville brought to Lehman, he was a hater, a venomous man who thrived on rumors, cabals, acrimony. "Before coming to Lehman Brothers," recalls Peterson, "I was told the firm itself was seriously divided and Jim Glanville was at once very productive in the energy area and perhaps the most divisive and even vindictive of the partners. I found both statements to be accurate. He constantly initiated charges, sometimes serious, against individual partners . . . Glanville created dissension at the firm's most senior levels and often attempted to involve Lew in his various schemes."

Glanville's angry missives became legendary around Lehman. Once, when Glanville asked the firm to make out a $5,000 bonus check to William Loomis, who worked for him, Peterson and the executive committee resisted. Bonuses, they said, were decided by the firm, not by individual partners. On July 21, 1977, Glanville wrote a one-sentence note to Peterson: "So it is to be war." The year before, when he disagreed with decisions taken by a new select salary committee, Glanville circulated a memorandum that said, in part: "The percent increase in salaries awarded to certain members of the Committee indicates to me that they behaved with the emotional maturity of a six-year-old turned loose in a candy store." He ended the two-page, single-spaced November 16, 1976, memo with a menacing, "I would not underestimate the importance I attach to this matter."

Peterson was not the only partner who felt Glanville pumped poison into the firm. Fairly or not, a number of partners believed he was an anti-Semite, despite his friendship with Glucksman. To them, a confirming piece of evidence was a March 26, 1980, letter Glanville wrote to former Under Secretary of State George Ball after Ball published a signed article in the Washington *Post* that was critical of Israeli policy. Two years after he and three partners had left Lehman to join Lazard Frères, Glanville wrote to his former partner: "My view on U.S. relations with Israel completely in line with yours (as they should be, as I learned from you) but I doubt if they receive much sympathy from the members of your Executive Committee. The members of that Committee are overwhelmingly of one ethnic persuasion with the exception of one gentleman who found it necessary to change his name in order to disguise his heritage. This is the same Committee that exhibited such glee over the opportunity to delete four Presbyterians from their list of partners."

Glanville says, in response to charges that he is anti-Semitic, "It is the sort of typecasting you give to someone when you can't figure out what to say about them. Peterson would go around waving that letter, which is outrageous." Lew Glucksman, for one, sides with Glanville: "Over the years I had two very close friends at this firm, Bob Rubin and Jim Glanville. People have said Jim Glanville is anti-Semitic. That's bullshit! He was a guy with lots of strong opinions on every subject in the world."

Glanville and three banking partners—"The Gang of Four"—left Lehman under murky circumstances in September 1978 amid angry charges and threats of lawsuits. Peterson says he learned, and brought to the executive committee, a report that Glanville and three partners were about to enter into a secret sweetheart real estate deal with the McMoran Oil & Gas Company, a Lehman client. At the time, in addition to representing McMoran, Lehman had a $2 million investment in the company, which partners wanted to withdraw; Glanville resisted. Six of the nine members of the executive committee confirm that there was a proposed sweetheart deal. The facts appear to be as follows: In order to raise cash, McMoran decided to sell and lease back an office building and discussed this plan with several Lehman partners, including the chief of the energy department, Jim Glanville. Instead, the three partners and Glanville proposed to buy the building themselves, a proposal that they did not disclose to their partners, as was required. "I was rather shocked at it," says former executive committee member Alvin E. Friedman, who had been a partner at Kuhn Loeb. "Something like this never would have happened at Kuhn Loeb. It would have been considered a 'misuse of corporate opportunity' to siphon business from the firm to a special group." It reminded Friedman of brokerage houses in the twenties—called "bucket shops"—where partners sneaked into the office in the morning to open the mail and pocket the checks.*

The executive committee, according to Peterson, "unanimously" authorized the chairman to confront Glanville. "If the transaction goes through," Peterson remembers saying, "I have the unanimous support of the executive committee to accept your resignation." Neither Rubin nor Glucksman share Peterson's recollection. "Glanville quit, he wasn't fired," says Glucksman. "The executive committee never gave Glanville an ultimatum." Neither Glucksman nor Rubin say they recall the McMoran real estate deal.

Two-thirds of the executive committee do recall the deal. Executive committee member Harvey Krueger confirms that the committee was upset by it and did discuss Glanville's possible resignation. "We asked Pete to work out the McMoran thing with Glanville," Krueger says. However, Krueger does not "recall" authorizing Peterson to accept Glanville's resignation because, "I think Glanville had already announced he was going to Lazard." Krueger is backed by former chief administrative officer and executive committee member David G. Sacks, who says it is "untrue" that Peterson was authorized to confront Glanville. "If McMoran is what caused Jim Glanville to leave, I'd be shocked and surprised," says Sacks. Nevertheless, two-thirds of the former executive committee agree: They were distressed with Glanville and the three other partners, and did inform Glanville and the three partners of their unhappiness. They differ only on whether Glanville was given an ultimatum.

*"There was a McMoran transaction," concedes former chief administrative officer and executive committee member David G. Sacks. "There was an incident that provoked irritation," confirms former partner Yves-André Istel, who refused to discuss details of executive committee sessions. "It was a real ethical problem," says another former member of the executive committee, who requested anonymity. "Can you visualize working for a firm where each partner took clients and did deals for himself? McMoran was a firm client not a Glanville client. What he proposed to do was totally inconsistent with the moral obligations of a partner."

Glanville has a totally different recollection. He dismisses the notion that the executive committee gave him an ultimatum as "a figment of someone's imagination. This is the first I've heard that story. Peterson never talked to me." What happened, he says, is that he met one afternoon with Peterson and two senior bankers, William Morris and Harvey Krueger, and told them he planned to go to Lazard Frères. "I offered to take them to my clients so they could secure the firm's continued relationship.* The next morning I was with a client in Tulsa and Pete called. He said, 'You're out now.' "

Did Glanville urge his partners not to unload $2 million in McMoran stock? "It is not impossible that I said that," he says.

Did Glanville plan to invest in a private real estate deal? "Not that I remember," he says.

It was like a divorce, says Morris, who succeeded Glanville as head of the energy department. "Divorces always start with an agreement to split the money, and things are relatively amicable. And they go downhill from there. That's what happened." Door locks were changed, credit cards were canceled. Glanville says of Peterson, "He canceled the bonuses of my secretary and of the other secretaries who were leaving." Peterson went to see the managing director of Lazard Frères, to warn him that Glanville was poison. Glanville retained former federal judge Simon Rifkind as his attorney. Missiles camouflaged as letters were lobbed back and forth.

In the showdown between Peterson and Glanville, Lew Glucksman sided with Peterson, rupturing his friendship with Glanville. Glucksman explains, "For the good of the firm I had to support the management here."

In the end, this crisis blew over. With Glanville gone, Peterson saw an opportunity to recruit Glucksman to his management team. Despite the tension between them, Peterson never wavered in his estimation of Glucksman's financial and managerial talents. And now Peterson felt he needed those talents.

Peterson had just gone through a difficult two years, and his troubles were not over yet. In August 1977 he had had surgery for a brain tumor, which happily turned out to be benign. And in 1978 Sally Peterson stunned her husband by asking for a divorce. Peterson was crushed. For all his worldliness, Peterson, at heart, is a surprisingly innocent man. He admits he was late to learn that his first wife was involved with a University of Chicago faculty colleague. Treas-

---

*Morris confirms this was a cordial meeting at which Glanville "offered to be helpful."

ury Secretary John Connally had elbowed him aside in Washington. Associates had to delegate Pete's good friend Dr. Mitchell Rosenthal to tell him that Sally was in love with her godson. And he was unaware of the rage bottled up within Lew Glucksman.

For a year and a half after Sally left, or until he began dating Joan Ganz Cooney in 1979, Peterson was distracted; he attended the dinners and cocktail parties of friends, and indiscriminately poured his heart out to anyone who would listen. Recognizing that he was distracted, Peterson looked for someone at Lehman to shoulder more of his burden. And when he looked about, the most capable manager he could find was the head of Lehman's fastest-growing division, Lew Glucksman.

In the autumn of 1978 Peterson approached Glucksman for a heart-to-heart conversation. "Lew, you've got to make a quality of life decision," Peterson recalls saying. "You've been operating in this environment so long you think it's a normal environment. Frankly, most business doesn't operate this way. We spend an immense amount of time here on internally divisive stuff. Lew, frankly, you're part of the problem." Glucksman told the chairman he wanted broader responsibilities. The chairman told him, "You're easily the most talented operational person around here, and we should have more burden-sharing around here."

Glucksman, who was wary of Peterson, profusely thanked the chairman for this vote of confidence. Peterson came away satisfied that with Glanville's influence over Glucksman removed, and with a little stroking and a little added responsibility, Lew Glucksman would join Peterson's team. Since many bankers were "resistant" to Glucksman, Peterson says he had to "build up Lew" gradually. The chairman assumed this precaution was reasonable; Glucksman, privately, considered it an insult—"a tip," he calls it. He believed Peterson was treating him as if he were a helpless insect, trapped first in Glanville's web and now in Peterson's.

But Glucksman said nothing. Over the next five years his responsibilities and power at Lehman grew. In 1979 he was made chairman of the operating committee; soon after, several divisions were directed to report to him; he was elevated to chief operating officer in 1980, to president in 1981, and in 1983 to co-CEO. Peterson proudly told partners that Lew had changed, had become less tempestuous, more measured, easier to work with. "Around me he was nearly always a perfect gentleman, deferential, supportive," recalls Peterson. "Even his worst enemies would admit a lot of his volatility of the seventies had moderated." But Peterson still had his problems with Glucksman, still was concerned about what he believed to be Glucksman's unwillingness to confront unpleasant situations, to speak his mind to Peterson or to concentrate on curbing overhead costs. But with Lew's surrogate son, James Boshart, serving as an intermediary, meeting daily with the chairman, interpreting Glucksman's moods and facilitating communications, Peterson was convinced he had succeeded, like professor Henry Higgins, in civilizing a raw talent.

The chairman had reason to feel content, for Glucksman went out of his way to appear respectful to Peterson, to play the grateful Eliza Doolittle. Soon after Peterson promoted Glucksman to president in July 1981, for example, Glucksman wrote a note, which read, in part: "What a nice place you have made this firm. I thank you for that and for the opportunity you have given me for self-expression."

But real differences persisted between the two men. It galled Glucksman to listen to Peterson's constant refrain about cutting costs, even when the firm was rolling in profits. Despite skyrocketing earnings in 1980, Peterson peppered Glucksman with cost-cutting memoranda. Repeatedly, Peterson asked for "a net reduction in personnel levels, particularly in those areas of our business where the earnings trend, rate of return, and prognosis has not been and is not favorable." This violated Glucksman's belief that trends in investment banking were essentially unpredictable and even irrational; one had to be prepared to move fast, and Lehman would be hampered if it focused more on dangers than on opportunities. Peterson's cost-cutting emphasis grated on Glucksman in another way: he thought Peterson took callous pleasure in contemplating the firing of employees. Glucksman could be ruthless, but he thought of himself as a sentimental man, a man who freely hugged and kissed co-workers. It enraged Glucksman to read a January 2, 1980, memo dictated by Peterson that referred to "marginal people"; the chairman conservatively estimated that at least 10 percent of these "marginal" employees could be identified and axed.

For his part, Peterson continued to fret, even as he entrusted more responsibility to Glucksman, that Glucksman lacked broad vision. Although Europe had become an important market for new business and a new source of capital to finance deals in the United States, Peterson was frustrated that Glucksman did not assign the same high priority to international business that he did. He remembers being taken aback when Glucksman was quoted in *Euromoney Magazine* as saying, recalls Peterson, "Doing business in London is like doing business in Indianapolis." Competitors in London, recalls Lehman partner Stephen Bershad, who was sent in 1981 to manage the London office, "were quoting that all over Europe," disparaging a "parochial" Lehman Brothers.

But Peterson and Glucksman's critics had twisted what Glucksman actually said. The full quote in the April 1981 issue of *Euromoney Magazine* reads: "I tend to look on international—without being parochial about it—the way I do Indianapolis, for example. We don't have a separate Indianapolis corporate finance office. International business is merged into our domestic business whether we look at banking or securities, because they all have the same common basis of support."

Still, Peterson was aghast. The comic-minded Bershad put up an extra clock in the London office. Now, in addition to clocks telling the time in London, Tokyo, New York, Chicago and San Francisco, sandwiched in the middle was a clock labeled, "Indianapolis."

Another underlying source of tension between the two was Glucksman's suspicion that Peterson was hoping to sell the firm before he turned sixty. "There was no question he was interested in selling the business," says Glucksman. "He was obsessed with money." But although Peterson had whispered to his wife of his desire to sell the business, he never said or did anything to give Glucksman solid clues. Glucksman believed he was too shrewd a poker player for that. He reasoned that for Peterson to talk openly of selling Lehman might cheapen the sales price.* What Glucksman and other partners remembered were occasional lunches around the partners' table in the dining room on the forty-third floor, where Peterson would solicitously listen to colleagues who spoke of bringing in an outside investor to add more capital to the firm, while Glucksman strenuously objected. They knew that Peterson believed that a full-service investment bank such as Lehman was striving to become would need additional capital to finance a broader range of client services and would need to take greater risks.

Glucksman is apparently correct that money was very much on the mind of many partners. Peterson, for example, concedes that by the spring of 1983 "the vast majority of the partnership wanted to sell

*Other partners also believed that Peterson wanted to sell, though they, too, offer little solid evidence.

the firm." His own mind, Peterson says, "was very open" on a sale; Glucksman's mind was closed.

Beyond fears that the sale of the firm might frustrate his developing dream of one day running Lehman Brothers alone, Glucksman harbored other anxieties. He was anxious to see more traders become partners and to increase their stock ownership. In 1982, for example, of Lehman's $122.8 million in profits, the trading divisions produced $2 in profit for every $1 produced by banking. Yet Glucksman knew that bankers then owned 67 percent of the approximately 100,000 Lehman shares; he knew that traders, whose departments contained most of Lehman's employees, boasted but twenty-eight of the then seventy-nine partners; he knew that the executive committee of the firm was dominated by senior bankers, not traders; and he knew that as profits soared so would the value of the partners' stock. Distribution of power and wealth within the firm was unfairly skewed toward bankers, and Peterson, too, recognized this, though he differed with Glucksman about how to alter it. As trading profits began to dwarf banking profits beginning in 1980, Glucksman began to press his partners to redistribute the firm's wealth; at operating committee meetings Richard Fuld, a protégé of Glucksman's, who then ran the commercial paper division, used to rant about "those fucking bankers" who hogged the wealth.

These pressures came to a head during the annual debate over bonuses and stock in 1982. It was different now from when Bobbie Lehman called partners into his office and asked them what their ownership share should be or alone decided how large a share to grant them. Now the various departments made recommendations to the operating committee, which in turn made recommendations to the executive committee. The executive committee, led by the chairman, decided on the size of each partner's bonus; the board of directors determined how to apportion shares among the partners. Glucksman, though he was president of the entire firm, behaved like an advocate for the trading divisions. He met with Peterson and recommended what Peterson considered a "radical plan" to redistribute the firm's ownership and bonuses. Glucksman believed that a partner's current performance, more than his seniority or record in past years, should determine the size of his bonus. According to Glucksman, even if a banking partner had had a good year, his bonus might slip in order to accommodate the trader who had a great year. Such a system would, inevitably, tilt the bonus schedule toward traders.

Peterson was stunned. He remembers that in the face of "record earnings and bonuses," Lew wanted to slash the bankers, particularly the shares and bonuses enjoyed by four senior bankers, Harvey Krueger, Peter Solomon, William Morris and Yves-André Istel. To reduce his shares, a partner sells back his stock to the firm at the current book value, which in late 1982 was about $1,250 per common share. These shares, in turn, are sold to partners designated by the board. What Glucksman wanted to do in September 1982 was to pare Krueger's, Morris's and Solomon's shares from 2,500 to 2,000, the same number held by less senior partners. He wanted to drop Istel below 2,000 shares. And he wanted to disband the executive committee, on which the four bankers sat.

Peterson remembers cautioning, "Lew, put yourself in the skin of Harvey Krueger, who was the president of Kuhn Loeb, or of Yves Istel, who was the president of Kuhn Loeb International." The proposal would, he said, polarize the firm. "Lew, I'm going to turn you down on this. It's much too sudden to cut the stock and bonuses of all bankers. We've got to have a five-to-ten-year plan."

Nevertheless, at the next weekly executive committee meeting Glucksman glared at the four senior bankers and exclaimed, "You guys have more shares than you deserve." The bonus schedule was still being considered by the departments, yet the word was out that Glucksman was on a rampage and was brandishing a radical plan to redistribute stock and bonuses. Banking partners were aghast, trading partners heartened. Rumors danced up and down the corridors, arousing violent argument. "It was like a bluefish-feeding frenzy," says Glucksman, who thought the bankers were being greedy; the bankers thought he was being vengeful. Peterson, exercising his corporate judicial function, tried to calm the waters. He said three criteria should be used to gauge bonuses—performance, corporate teamwork and seniority. When Peter Solomon privately complained that his bonus was to be only $250,000, much lower than expected, he recalls that Peterson privately cautioned, "Don't get in a fight with Glucksman. It's only a couple of hundred thousand dollars. I'll make it up to you."

Just three years before, mindful of disparities in ownership, Peterson, who in 1979 owned 5,750 shares, voluntarily slimmed that number to 3,500, selling his shares back to the firm. Glucksman also voluntarily pared his ownership from 4,300 to 3,500 shares. The 3,050 shares they had thrown into the pot were to be divided among the other partners. Since the total pot was only 102,000 common shares to be divided among a total of almost eighty partners, Peterson and Glucksman were trying in their own way to redistribute income.

Soon after they made this financial gesture, however, each man complained to the board that the number of shares he owned was not commensurate with either his broad responsibilities or with what the two top partners at competing firms retained. Responding to complaints from Peterson and Glucksman, in 1981 an internal committee was appointed to review this matter. The committee concluded that Peterson and Glucksman had penurious pension plans, providing them with an annual retirement payment of just $9,000. As a substitute, the committee recommended that the board award each man deferred compensation equal to 1 percent of the firm's net profits, beginning in 1982. This 1 percent would be placed in an interest-bearing account, not to be touched until 1986. In the event the firm lost money, 1 percent of the net loss would be subtracted from their account. In the event the firm was sold, the buyer would be required to honor the contract. Board members were not pleased to cede 2 percent of the firm's profits, but they went along with it.

Now, in September 1982, Peterson, hoping to temper conflicts within the firm, told the executive committee that Glucksman was right about the inequitable distribution of stock, and warned partners that they had to be prepared for change. He singled out Henry Breck, a banker, and said that he was too passive and that his bonus should be kept low. Then, just as he thought compromise was at hand, he learned that Glucksman had made what partners referred to as a "deal" with his friend Bob Rubin, who was a good analyst but not a good business producer. Rubin would receive two-thirds the amount of whatever bonus Glucksman got. Such a decision, Peterson felt, would disrupt the tenuous peace. Since Glucksman desired a bonus of $1.25 million, this would mean Rubin would receive about $900,000, while Solomon, their premier investment banker specializing in the retail industry, received only $250,000. To bring Rubin's share down, Peterson voluntarily reduced his own bonus below Glucksman's, to $1 million. This was a clever tactical move, which flattered Glucksman. Since the chairman was taking less, he could now pare Rubin to $700,000, while elevating Solomon and some of the other bankers.

Many partners applauded Peterson's shrewdness and generosity. The chairman was satisfied. He believed he had maneuvered the firm past the shoals of this controversy by being firm with the partners and with Glucksman. And, clearly, because of his intercession Glucksman did not get what he had wanted. But the way Peterson deferred to Glucksman and the passion with which Glucksman presented his case left many partners with the feeling that the currents were moving Glucksman's way. "Like all of us, Pete Peterson likes to think he was firmer than he was," says Harvey Krueger. "Lew was on a roll." Everyone, from Peterson on down, wanted to placate the man with the golden business touch.

To further satisfy Glucksman and to right what he perceived as an internal wrong, Peterson made one other decision related to the 1982 bonus battle. He agreed that the executive committee was unrepresentative, composed as it was of four senior bankers, as well as Rubin, Peterson and Glucksman. Dick Fuld and Shel Gordon, the firm's principal traders, were not members, nor were any of the three men then jointly running the banking department—Roger Altman, François de Saint Phalle or Vincent Mai. Nor was the chief of money management, Edmund Hajim. So Peterson agreed in October 1982 to expand the duties of the board of directors to include those of the executive committee. He announced that the board would henceforth meet more than once a month. This accomplished, he placed the executive committee in limbo; instead of reconstituting the committee, as Glucksman wished, the chairman simply refrained from calling meetings. The disbanding of the committee, according to members, was more a loss of status than a real blow to the firm. "The committee met weekly and talked about nothing," says one former member. "Pete would come in and say, 'I'm going to meet with the chairman of this or that company today. What do you guys think of that?' It was anything that was on Pete's mind. The committee was useless. If there was an operating issue, it was settled by the operating committee. If it was an important issue, Lew and Pete settled it." This banker believes that in light of what would later happen, Peterson's decision to phase out the executive committee was a fateful one. "In the end, when Pete wondered where the executive committee was, ironically he had allowed it to disappear."

Peterson alone was CEO, the final authority, but he was not the boss. A partnership, he learned when he came to Wall Street, is not a corporation like Bell & Howell, with a pyramidal structure. Decisions often had to be made consensually. Moreover, the very nature of the marriage of convenience between Peterson and Glucksman necessitated compromise. Peterson looked upon Glucksman as a tempestuous personality, as a center of power to be placated, rather than as a true partner.

In late 1982, Peterson appointed a cost-reduction committee chaired by a protégé, mergers and acquisitions specialist Stephen Schwarzman. By early 1983, Schwarzman had unearthed $10 million in potential savings, including wasteful across-the-board pay hikes, unnecessary taxis, padded expense accounts, employees who neglected to use the tie-line to London and instead telephoned through an operator. Schwarzman, who had been forewarned of Glucksman's wariness of cost-cutting schemes, privately visited him and ticked off the areas of waste. Glucksman, Schwarzman recalls, exploded, saying it was "chicken-shit" and would divert the firm's energies. Schwarzman went to Peterson expecting to be supported. After all, $10 million was a lot of money. Instead, Peterson allowed the cost-reduction committee, like the executive committee, to fade away. Peterson said he did not want to confront Glucksman, did not want Glucksman to feel undermined. He spoke privately with James Boshart, the partner who served as their go-between, and remembers saying, "Let's do this quietly. All we have to do is inspect a few expense reports and word will get out."

Peterson believed that this technique would curb costs and mollify Glucksman. Partners groused that Peterson's decision had more effect on Glucksman than on costs. Still, this was not a major issue. Lehman's profits were rising. Most partners were drowning in work. And as Lehman moved into 1983, partners sometimes sensed tension but rarely saw signs of trouble between the chairman and the president. Everyone had pretty much come to accept this odd couple. Richard Bingham, who ran the mergers and acquisitions department, put the relationship into perspective: "There was constant tension. The reason for it was that these were dramatically different personalities. Peterson was a corporate businessman, a broader strategic thinker. He had certain management principles he thought ought to be applied to investment banking. Lew was more an instinctive operator and trader, and a very good one. Pete had come from the West, Lew from the East. Lew was happier inside the organization, Pete was happier promoting it on the outside. The two of them working together were outstanding. The strengths and weaknesses of both men complemented each other."

Peterson was aware of these differences; he was not aware of deeper currents gathering force within Lew Glucksman. As in any insincere relationship, each man responded to shadows. To Peterson,

Glucksman was a checklist—*check with Lew* that it is okay, *check that Lew knows about this.* Glucksman's smoldering resentment of Peterson was so intense that emotion sometimes warped his memory of events. Such was the case with O.P.M. Leasing Services, once one of the nation's premier computer leasing companies. O.P.M. served as a middleman, purchasing computers and then leasing them to their eventual users. After a sensational rise, the company filed for bankruptcy in 1981, leaving behind a trainload of blue-ribbon creditors, scores of lawsuits, and allegations that O.P.M. employed bogus leases and phony bills of sale in order to secure loans that allowed the firm to carry its bad debts. The U.S. Attorney launched an investigation, and lenders filed class-action suits against O.P.M.'s investment banker, charging that it should not have lent its good name to the company and should have known of the fraud. The investment banker was Lehman Brothers.*

Lehman agreed to an out-of-court settlement, in effect acknowledging its fiduciary responsibility and failure to monitor what O.P.M. was doing. In the fall of 1982 the Lehman board agreed to pay $23 million to settle the civil lawsuit. Glucksman was immersed in the case, chairing meetings, ascertaining which Lehman employees had been lax, giving sworn depositions. Peterson, however, had been so uninvolved in O.P.M. matters that he was not even asked to be deposed. Yet when the papers settling the O.P.M. case were to be signed in March 1983, Glucksman says he was enraged. As president, Glucksman signed the papers and he says he assumed Peterson, as chairman, would also sign: he says he was shocked when Peterson refused. The matter came up in one of the regular meetings the two men held once or twice a week in Peterson's corner office on the forty-third floor. "I brought it up and it got dismissed," says Glucksman. He recalls that Peterson had said, "Lew, you are the one who assumed working responsibility for O.P.M. No one could believe that Peter G. Peterson could be involved in something like that."

To Glucksman it was typical of Peterson to be preoccupied with his image, to worry more about his good name than that of the firm. It symbolized to him Peterson's growing noninvolvement with Leh-

*Like other investment banks, Lehman received its share of lawsuits charging malfeasance or worse. By the spring of 1985, several former customers had brought suit, charging that in order to inflate their commissions Lehman salesmen "churned" customer accounts excessively. One Chicago businessman, Francis Wagner, filed a suit contending that such deliberate "churning" cost him, according to the April 5, 1985, *Wall Street Journal,* "more than $1.7 million in interest, commissions and lost interest capital."

man Brothers, his preoccupation with the outside world, with such activities as the Bi-Partisan Budget Appeal or the Third World debt crisis. So Glucksman vented his rage to Bob Rubin, who as a long-time member of the board offered to affix his name to the document. "Bob Rubin signed because he was unwilling to let me be the only name there, for clearly it was not my responsibility," says Glucksman. Rubin, who during this period had been more open than Glucksman about his disdain for the chairman, says, "Lew thought Pete's behavior was unconscionable. You have to take responsibility for the mistakes of your organization." Both Glucksman and Rubin say that O.P.M. was one of the critical issues that gnawed away at Glucksman and led to his July 1983 explosion.

Peterson's recollection of this event is diametrically different. "Lew never asked me to sign that piece of paper," he says. "To say he did is an absolute lie!" He recalls that when the matter came up, Glucksman said, "Pete, this is an immense source of embarrassment to me. I signed it. I didn't see any reason to get you involved in this thing." If Glucksman was unhappy, he wonders, why didn't he say anything at the time to the board of directors or to the head of the audit committee?

That is a question asked by other partners as well, who are puzzled by Glucksman's recollection. The head of the audit committee, Harvey Krueger, says that Glucksman never said a word to him expressing anger at Peterson's handling of O.P.M. And Shel Gordon, who then worked directly for Glucksman as head of equity trading, says, "My understanding was that Lew had really been handling the O.P.M. thing as chief operating officer and that Pete really wasn't involved. When it came to the signing, if my recollection is correct, Lew said he really didn't want Pete to sign because of who Pete was and because he really wasn't involved. My recollection is that Rubin said to Lew at that time, 'I'm not going to let you sign alone.' "

What is not disputed by either Glucksman or Peterson is that Glucksman did not register his complaints with Peterson; in fact, he said nothing. That two partners might have business differences is hardly unusual. What is unusual is that Glucksman could be so angry and yet not betray this anger to Peterson. Such silence suggests the chasm between the two men. It also suggests that just as Peterson stroked Glucksman and feared his estrangement, so Glucksman often feared offending the chairman. Lew Glucksman enjoyed his reputation within the firm as a man who motivated people through a combination of fear and love. But with Peter G. Peterson—one of *them*—he was usually respectful, and brooded silently.

The two men, as the O.P.M. matter suggests, were uncomfortable with, even afraid of, each other. They met alone, by Peterson's count, only twice weekly. Much of their business was conducted through intermediaries like Jim Boshart, who usually met with Peterson two or three times daily. Peterson was insecure about his knowledge of trading operations, Glucksman about his relations with bankers and the establishment. Peterson was insecure about losing Glucksman, and thus being forced to return to managing daily operations, which he dreaded. Glucksman was insecure about his relations with the banking department and the outside world. Within Lehman it is much remarked that Glucksman was out to prove something and was at bottom a profoundly insecure man. But some partners believe that Peterson, despite his brusque manner, was also insecure. "Pete is a very insecure guy," says one former partner whom Peterson considers a friend. "Look at the way he treated people and wanted to subordinate them. He made people feel like second-class citizens around him. He would be an intensive name-dropper and say things like, 'Lew, I want you to ride out to the airport with me.'" Though Peterson condescended to Glucksman, as he did to others, deep down perhaps he was afraid of Glucksman, certainly afraid of alienating him, which is why he asked Jim Boshart to serve as an interpreter to him of Glucksman's true feelings. "One of your jobs," he would tell Boshart regularly, "is to be sure that nothing happens to sour relations between Lew and me." When he noticed that Lew seemed moody, Peterson would say to Boshart, "I noticed that Lew seemed distracted. Remember, Jim, if there's any problem, be sure I'm the first to know." Often he would simply ask Boshart, who was like a son to Glucksman, "Is Lew happy?"

The chairman would nevertheless mix solicitude with condescension, not thinking twice about lecturing Glucksman about the stains on his ties, his obesity, his unfashionable clothes—about how his personal appearance harmed the firm's image. And when, beginning in late 1982, Glucksman lost about seventy pounds, Peterson would boast to insiders and outsiders alike how "proud" he was of Lew. Glucksman turned the other cheek, but says he seethed inside.

Peterson remained blind to Glucksman's rage. However odd a couple they might be, he believed there were rational advantages for him and Lew Glucksman to work as partners. The bottom line was his proof—since 1978 the firm had had consecutive record-profit years. During the first nine months of the 1983 fiscal year, Lehman had enjoyed higher earnings than at any other time in the firm's one-hundred-and-thirty-three-year history; by the end of that fiscal year, pre-tax and pre-bonus profits would climb to $148 million and Lehman was on the brink of breaking into underwriting's elite of so-called "special bracket" firms—the five leading banking houses of Goldman, Sachs; Salomon Brothers; Merrill Lynch; Morgan Stanley; and First Boston—a ranking destined to attract even more business.

Peterson had served in the Nixon Administration and knew the men who had behaved so irrationally after their landslide victory in 1972, but this encounter with human frailty did not alter Peterson's confidence in the power of reason. He understood that Glucksman could be excessive, could flare at partners, but he was convinced that he had tamed Lew.

Peterson's approach to life is cerebral. He prides himself on no longer being "a stranger to one's subconscious," as he puts it. For Peterson, this meant that he now tried to isolate personal weaknesses and will them to cease; he spent more time with his children, he controlled his anger, he learned to be self-deprecating, to be more deferential to Lew, insisting that Lew be included in any Lehman picture the chairman posed for. The trouble with such a rational approach is that it is self-centered. Peterson isolated and corrected those weaknesses that *he* perceived, not necessarily those perceived by others. And when he did reach out, he tended to rely on what others said, not on his own intuitive radar.

With the benefit of hindsight, one former Lehman partner thinks Peterson had been naïve, even foolish: "There's blood in the sea and a shark is circling and he'd ask the shark, 'Have you had enough to eat?' The shark said, 'Yes,' and Pete said, 'I'm safe!' "

Peterson felt so safe that he had begun to toy with the idea of elevating Glucksman to co-CEO. On September 10, 1981, he invited John C. Whitehead and John L. Weinberg, co-CEO's of Goldman, Sachs, to join him and Glucksman for breakfast at Lehman. Such meetings between competitors are not uncommon on Wall Street, particularly since firms co-manage various underwritings. Whitehead and Weinberg, however, were special, for they not only ran what is widely considered to be the premier investment banking house but also performed as true partners. At this breakfast, Whitehead recalls that Peterson pressed them to explain how they divided responsibilities and how they dealt with compensation: "I remember questions such as, 'Do you and John have the same percentage?' 'How much of a gap is there between the top two persons and everyone else?' "

As usual, Peterson had a game plan. He was thinking about the eventual succession at Lehman. In the short run, he wanted, as he told associates, "to build up Lew." In the long-term, he had his eye on three younger prospects who were developing broad familiarity with all aspects of the business, and he hoped one of them might eventually manage the firm. The leading prospect was probably Sheldon Gordon, then forty-seven, a Harvard-trained economist who had received an M.B.A. from the University of Pennsylvania's Wharton School, completed his course work for a doctorate in economics, and served on the Wharton faculty before launching a Philadelphia-based economic analysis and portfolio management company. After merging this company with the Philadelphia Life Insurance Company, and becoming president of their asset management subsidiary, in 1972 Gordon gave it all up. He decided to accept a faculty appointment at the Wharton Graduate School. This move, which impressed his Lehman partners, helped stamp Gordon as a man of inner calm, a man who did not lust for power or money. He joined Lehman in 1975 and became president of its investment management division, moving on to run the corporate bond department in 1979, to head the equity division in 1981, and then joined both the operating committee and the board.

Working in the trading area, Gordon became known as a Glucksman protégé. But unlike some protégés, Shel Gordon was not a polarizing figure. His relaxed manner, his ability to listen, to speak only after careful deliberation, his gentle skills as a manager—all conspired to make Gordon a popular figure. In the simplified war zones of Lehman, Shel Gordon was cast as a "trader." Yet Gordon, unlike most of his colleagues, was able to rise above the fractiousness at Lehman. Like Talleyrand, Shel Gordon did not break, he bent. It was Peterson's tentative plan to make Gordon head of the banking division, thus broadening his platform for the future.

The second partner the chairman had his eye on was Roger Altman, then thirty-seven, a man who shared Peterson's intense interest in public life. While studying for an M.B.A. at the University of Chicago in 1968, Altman took a leave to labor on behalf of Robert F. Kennedy's quest for the presidency. He came to Wall Street in 1969 and joined Lehman's banking department, eventually becoming the firm's youngest partner. But government and politics beckoned, and in 1977 Altman moved to Washington as one of four assistant secretaries of the Treasury (for domestic finance). While overseeing the federal loan guarantee program for New York City and the Chrysler bailout, the lean, dark-haired and boyishly handsome Altman was popular among the various combatants, in part because he is a pleasant man who cultivates a network of relationships, in part because he can articulate and frame issues well, in part because Roger Altman does not make waves.

When Altman left the Carter Administration in 1980, Peterson at first encountered resistance when he tried to bring him back to Lehman. Bob Rubin, among others, protested that he was a better salesman or "politician" than banker. Peterson finally succeeded in placing Altman in charge of new business development, which made him familiar with Lehman's various divisions. Then, in 1982, when William Morris was relieved as head of investment banking, Altman and two colleagues—"the troika," as it was called—were put in charge of investment banking. Altman was made a member of the operating committee, and because of his relationship with Peterson he was perceived as a comer at Lehman. Yet his deep involvement in Walter Mondale's presidential quest, beginning almost as soon as he rejoined Lehman, the pictures arranged on his office wall—Altman shaking hands with President Carter, Altman standing with former Treasury Secretary Michael Blumenthal, Altman with Mayor Edward Koch—hinted at his true love and no doubt fueled the resentments of partners who thought him "too political."

Another member of the troika, François de Saint Phalle, also then thirty-seven, was the third partner singled out by Peterson. He was a senior at Columbia University when the 1968 student riots closed the school. He decided to leave, and landed a job as a part-time researcher at *Newsweek*. This son of a French textile-company owner decided not to return to Columbia for his degree. He joined Lehman that fall and, after a time, was placed in the syndicate department. His job was to decide what type of security to issue on behalf of a company wanting to raise funds, to decide how much could be raised, set the market price on each public offering, join with other investment banks to forge an underwriting syndicate and determine when to go to market. In this capacity de Saint Phalle was often on the trading floor, where he got to know Lew Glucksman. He became one of those who sat around Glucksman's glass office at seven each morning and was considered a member of his "team." De Saint

Phalle was part of that growing army of bankers who worked on the trading floor and, unavoidably, blurred the distinction between "traders" and "bankers."

In 1975, de Saint Phalle was named head of the entire syndicate department; in 1982, he became a member of the operating committee. "France," as he is called, is six feet tall and muscular; his blond good looks were highlighted by bright suspenders, round gold-rimmed glasses and thick cigars. Both Peterson and Glucksman agreed: France was a real financial whiz, "a pro," as they referred to him. If he had a weakness, apart from his not being acquainted with all aspects of the business, it was that he could be gruff with younger associates and withdrawn from his partners. De Saint Phalle was more a loner than Gordon or Altman.

Peterson's immediate plan began to unfold in the spring of 1983, when he quietly polled a handful of board members about the idea of elevating Glucksman to co-CEO. Outside public activities, including the Bi-Partisan Budget Appeal, were now claiming more of Peterson's time. Thinking decades ahead, as he liked to do, Peterson had come to believe fervently that the nation's mounting deficits would drive up interest rates, crippling productivity growth, and thus the economy as a whole. Interest charges on the cumulative federal deficit already consumed over 10 percent of the federal budget.* Peterson decided to act on his convictions and organized a powerhouse group of business leaders and others to apply pressure on the President and the Congress to adopt a policy of short-term pain for long-term gain. Consisting of himself, five former Secretaries of the Treasury, including his old nemesis, John Connally, and a total of five hundred or so business, government and academic leaders, the initial group was announced in May 1982. By January 1983, with Peterson taking responsibility for the details, they had carefully delineated $175 billion in spending cuts and tax increases, which they urged on President Reagan and the Congress for fiscal 1985. The Bi-Partisan Budget Appeal had caught the attention, if not yet the support, of the President and the Congress. The group issued alarmed statements, which were prominently displayed by the media. These pronouncements were drafted by Peterson. A May 1983 statement warned:

*Interest on the national debt was projected to cost $155 billion in the budget year ending September 30, 1985, a sum greater than the entire 1966 federal budget.

Massive Federal borrowing will consume savings urgently needed for investment in new plants and equipment, new infrastructure and new jobs and training. Overvalued dollars will crush export industries. Real long-term interest rates will remain high for the foreseeable future, smothering capital-intensive sectors and causing the recovery to sputter and stall. The long-term result will be even more painful than the steps that avert it.

As he thought about the future of Lehman, Peterson believed his chief value was his strong strategic sense, his ability to market and sell ideas, his detailed grasp of marketing and recruiting new business, his role as the firm's Mr. Outside. But he also understood Glucksman's value as Mr. Inside—handling most day-to-day details and juggling the various egos. Keeping Glucksman happy became a Peterson obsession. He received signals through intermediaries that Lew "wanted more recognition" and more managerial freedom, and honestly tried to give him both. He tried to assuage Glucksman by cooling his cost-cutting ardor. He tried, none too gracefully, to compliment Glucksman about the weight he had lost, about his new tailor. On one of the infrequent occasions that she encountered Glucksman, Joan Ganz Cooney recalls this whispered advice from her husband, "Be nice to Lew."

In one of their regular meetings in May 1983, Peterson asked Jim Boshart, "Is Lew happy?" Boshart remembers responding that Lew had some frustrations, particularly about the credit he did not receive for managing the day-to-day affairs of the firm.

"The right thing to do is to make Lew co-CEO. My ego can handle it," said Peterson. "In every sense we'll be co-CEO's." He cited the co-equal team of John Weinberg and John Whitehead, at Goldman, Sachs. He knew that at First Boston, Peter T. Buchanan, a former trader who had become president and CEO, divided responsibility with the chairman, Alvin V. Shoemaker; even at Morgan Stanley, where trading and distribution were sneered at for years, Richard B. Fisher, a man who had spent the last decade as a trader, was on the rise and would (in January 1984) become president. After the meeting with Boshart, Peterson went about drafting a logical and orderly division of responsibilities.

Determined to proceed, Peterson met alone with Glucksman. "Lew, look, I think we have a common set of goals," he recalls saying. "We always talk about the institution first. I have talked with you about how I have wanted to build you up and build a team that can succeed us. I get too much of the credit. We're the same age. You've worked so hard for so long that fairness in terms of sharing the glory and the credit means that you should share the job. Also, if something happens to me, the institution requires a clear succession. Until now, if an ultimate decision needed to be made, I made it. Now there will be two of us making decisions."

Glucksman seemed pleased: "I think that's very fair of you, very generous of you. I never wanted to be chairman. I don't have the right talents to be chairman."*

Peterson then reviewed the May 16 memorandum of understanding he had drafted. After praising Glucksman's contributions, the draft memo to all Lehman employees said that while both men would retain their respective titles as chairman and president, "effective immediately" they would "share the chief executive responsibilities as co-chief executive officers." The move permitted them to define "areas of primary as well as shared responsibility." Peterson would "focus more time on a number of future initiatives—such as future business strategies and development, and a much expanded special investment activity—in addition, of course, to continuing to work with investment banking clients." Glucksman's primary responsibilities were defined as "exercising principal day-to-day responsibility for our various operating divisions and departments." And, together, "we will continue to share in basic organizational and strategic decisions, and will maintain our ongoing involvement in strengthening the firm's client relationships." Peterson arranged for Glucksman to receive the same $225,000 salary reserved for the chairman.

The chairman felt satisfied, felt he had behaved magnanimously, thinking first of the long-term interests of Lehman, as he did when he coaxed Glucksman to join his management team in 1978. Pete Peterson had mastered his own ego.

Glucksman feigned pleasure, effusively praising Peterson, but says he felt no gratitude. What Peterson saw as generosity, he saw as necessity; what was compassion to Peterson came off as condescension to Glucksman. Peterson thought he was offering recognition to a talented man who could never, on his own, run the prestigious House of Lehman; Glucksman thought he was truly running Lehman already and resented the need to defer to a self-important chairman he disliked. "Peterson resisted ever making me president until

---

*Glucksman admits he acted as if he were pleased, but wasn't. And: "If I did say I didn't have the right talents to be chairman, I would have been lying."

I forced the action," Glucksman says today. "I was very unen-
thusiastic about this co-CEO thing. It was a slap in the face. Another
example of Pete's unwillingness to let go when his interests were
outside the business." What he really wanted, Glucksman now says,
was for Peterson to announce plans to step down eventually, as he
thought Peterson planned to do when he wrote the memo in 1980
alerting Rubin and Glucksman of his thoughts about a "transition"
at Lehman.

Glucksman had reason to believe Peterson was thinking about
stepping aside one day soon. Even Peterson's close friends interpreted the co-CEO announcement as a move in that direction. After ten
years at Lehman, says Peterson's good friend Eli Jacobs, "Pete had
felt he had done his job." This successful venture capitalist remembered a drink he had had with Peterson at the River Club in June
1983, when Peterson suddenly said, "I wish I could be doing what
you're doing." The two men then talked about one day going into
business together. Jacobs assumed Peterson wanted out. Glucksman's friend Bob Rubin got the same signal: "I think Lew took the
May statement for what it said, which was that 'I, Lew Glucksman,
am going to be responsible for running the business, and Pete won't
meddle. I'm not going to be frustrated anymore by pretending we're
doing it together.' "

Peterson called a board meeting at eight-thirty in the morning on
May 16, 1983, to ratify the change. The board unanimously approved
the resolution, though afterward Peterson remembers a few partners
whispering to him, "Are you sure this is what you want?" Peterson
said he was sure.

At eleven all seventy-seven partners were invited to sip champagne
and celebrate in the partners' dining room. Warm toasts to Glucksman and Peterson and the *team* were made, but Jim Boshart could
sense that Lew was restive. He seemed subdued. "I could tell he
wasn't thrilled," says Boshart. "He said nothing. The sense I got was
that he felt it was anticlimactic. That he deserved it before. He felt
that way when he was made president. He felt it was anticlimactic.
Almost like, Okay, you've been a good boy so you get a pat on the
head."

The co-CEO announcement was made that afternoon. After reviewing Lehman's impressive growth, the two-page Peterson memorandum to all Lehman employees and the press, which followed
word for word Peterson's draft, concluded: "I doubt that this move
will in fact result in Lew and I working more closely together in the

future than we have in the past, for that would hardly be possible."

The board and most of the partners were pleased, believing the new titles merely confirmed the reality that Glucksman was truly in charge of day-to-day operations at Lehman. No matter how crude some partners thought Lew was, he was a proven moneymaker. Even board member Peter Solomon, who detested Glucksman and, as on most matters, did not camouflage his emotions, was satisfied. "It was okay with me," he says. "I thought everything was terrific. We were in the middle of a bull market. I was banging out deals."

Oddly enough, a lonely dissent was uttered by Joan Ganz Cooney, Peterson's wife. She recalls once saying to her husband, "You never talk about your work. You talk about what you did in government. You talk about Bell & Howell. You talk about the economy." She doesn't remember his precise answer. "But it was to the effect that Lehman wasn't 'a pleasant place to work. It's a troubled partnership.' I once heard him say, 'I don't know what Lew would say to that.' " She wondered why her husband, the chairman, had to be vexed by such things. She also knew that Pete and Lew had had differences over the years. She knew that Glucksman was violently opposed to the idea of selling the firm, while it was Pete's private hope to sell Lehman before he reached sixty. "Pete certainly hoped it would sell in that period, and we'd have no money worries," she says. She remembers that when Pete first talked to her in May about a promotion for Glucksman, she warned, "Pete, you give him a fingernail and he's going to take an arm."

G LUCKSMAN BEGAN TO NIBBLE AT PETERSON'S AUTHORITY. Instead of consulting Peterson on personnel decisions, he began to act unilaterally. Within days of Glucksman's appointment, a stunned Edmund A. Hajim, chairman and CEO of the Lehman Management Company (Lemco), appeared in Peterson's office. The chief of Lehman's money management arm told the chairman that Lew Glucksman had terminated him as CEO of Lemco, and was transferring him to the banking department. Peterson says he was flabbergasted. How could Lew remove Hajim? By every bottom-line measure, Hajim was a success. When Peterson became chairman in 1973, money management was viewed as an auxiliary business at Lehman. Peterson had the vision to significantly expand this effort. Within six years, Lemco controlled $2 billion in assets. Since Hajim assumed command of this division in 1980, the assets Lemco managed climbed from $2 billion to more than $10 billion; revenues tripled; and the mutual funds he supervised performed in the top 3 percent of all mutual funds. Yet here Hajim stood—a member of the board of directors, a man Glucksman himself had recruited from E. F. Hutton—and informed Peterson that his new co-CEO had removed him.

Hajim protested that Glucksman offered no criticism of his performance, instead emphasizing that he liked to move people around, and adding, "We need you in banking." Glucksman remembers he told Hajim, "You're growing the business too fast. There are no clear management controls." Glucksman wanted firmer management at Lemco and throughout Lehman.

Equally appalling to Peterson, Glucksman intended to replace Hajim with investment banker Henry Breck, then forty-six, a friend of Bob Rubin's who had befriended Lew Glucksman. Peterson believed that Breck's management skills were untested and that he had not proven to be a dynamic banker. He remembered how in 1982, with Glucksman's concurrence, Breck was awarded a mere $250,000 bonus. Like some banking partners, Peterson was never comfortable with Breck. He seemed so controlled, so wary, so distant, reminding partners of his mysterious C.I.A. past and prompting some to refer to him as "the spook."

"This was the first indication I had that he was not following our written agreement of May 16, in which all significant organizational changes were to be reviewed in advance," says Peterson. Peterson says that Hajim had performed ably and that Glucksman's conversations with Hajim came as a surprise to him. Glucksman insists that he spoke first to Peterson. "The facts are that we discussed the need to replace Hajim because we felt the business should grow more slowly," he says.*

---

*Peterson later amended his earlier recollection, saying he knew that "Lew hated Hajim," and therefore he was not completely surprised by the move.

Peterson accepted the decision. Since Hajim reported to Glucksman, he says good management practice left him no choice but to accept. Now his concern was twofold: Who would replace Hajim? And how to use Hajim's talents? The chairman spoke with Glucksman and protested that Henry Breck, who joined the firm as an investment banker in 1968, lacked management experience and that since he was a friend of Lew's, his appointment smacked of cronyism. He tried, and failed, to persuade Glucksman to rescind his decision. But he did induce him to install a more experienced manager, Robert Arkison, as president and chief operating officer under Breck. He also induced Hajim to report to the banking department, and got Glucksman to agree that Hajim's stock ownership would not be cut and that he would remain a member of the board. Finally, Peterson had Glucksman set up a meeting between the co-CEO's and Breck. Peterson remembers telling Breck what was expected of him; Glucksman remembers that Peterson "spent one hour ungraciously telling Henry of his faults."

Peterson's allies, including Hajim, were disappointed; they felt he sacrificed Hajim to appease Glucksman. Many partners thought the move made no business sense. It was, says senior banker Harvey Krueger—called "Uncle Harvey" by colleagues because of his avuncular manner—"an error in judgment to pull Hajim out of the job." The less reverent Peter Solomon put it differently: "The Ed Hajim thing was whacko!"

Glucksman's appetite for power grew, and soon he made another unilateral decision, appointing Michael Schmertzler as chief financial officer. Glucksman says, "I'm positive I consulted Pete first," and remembered that Peterson asked, "What experience does he have?" Peterson was troubled that the decision to elevate the thirty-one-year-old Schmertzler was sprung on him and that he was not yet a partner, a man with "no comptrollership experience." Yet he was being asked to fill the shoes of former partner Arthur Fried. Privately, Peterson wondered, Will Schmertzler stand up to Glucksman the way Fried would? It could not have pleased Peterson to hear Schmertzler tell partners that Bob Rubin would be "the de facto chief financial officer." And yet Peterson went along, he says, because he believed Glucksman had the right to select his own deputies and because Schmertzler enjoyed a reputation as a bright young man.

Another point of friction became Mario d'Urso's status as a banking partner. A lean, suave and charming international banker, with shiny black hair combed straight back, his face perpetually tan, the forty-four-year-old Naples-born d'Urso came to Lehman in the merger with Kuhn Loeb. His aristocratic father had been a friend of Bobbie Lehman's, and between trips to Rome, Zurich, London, the Philippines and Manhattan, Mario had established his own impeccable political and social credentials. He could be seen at cocktails with Henry Kissinger, dining with Marietta Tree, William Paley, the Agnellis, Imelda Marcos, jogging in Central Park in a red velour running suit, coming to work late and then taking a leisurely lunch with such close friends as Enrico Braggiotti, the Milan banker who served on Lehman's board and was its sole outside investor. D'Urso did not believe the firm should be gambling its money guessing interest rates or engaging in risk arbitrage; he believed in trading only to accommodate the banking clients. To Peterson, d'Urso had valued international business and social contacts. To Glucksman, he was a dandy, the personification of a lazy banker to whom the office was a place to rest his hat and coat and receive telephone messages between lunch and cocktails. Beginning in the winter of 1983, d'Urso became a fixation of Glucksman's. "He asked me to leave the firm," says d'Urso. "He said he was prepared to tell me the reason in two years."

Glucksman's face would redden at the mention of d'Urso, but each time Glucksman tried to fire him Peterson would intercede, testifying to his value as a banker and his value as a friend of Braggiotti's and others. Braggiotti, who intervened in February to spare d'Urso, recalls saying, "D'Urso is the best public relations man in the world. He is very good to put people together." Glucksman backed off, but he believed relationship banking had died with the Lehmans and Loebs; he thought that Peterson, like a boy from Nebraska whose head had been turned by the big city, was too easily impressed by glitter.

Peace reigned for a few months, and then Glucksman went after d'Urso again. In one meeting he told d'Urso to "shut up." In the spring, recalls Peterson, "To my astonishment and embarrassment, Lew called Mario a liar in a meeting with Enrico Braggiotti." Peterson thought he was once again witnessing the irrational Lew Glucksman of what he refers to as the "Glanville era." D'Urso was not in attendance, but he remembers, "Braggiotti was so shocked he told me he would not tell me what happened. Afterwards we had lunch." The issue festered. "Lew had strong feelings about d'Urso, and Pete stood in the way and didn't want Mario to leave," says Jim Boshart. "It became a symbolic issue, proof that Lew really wasn't running the business." Finally, in June, Glucksman got his way—d'Urso left to run for the Italian Parliament. "It was not a Glucksman decision," says Glucksman. "It was a consensus view of a substantial number of the firm's managers." Peterson dissents: "That is not true. There may be some people who felt Mario had too many shares. But a lot of important people around the world didn't like his departure at all." On this issue, many Lehman bankers stood, uncomfortably, beside Glucksman. A senior banking ally of Peterson's, who was consulted, supports Glucksman: "A substantial number of us felt that if shares were scarce, as they were, then they ought to come from d'Urso before they came from others."

Yet another point of friction arose at a May 31 luncheon Peterson was to host at the River House for Japanese Prime Minister Nakasone. As was often the case with Peterson's public activities, he carefully circulated a memo to select partners asking for suggested corporate clients or prospective customers to invite. When the internal responses came in, Peterson noticed that every partner had responded—except Lew Glucksman. Invited to the luncheon, in addition to twenty-four Japanese officials, were the chairmen of Citicorp, Manufacturers Hanover Trust, PepsiCo, the Ford Motor Company, Johnson & Johnson, ITT, ABC, RCA, Revlon and the chief executives of several Wall Street competitors. Glucksman complained to friends that Peterson had not thought to invite him. Glucksman noted that Peterson did think to invite a Lehman senior adviser, Richard C. Holbrooke, a former Assistant Secretary of State for Asian Affairs. Peterson says the "guest list was totally under the control of the Japanese Ministry of Foreign Affairs. I gave them a list of top executives. They then gave me back an approved list." Peterson says he suggested Glucksman's name. Holbrooke, who helped organize the lunch, blames himself for not being "sensitive" enough to suggest that Glucksman be invited.

Most Lehman partners applauded such outside activities of Peterson's, and appreciated how diligent the chairman was in soliciting their suggestions for clients to invite. However, at least two partners were angry about the lunch. One was Peter Solomon, who recalls, "I was upset I wasn't invited. I had been to Japan six times for Lehman Brothers. Holbrooke was there; I should have been." Peterson might dismiss Solomon's anger as vanity. At Lehman, Solomon's manner was often either outraged or prankish, which is why some partners called him "the brat." But Glucksman was something else. His anger, unlike Solomon's, was rarely leavened with humor. Peterson was aware that Lew had not responded to his memo. This was, he told friends, the "first time" he became aware of personal tensions with his co-CEO. The other disagreements he considered business differences; this seemed more personal, for Glucksman seemed to be unusually quiet, curt, testy. Asked why he failed to respond to the chairman's memo, Glucksman says, "I didn't have to be a flunky!" A year after this incident, the fire within Glucksman still burned, for when he was asked whether he was upset that he was not included, he raged, "No. Want to know why? Those lunches were dipshit! A waste of time. Grease for his vanity. Lehman didn't count for anything in Japan, and we weren't going to count for anything in Japan."

Still other differences of opinion or procedure surfaced. "Glucksman became more gruff," explains Peterson's executive assistant, Melba Duncan. "He wasn't as controlled as before. He was now co-CEO. Just like Peterson. He had very little time to say good morning." Tensions were "palpable," recalls James Hood, who joined Lehman in September 1982 to coordinate all marketing and public relations, and had a box seat across from Peterson's office on the forty-third floor. Parading before him, says Hood, were "rivaling sports teams—the Bankers versus the Traders." Hood noticed that with Glucksman's ascendancy employees in the trading divisions grew more assertive, while bankers became more defensive. Traders spoke of how "we" do this, while bankers receded, became more self-conscious. Working closely with both Peterson and Glucksman, Hood began to notice that the co-CEO marriage partners no longer pretended to be in love. In private meetings that spring, Glucksman told Hood, "Pete won't be much help on the details of that, so talk to me about it." And Peterson, when speaking of strategy, told Hood, "Well, you and I have to work this one out because Lew is only dealing with day-to-day operations."

Glucksman's ascendancy frightened many bankers, yet few saw Peterson as their champion. As the tenth anniversary of his chairmanship of Lehman neared, Peterson had worn thin his welcome. In reflective moments, many partners would concede that he had saved the firm in 1973, that he was a brilliant strategist, an effective cost cutter, a terrific business getter, a superb salesman and public face for the firm. But the words most used by partners (including many whom Peterson considers friends) when describing Peterson are "condescending," "self-centered," "vain," "uncaring."

By the spring of 1983, Peterson seemed to be out of the office more and more, while Glucksman was in charge. By then, says former senior banker and board member George Wiegers, who announced prior to that summer that he was moving to Dillon, Read, "Pete had little support among the senior banking partners. Peterson was frustrating to most of the partners. He was a very demanding and self-centered man. His allocation of time and resources always preempted everyone else's." Senior banker and board member Peter Solomon, who would have supported Peterson in a showdown with Glucksman, says of Peterson, "He doesn't have the milk of human kindness passing through his veins." William E. Welsh, who headed special projects and also served on the board, and who was a cheerful man, popular among most of his partners, says, "Pete was very standoffish. He was interested in himself. If you met him as an individual, you'd witness a monologue." In the end, Peterson was thought to be close to only a handful of partners—Roger C. Altman, mergers and acquisitions specialist Stephen A. Schwarzman, banker Steven R. Fenster, among them. Yet one of these men, who admires Peterson's talents, concedes, "Pete was apersonal. Over time he did not have a lot of friends at the firm."

It rankled partners that the chairman often treated them as coldly as the numbers on his yellow pad, that he rarely remembered their wives' names, that they were often summoned without notice to ride uptown with him, that he read memos in meetings with their clients, that he preferred to dine in a private room he had constructed adjoining his office and rarely ventured into the partners' dining room, rarely took time to schmooze, seemed preoccupied with his own press notices.

Partners collected anecdotes about Peterson's brusqueness: for example, about the time Peterson had a cold and was visiting the London office, and how he matter-of-factly turned to the nearest partner and commanded that he go fetch him some aspirin. Henry Breck remembered a hot summer day in 1977 when he and Peterson were in George Ball's office at One William Street, having returned together from lunch. They were reviewing a banking matter when, suddenly, Peterson rose from the couch, his face white, his eyes rolled back, and he fell like a tree. Peterson was having a seizure. Ball rushed to summon a doctor. Breck rushed to jam a wooden ruler in Peterson's mouth, preventing him from swallowing his tongue. After days of tests and an operation on his skull by a specialist recommended by Henry Kissinger and Averell Harriman, a tumor was located, pressing on Peterson's brain. It was benign. Peterson quickly recovered and was out of the hospital in two weeks. Yet what still rankles Breck, eight years later, is that Peterson never once thanked him or even acknowledged his presence that day.

One former partner remembers how brusque Peterson could be with partners and sometimes with clients: "Pete's head was a little bit up in the clouds. Even with clients he'd come into a luncheon and start reading his notes for something else. Clients like you to try and pay attention. He's so quick that when the client started talking, he'd catch right up." A friend and business associate of Peterson's observes, "Pete in some ways is like Henry Kissinger. He never got over being in government. I believe everything that has happened to him since is like a way station to going back either as Secretary of the Treasury or Chairman of the Federal Reserve."

This brusqueness is placed in a somewhat different though not necessarily endearing light by Peterson's friend and former partner Warren Hellman, who now lives in San Francisco: "Pete is a guy who gives enormous attention to business. Once he came out to San Francisco and we were going to have a social dinner. We went to Ondine's for dinner, a very elegant restaurant. It was just the two of us. As soon as we sat down Pete said, 'Can we order the whole meal now?' We were out of there in forty-five minutes!"

Peterson was largely unaware that many of his partners found him imperious. He believed that as the chairman he often had to make painful personnel choices (when bonuses and shares were distributed in September, when promotions were granted) and that to maintain the appearance of fairness he had to keep distant, like a judge—"like De Gaulle," his wife explains. Peterson also says, "I wasn't running for office. I had a partner. Lew wanted to run operations. I didn't think he would appreciate it if I was in touch with people."*

Nevertheless, there are those who look at Peterson and instead of seeing coldness, see shyness and warmth. Peterson can be awkward in a social setting, and on weekends in the Hamptons he is most comfortable seeing a few close friends. He is now more attentive to his five children, whose pictures are sprinkled throughout his homes and office. He dotes on his wife Joan, and eagerly discusses her work as president of the Children's Television Workshop, her membership on five corporate boards. Some may think it was insensitive of him to have had a secretary call for a first date to the ballet, as Pete did with Joan in 1979. "He probably had fears of rejection," explains

---

*It is possible that with the passage of time, and the outcome of the turmoil at the firm, partners today project greater hostility toward Peterson than they felt then. It is also possible that the polite things many said at the time were unfelt.

Joan. "He is somewhat shy. And having your secretary call is totally appropriate in the business world." She turned down the initial offer, thinking he was still married. His failure to glimpse Glucksman's hostility is seen by Joan as a virtue, not a vice. "Pete was totally trusting of Lew's compliments," she says. "He wanted to believe Lew had changed."

Although Peterson's fastidious concern for appearances is often remarked upon, it is also true that he suffered openly after Sally Peterson left him in 1978. "He was a basket case," says Joan, who spotted him at a party at Linda and Morton Janklows'. "Pete was in a corner telling his troubles to Barbara Walters, who is a close friend. And Linda Janklow was coming by and saying, 'Joan, Joan. Talk to Pete.' " She avoided him because he was so downcast. After their first date, arranged by the Janklows, Pete pursued her with a single-minded intensity. "Pete is like a horse with blinders," she says. He can be obsessive. Soon, like a thrilled, innocent adolescent, Peterson announced to friends and acquaintances, "I'm going steady." He waited until their fifth date to kiss her.

Melba Duncan, who went to work for Peterson as a secretary in 1976 and rose to become his executive assistant, saw a kind, not remote man. She recalls that on the morning of his brain surgery, he telephoned and said, "I just want to say how much I appreciate all you've done. You're a terrific person. And if I don't come out of this, I want you to know that."

The first word that comes to former Senator Charles Percy's lips when Peterson's name is mentioned is "friend." He explains that when his daughter Valerie was murdered in the mid-sixties, Peterson was "among the first to arrive at our door that fateful Sunday morning not only to offer sympathy and help but also to take over many of the difficult situations imposed upon us as a family."

As is the case with Lew Glucksman, there is more than one truth about Pete Peterson's personality, depending on whom one talks to. Sometimes partners had contradictory impressions of him, none of them frozen, each impression changing from day to day. Sometimes people hid their true feelings, which is another reason that Peterson may have missed the gathering storm. After all, Glucksman did help organize, on June 6, 1983, a tenth anniversary luncheon honoring the chairman, at which he served as host. Holding aloft a glass of champagne, Glucksman offered an effusive toast about what a great honor it had been to work beside Pete and how he looked forward to working beside him for many more years. On behalf of the partnership, he presented to the chairman a $25,000 Henry Moore charcoal drawing. Senior banker William Morris, whose dislike for Peterson was well known, had to be persuaded by Glucksman to attend the lunch.* Morris stunned many of his partners by adding his own tribute to the chairman.

This was not the only occasion on which Glucksman was insincere. Over the Memorial Day weekend that year—six weeks before Glucksman presented his ultimatum to the chairman—the Petersons were dining at the Palm Restaurant in East Hampton with another couple and they bumped into Inez and Lew Glucksman and their two daughters. They stopped to say hello. Later, Glucksman came over to their table, where he lingered for about five minutes while the food was on the table, heaping encomium after encomium on Peterson. In an interview a week or so before he confronted Peterson, Glucksman told Lenny Glynn of *Institutional Investor,* † "If I were to devote my energies to being on the outside, I could not manage this business on a day-to-day basis. Pete takes responsibility for maintaining relationships with hundreds of clients. One man couldn't do both jobs."

Months later, when asked why he had hidden his true feelings, Glucksman said, "I'm a great actor. I tried to make the place work, despite whatever feelings I may have frequently had. Life isn't exactly like an Al Capone dinner, where you stand up and beat an associate to death."

Peterson's friends say if he is to be faulted for missing the rage building within Lew Glucksman, it is because he was too trusting; detractors say he was a fool to be so blind. Peterson says it wasn't until about mid-June that he became aware that Lew was always "tense." And yet he did not confront Glucksman. Instead, he continued to rely on James Boshart, and said he hoped that if anything was bothering Lew, Jim would keep him informed.

Peterson, too, tells friends his vice was really the virtue of being too trusting. In a reflective moment in the summer of 1984, Peterson probably best summed up his weakness when he said, "I saw a movie last night. It was Robert Redford in *The Natural.* At one point he said of the woman who shot him, 'I should have seen it coming, but I didn't.' "

---

*As did Harvey Krueger, who had grown tired of the chairman's monologues.
†Glynn's compelling piece, "The Big Power Play at Lehman," appeared in September 1983.

"JOAN, I HAVE JUST HAD THE ULTIMATE CONVERSATION WITH Lew Glucksman," Peterson told his wife on the telephone late on the afternoon of July 13.

"What do you mean?"

"I will tell you when I get home," he said.

Peterson was staggered by his five-hour meeting with Glucksman, absolutely flabbergasted when Glucksman launched his monologue about ships and the joy he gets at the helm of his own boat and announced that he wanted to captain Lehman alone.

Before Peterson could go home and share this experience with his wife, he first had to join Lew Glucksman for cocktails and dinner in honor of Arthur (Artie) Weigner, chief of all over-the-counter trading, who was celebrating his fiftieth year at Lehman, where he began as a $14-a-week errand boy/runner in a trading room employing three people. The party was held in the partners' dining room, a magnificent room with treasured Impressionist paintings on the walls and coral silk covering the windows. Attending were twenty-nine Lehman employees, mostly from the sales and trading side of the business. Fresh flowers filled the room, as they do each day at Lehman. Heavy silverware was neatly arranged at each place, with the "LB" monogram facing up.

It was a festive evening. At the three-pedestal mahogany table, warm toasts were offered between courses of smoked salmon, roast beef and chocolate cake. After dinner, cognac was served, along with a selection of expensive cigars. Weigner sat between Glucksman and Peterson, and the only unusual thing he noticed was that Glucksman "had fish because he was on a diet." It was, says partner William Welsh, who organized the dinner, a "warm, friendly evening, with Lew and others offering toasts to Artie."

Only four people in the room were aware of the conversation the co-CEO's had had just hours before: Glucksman, Peterson, Bob Rubin and Jim Boshart. And, aside from the brief telephone call to Joan, Peterson had spoken to only one other person, Jim Boshart. Soon after Glucksman briefed him and Rubin on the confrontation, Boshart climbed the stairs to Peterson's office. They were both late for the dinner, so there was little time to talk, but from the few words Peterson offered as they rushed to dinner, Boshart knew Peterson wasn't sure whether Glucksman meant what he said. He could tell Peterson was hurt. Still, as Boshart looked across the table, he marveled at the aplomb of the two men who sat just inches away from each other: "If I hadn't known what was going on, I could not have told what was going on. I was watching Pete. He did not seem preoccupied. Nor did Lew. They seemed very relaxed. A remarkable performance."

Later, when the events of this day became public, Weigner remembered a conversation he had with Glucksman before dinner, when he reviewed with his friend how he planned to stand up and roast former and present partners.

"What about Peterson, can he take a joke?" Weigner asked.

"Yeah, but not too rough. I don't think this is the right time," said Glucksman.

That night, when Peterson arrived home, he told his wife of his confrontation with Glucksman. He was glum, and stared out at the East River, which flows below their apartment. "What are you going to do?" she remembers asking.

"He's capable of being very excitable," he said. "I have to find out if he's upset momentarily or if this is the real thing."

"I don't understand why you don't tell him to go to hell," she said. "You're the chairman. You're senior!"

They discussed how a partnership is not a pyramidal structure the way most corporations are, and what his options were. If Lew was serious, Pete said, then perhaps they could compromise and agree to a transition period in which he would eventually leave. Such a plan would spare the firm and everyone else embarrassment.

The next morning Peterson had an eight o'clock breakfast at the River House with partner Steve Schwarzman and a client, the Continental Group, followed by a ten o'clock meeting at Lehman with international banker Yves-André Istel and BMW. He said nothing to betray what had happened the day before. In this crisis, Pete Peterson was cool, according to those who saw him that morning and afterward. As always, he kept his eye on the big picture and thought out the ramifications of every step he might take. And at this point he still wasn't sure whether yesterday was real or only a passing storm.

Soon after he arrived at the office, Peterson learned that this was in fact "the real thing." There was an urgent message that Jim Boshart needed to see him. The tall, wholesome young man with longish, parted blond hair solicitously said he was concerned that the conflict could damage the firm. Peterson concurred. Boshart praised Peterson for trying to work with Lew. He said he was taken totally by surprise, was shocked that matters had come to this point.*

---

*Both men concur about the dialogue that ensued.

In an odd way, Peterson was comforted by Boshart's shock, by his grief. Surely, if Lew's surrogate son was taken totally by surprise, there was reason to believe Glucksman had acted on impulse and not according to a plan. Peterson reviewed the five-hour conversation of the day before, and said he wasn't sure whether Lew was being impulsive or firm.

He waited for a signal from Boshart, which is what Glucksman had anticipated. "Lew always says that in conversations people hear what they want to hear," Boshart said later. "Glucksman had no doubt he was clear with Pete. He wondered whether Pete had heard him. So he suggested that I talk to Pete."

The chairman probed, asking Boshart, "Tell me, what did Lew tell you?"

"He told me his feet are set in cement," responded Boshart. "He wants to take over on September 30."

The words struck Peterson with the force of a punch. There was no mistaking that Boshart was acting as Glucksman's appointed messenger. Peterson stiffened, and said, "Jim, at this point let me just say this: That was not my understanding, and in any event it is clear that we must think this through very carefully and must have additional discussions." As a damage-control effort, Peterson said this matter must, for the time being, be kept from the partners and the public; a leak would be devastating. He suggested that former partner George Ball, a close friend who was also respected by Glucksman, be asked to serve as an intermediary. Boshart thought this was a good idea.

When Boshart left, Peterson placed a call to Ball in Princeton, New Jersey, where he maintains a home and office. After Peterson informed Ball of the confrontation with Glucksman, he said, "You know Lew and he likes you and respects you. You're an obvious choice to sit down with him and see what's on his mind. This thing has enormous implications and it is important that we don't allow it to escalate out of control." Ball was scheduled to enter the hospital for prostate surgery, but agreed to delay the operation.

After speaking with Ball, Peterson telephoned Glucksman. "Lew, I think it's important that we maintain the best possible relationship and that we pick someone we both trust to try and understand this situation. George Ball is my candidate."

"Fine. Have George call me," said Glucksman.

This was the last conversation the two men would have for the next thirteen days.

Thursday afternoon Joan and Pete Peterson flew out to East

Hampton for a long weekend of soul-wrenching conversation. Their house on Georgica Pond, with its own tennis court and pool, was special to them, a getaway nestled among tall pine trees. Here they could think clearly, which was necessary this weekend.

Joan was full of fury. To her, Glucksman was an animal. He was committing a *lawless* act. He had no right to push Pete out. She wanted Pete to declare war, to crush Glucksman.

As distraught as Pete was, he was logical, precise. He remembers puzzling out the options this way: If I declared war on Glucksman —one of us must go! The firm might be destroyed. If Glucksman loses, he might take the heart of his trading operations to a rival firm. If I win, I will once again be stuck, as I was ten years before, with the task of rebuilding Lehman Brothers. And I don't have the energy to repeat that arduous task. If I forced Glucksman to agree to a one-year transition period, I will then be a lame duck asking the board to vote against the wishes of its future CEO. If Glucksman is an animal, as Joan thinks, won't he seek retribution against those who sided with me? It seemed like a Hobson's choice. And yet the only rational choice, for Peterson, seemed to be to work out an orderly transition, one that would allow Glucksman to take command within a certain period. And at the same time preserve Peterson's dignity.

That alternative seemed logical. Yet Peterson was haunted. Glucksman's behavior seemed so mindless to Peterson, so . . . Nixonian. Now he made the connection between Glucksman and Nixon. Now he remembered the former President's irrational Watergate behavior, which came right after winning the second greatest electoral landslide in history. If only Glucksman had said something in May, prior to the co-CEO announcement. Perhaps they could have worked something out. Now, after that public expression of mutual respect, there was no way to avoid public humiliation. How could Glucksman be so selfish? How could one man's whim bring seventy-seven partners to this precipice? Over and over again that weekend, Joan and Pete Peterson would have a variation of this conversation as they struggled to determine their next steps. For them, a course of action hinged on what would happen between Ball and Glucksman, who were to meet Friday morning in Glucksman's cramped, windowless chart room office on the forty-first floor.

The meeting between Ball and Glucksman lasted three hours, and was attended by Bob Rubin. Ball says he was startled by the vehemence of Glucksman's diatribe against Peterson. Glucksman, he recalls, railed against Peterson's long-winded speech about leveraged buyouts and merchant banking just two days before at the Equitable lunch. "Peterson doesn't understand these things," Glucksman said. "He wasn't professional. He is an embarrassment to the firm. I have to keep stepping in to save him." Glucksman said he could "heal the wounds," could bring about more rigorous management. Glucksman says, "I wasn't highly agitated. I was controlled." Nevertheless, he concedes he was pretty rough on Peterson but says he regrets only one thing he said: "I referred to Pete at Bell & Howell—where I don't think he was very good. He sold off things they should not have. I wish I hadn't brought it up."

At one point Bob Rubin, who said little throughout, admits he interceded to gently prod his friend to ease his verbal onslaught.

"Glucksman went on and on about how he was frustrated to have Pete run the firm and how he could do better," says Ball. "It wasn't very coherent. He was angry. He was jealous. I sat there in a state of considerable surprise because he seemed so incoherent. I could only think of Macbeth's line: 'O! full of scorpions is my mind . . .' "

Ball explored the possibility of an orderly transition. What if Pete stayed as co-CEO and chairman for a period of time? This was reminiscent of the graceful exit Peterson had offered Fred Ehrman in 1973. But, like Erhman, Glucksman was closed to compromise.

"I'd have to be the dumbest guy in the world to accept such a transition," Glucksman recalls saying. "The die is cast, George. Our relations are bad. After this, there is no way we could work together." He said he believed Pete was prepared to leave, and the best interests of the firm would be served if he exited quickly.

Two or three times Ball heard Glucksman say, "We've got the votes. The board is totally on our side." He heard Glucksman say, "I have all the votes . . . I am asking Cleary, Gottlieb to represent me." The firm of Cleary, Gottlieb, Steen & Hamilton was one of two principal law firms that regularly represented Lehman Brothers; it was where Ball had once been a founding partner. Hearing this only strengthened Ball's suspicion that Glucksman had first lined up the votes. (Edwin B. Mishkin, the Cleary, Gottlieb partner who would negotiate for Glucksman, says he was not summoned until the middle of the following week. However, Mishkin had the same impression Ball did: "It was my impression that Lew either polled the board or in a scientific or unscientific way knew there was no question the board would approve his becoming chairman.") Glucksman denies implying that he had polled the board; he admits to saying something that could have left that impression: "I think I may have said the following—and I'd say it again—'You put it to a vote and it's a laydown.' "

"Money's no problem," Rubin recalls saying. "We'll be very generous." It was the first time the issue of a financial settlement for Peterson was raised.

Shaken, Ball walked away from this meeting convinced that compromise was fruitless. He telephoned Peterson in East Hampton and reviewed the meeting. No doubt strongly influenced by Joan's hawkish views, Peterson had itemized five options. One was to take the fight to the board. Two was to press for a transition that would allow him to remain as co-CEO for two years and then another year as chairman. Three was to stay one year as co-CEO and one additional year as chairman. Four was to stay one year as co-CEO and two additional years as chairman. Five was to stay through May 1984, the anniversary of Glucksman's appointment as co-CEO. Peterson said he preferred option two, which would permit him to stay as co-CEO for two years and then as chairman for one year. He could then retire with dignity at age sixty.

Ball, who had been a dove in his advice to President Lyndon Johnson during the Vietnam war, thinking Johnson was avoiding reality, now gently tried to introduce the reality he saw at Lehman Brothers. He said he feared that Glucksman had the votes of the board in his pocket. He recalls offering this advice to Peterson: "If you choose to fight, partners will have to make a calculation who would win. I'll tell you how I would calculate were I a young man. I would say, 'If I vote for Glucksman and Glucksman loses, I can probably make peace with Peterson. If I vote for Peterson and Glucksman wins, I'm dead.' On the other hand, if you remain as chairman and Glucksman is the chief executive, your life would be unbearable. If Glucksman is unhappy with the co-CEO situation after two months, he will be unhappy with this arrangement in two months. And by then, Pete, you would have given away bargaining points." Ball urged Peterson to think about a graceful retreat, one paved with a generous severance settlement.

Joan remembers Ball's parting words this way: "I think you should prepare to leave. We should think of putting the best face on it. Think of them putting a $20 million investment in a new business of yours."

Peterson thought $20 million was too steep and told Ball this. Peterson asked Ball to check Lehman's bylaws, in case he wanted to take a challenge to the board or even to the full partnership. They agreed to meet Sunday night for dinner and further discussion. Joan and Pete Peterson resumed their dialogue.

Meanwhile, that Friday afternoon Glucksman drove alone with Jim Boshart out to his home in Three Mile Harbor, not far from where he docked his thirty-five-foot Delta Sportsfisherman and just a few miles from Peterson's more glamorous setting on Georgica Pond. On Saturday and Sunday, Glucksman and Boshart went fishing at five-thirty in the morning. They reviewed the stunning events of the week. They talked strategy. They tried to anticipate what Peterson's next move might be. They talked about bluefish, with Glucksman boasting, as he often did, that he charcoaled bluefish as well as anyone. They talked about Glucksman's concern that he had been too harsh in what he said to Ball.

Glucksman was feeling contrite. Boshart, whose instincts are non-confrontational, encouraged this guilt. Perhaps the tie between Glucksman and Peterson could be severed gently, he thought. Perhaps a generous severance would help. "My principal concern," says Glucksman, "was that the best thing that could happen would be an orderly and a quiet transition to benefit the business. I wanted to do it quickly. The key in any financial deal is to keep the momentum going." In addition to hauling in bluefish, Glucksman and Boshart focused most of their attention that weekend on how to keep the "momentum going."

Sunday evening George Ball arrived for a drink at the Petersons' apartment. Joined by Joan, they walked the few blocks to Xenia restaurant on First Avenue. George sipped a Scotch, Joan a glass of wine, and Pete, who gets wobbly on two glasses of wine, had iced tea. They ordered shish kebab, a Peterson favorite at this Greek restaurant. Ball spoke first of the Friday meeting with Glucksman. "Pete, he ripped apart every aspect of your person," Joan recalls Ball saying. "It is dangerous for your reputation for you to remain in that situation. I think he has probably sampled the board."

Ball reviewed the bylaws, explaining, "You can call a partnership meeting. You have the authority. And if you choose to fight, you can win there."

Peterson had moved away from that option. "George," he said, "Joan and I talked and I figure I could step aside next June 30 and maybe remain chairman for a couple of more years." He said it was inconceivable that Lew would not take into account that he was abrogating their carefully worked-out agreement of May 16, or that

"Lew would seek to further his own ambitions with absolutely no regard for the institution."

"Pete, don't even consider it," said Ball. "He will make that the most miserable year of your life. And he will hurt your reputation as a businessman. And Pete, he will humiliate you at Lehman. You will be responsible for decisions he won't consult you on. I am telling you, you must get out now!" Ball praised Peterson's generosity, but said he was being too rational in an irrational situation. For years Glucksman had had the power, now he wanted the recognition. By slaying Peterson, he was getting back at him and perhaps at Bobbie Lehman and all those who had blackballed him from the New York Athletic Club or called him "pushy." What Peterson had to do, Ball said, was get a lawyer to negotiate a severance agreement.

Ball remembers that Peterson was shocked, and several times repeated, "This is not the way people deal with one another." Nevertheless, he reviewed the options precisely, logically, coolly. Joan was not ready to. She was enraged. "I frankly thought Lew Glucksman was a dangerous animal that you threw meat at," she says. She kept pressing, "Why don't you discuss this with the partners? Why don't you tell him to go to hell?"

She worried that her husband's reputation would be mangled. "Pete would have been willing to leave for nothing if he allowed him a graceful way out," she says.

Ball's parting word of wisdom was, "Pete, you have a serious problem. One of you has to leave."

Intellectually, Peterson knew that Ball was right. But as he later said, he could not then accept this conclusion emotionally. "George, Joan and I have to go home and do some real thinking," Peterson recalls saying. "What you're saying is that no transition will work."

"It breaks my heart to say this, Pete, but it won't work."

Ball got into a cab, which took him to his East Seventy-ninth Street apartment, where he would stay during much of the next nine days. As the Petersons walked home alone holding hands that night, Pete's thoughts tumbled out in whispers: A public donnybrook would tear Lehman apart; if he won, he would again be consumed with day-to-day management of Lehman, and he would probably lose the valuable services of Glucksman; if he lost, he would be humiliated, and partners forced to choose sides might suffer retribution. "It's a battle I couldn't afford to win," Peterson said. They talked about the fatalism they shared, and about the illnesses they had survived. During the past eight years Joan had survived a radical mastectomy and three subsequent biopsies (no malignancies were found); Pete had survived a brain operation from which he did not expect to awake.*

"When people ask why we didn't fight last summer," says Joan, "I say to them that we are different from people who haven't seen the horizon. It always hangs over our heads. Pete always says, 'Who knows how much time we have. Let's do what's right for us.' "

"When we walked home we thought it was over," says Joan. What became "right" for them was to negotiate a generous divorce settlement from Lehman Brothers. But Peterson did not communicate this decision to his associates. Instead, when they got back to the apartment he telephoned his friend and attorney Morton L. Janklow, told him what had happened, asked him to think through the options and join him for breakfast at River House the next morning. Then Peterson called venture capitalist Eli Jacobs, another old friend, with whom he had some joint investments and who was in town from his California home. Peterson reached him at his Carlyle Hotel suite. "There are major problems at Lehman Brothers," Jacobs recalls Peterson saying. "I think it may end up with my leaving the firm. If I do, could we be partners?"

"Yes. Can I be of help?" Jacobs replied. Peterson asked him to think of what his options might be and made a date to meet the next day, Monday.

For the next few days Joan and Pete Peterson's position would shift back and forth as they tried to integrate cold logic and hot emotion. "I would get it for a little while, the way you glimpse an answer to a complex mathematical problem," explains Joan. "Then I would have to have it explained again."

Monday morning Peterson was joined at breakfast by Janklow and Ball, where they reviewed many of the same options Ball had dismissed the night before. "Pete's instinct was not to fight," recalls Janklow. "But we didn't know if we could make a deal. My view is that you don't make a good deal unless you're prepared to fight. I wanted to be prepared to go to the mattresses. At this point we didn't have any proposals from Glucksman." Janklow, who earned his way through college and law school as a professional card player, was prepared to bluff. But he knew, he recalls, "If Pete had gotten mad and started a fight, he would have destroyed the entity. It's like atomic war."

*Today, both say they are free of life-threatening illnesses.

Within a few hours Peterson would receive the first proposal from Glucksman. Immediately upon arriving at Lehman, Peterson canceled the board of directors meeting scheduled for that day. Then he saw Jim Boshart, who had left a message that he wished to confer. As part of what Boshart calls his "damage-control exercise," he told Pete that Lew felt badly about some of the things he had said to George Ball and wanted to get together immediately to apologize. Firmly, Peterson told him a meeting between them made no sense at this time. Too much emotion was invested, and the firm could be the loser if there was an explosion. "Pete understood that his hand was strengthened as long as Lew felt guilty," says Joan Ganz Cooney.

Peterson wanted to address one and only one question, the same question he had raised with Boshart the week before. Looking straight at Boshart, Peterson recalls asking, "Jim, there are few questions you will ever be asked about this firm that will be more important. Do you believe there is any kind of transition that would be acceptable—like next May—which is the anniversary of Lew's becoming co-CEO? George Ball gives me the impression this won't work. Will it work?"

Both men were standing. Boshart circled a chair twice, then stopped and said, "Pete, oh, how I wish I could give you any other answer, but I just know there is only one honest answer. He is absolutely set in cement. There is no transition that is acceptable. It must be September 30."

It was at this moment that Peterson exploded for the only time during the thirteen days of negotiations. "I want you to know that is not acceptable," he shouted. "It is mindless! It is unnecessary! It is destructive!"

Boshart tried to soothe the chairman, acknowledging that it would be a shock to people but that too much blood had already been spilled. Then, to keep "the momentum going," Boshart made what amounted to a proposal. "Money is no problem," he remembers telling Peterson. He quickly added that Glucksman and Rubin knew he had poured his life into Lehman and was owed a lot. They were prepared to be generous, knowing that the Lehman pension plan was modest. They were prepared to invest money in a new Peterson venture, though Boshart said the $20 million figure Ball tossed out was too rich. They thought, Peterson recalls Boshart saying, that the public relations exposure on this event was minor, perhaps a page-three business story. They wanted to say nothing to the press, which Ball had warned would "look like Peterson was kicked out."

"I knew then that it was all over and my own nightmare was beginning," says Peterson. "I also knew that we would need to finalize my transition arrangements promptly before there were leaks."

This meeting toughened Peterson's stance. He remembers telephoning Ball, who was scheduled to see Glucksman again that day, and instructing Ball, "Tell them that a complete, full disclosure statement by Lew on what he had done was a nonnegotiable minimum requirement for any solution acceptable to me—and that if I found he had told anyone other than Bob Rubin and Jim Boshart about these discussions, the entire issue would be reopened." Peterson had one other requirement, as recounted by his wife: "At that point our sole interest was in getting as much money as we could." Her husband, she explains, had to start a new business from scratch and had scarcely any retirement provisions to show for his ten years at Lehman. Actually, that wasn't quite true, since as we've seen, starting in 1982 Peterson and Glucksman had placed in an interest-bearing account 1 percent each of the firm's profits, to be available in 1986. In its first two years, this account had accumulated over $1 million for each man. What wasn't clear, however, was whether this contract carried over if Peterson left the firm.

The meeting with Boshart apparently convinced Peterson that he had no choice but to leave. For when he met at midday with his friend Eli Jacobs, he said, "If I win in a board showdown and Glucksman leaves the firm, then the firm loses and I lose. If I fight and lose, then I lose. There are some victories too costly to win!" There were two other factors in Pete's thinking, says Jacobs. After a decade at Lehman he was tired, ready to try something new. And though he was then earning the after-tax equivalent of almost $5 million annually,* "Pete had also wanted a chance in life to make more money."

While Peterson and Jacobs met, Ball huddled with Glucksman in the chart room and indicated that Peterson might be prepared to leave. Ball recalls, "I said I was advising Pete to leave under the following terms"—strict secrecy until an agreement was reached, full

---

*Salary, bonus and dividends are taxed at ordinary income rates (57 percent), while appreciation of the worth of Lehman stock is taxed at capital gains rates (25 percent). The $5 million figure represents the amount of salary and bonus income an executive would have to receive to obtain the same after-tax sum that Peterson did in 1983.

disclosure to the press of the reasons for Peterson's departure, and a generous financial settlement. "I said I didn't know whether I could convince him." Ball later reported that Glucksman again was volatile, one moment storming at Peterson, the next sweetly reasonable. By the end of their meeting, Glucksman had agreed to each provision, subject to detailed negotiations.

Over the next several days Ball tried his hand at drafting a press release, as did Janklow, with the team of Peterson, Cooney, Ball, Janklow and Jacobs reviewing and constantly amending this draft; there were daily strategy sessions in this group, as well as between Glucksman, Rubin and Boshart, and, beginning Wednesday, between Glucksman and Ed Mishkin of Cleary, Gottlieb; Ball and Glucksman negotiated several more times that week. The overriding fear of each participant was a leak to the partners and the press. "The first week it was like the first week we learned the missiles were in Cuba and the world didn't know it," says Ball, who as Under Secretary of State had been immersed in that 1962 world crisis. "We had to keep things to ourselves because the damn thing would have leaked before we had a plan devised." Ball kept thinking of a conversation he and former Defense Secretary Robert McNamara and former National Security Adviser McGeorge Bundy had once taped for Alfred Sloan Foundation on the missile crisis: "We all agreed that it took one week to analyze our reaction, and our reaction to the Russian action, and their reaction to our reaction. The three of us agreed that if we had made a decision in the first forty-eight hours after we learned the missiles were in Cuba, we would have made the wrong decision."

By Friday, July 22, there were draft documents of a press release and a severance agreement, and Janklow sat with Ed Mishkin for the first time to commence their negotiations. Janklow was deeply distressed, he remembers, "about the propriety of Cleary, Gottlieb, as the counsel to Lehman Brothers, representing Glucksman, since it was possible that the interest of Lehman Brothers and Glucksman would not always be identical." How could Glucksman speak for the partners? Did he poll the board? Did Mishkin ascertain that? (Mishkin says, "When I got in the picture Lew and Pete had already come to an understanding in principle." It was, he says, "a done deal.")

Janklow expressed none of his misgivings to Mishkin. He had come to feel contempt for Glucksman, and as an experienced negotiator, felt he was in a commanding position: "I ultimately concluded that this was not a rational act. This was a guy [Glucksman] sitting with a pair of deuces in a poker game and bumping a guy [Peterson] who had three aces showing."

All through that weekend Janklow and Mishkin negotiated at a dining-room table in the East Hampton home that Linda and Morton Janklow had rented that summer. They would break from time to time, allowing Mishkin to travel the few miles to Glucksman's Three Mile Harbor house, and for Janklow to speed around Georgica Pond, where Peterson was waiting at home. The Petersons had previously invited houseguests that weekend—Sally and Jerome Goodman (who, as Adam Smith, writes on economics and finance and appears on public television)—who knew nothing of the negotiations. Often, Peterson would slip into a back room to meet with Janklow, or be on the telephone. "We just kept smiling all through this," says Joan.

For two days Janklow and Mishkin discussed and argued about the draft press release and the financial terms of Peterson's severance. "We spent as much time on the press release as on the terms," says Janklow, because they hoped "to make it look less painful to the firm's reputation and to Pete's." Peterson's instructions to him, he recalls, were simple: "We have to tell the truth because no one will believe us otherwise." Peterson, remembering the nightmare of Watergate, kept saying he would not go the "limited hangout route."

Janklow and Mishkin argued over whether the press release should say Glucksman "confronted" Peterson. Mishkin tried to soften the language; Janklow pushed, he recalls, for "a press release which reflected the truth as much as possible and at the same time put the best possible face on things." Meanwhile, they wrestled over the six main points of the severance agreement.

By Sunday afternoon Janklow, exhausted, decided to clear his head by taking a walk on the beach. Strolling alone, he was startled to bump into John S. Levy, a Lehman partner. "How are you Mort?" asked Levy.

"I've had to work all weekend," said Janklow.

"Why? You should be enjoying yourself out here," said Levy.

Janklow shrugged and kept moving. "I walked away thinking," says Janklow, "that he's sunning and relaxing—and it's his life I'm dealing with!"

W ILLIAM WELSH WAS IN THE POOL AT HIS WESTHAMPTON Beach house, enjoying a vacation, when Lew Glucksman called Monday afternoon. "There's a special meeting of the board tomorrow at two," he remembers Glucksman saying. "I want all directors to attend. It is not for the sale of the firm." Glucksman would not say why the meeting was called. Welsh drove in the next morning and upon arriving in the office, asked his fellow board members, "What's going on?" No one knew. Each board member had received, the day before, a one-sentence memo announcing "a Special Meeting of the Board" to be held Tuesday, July 26, 1983, at 2:00 P.M.

Aside from Peterson, Glucksman and Rubin, only two board members say they suspected that Peterson was to be ousted. One was William Morris. "I knew there were some discussions going on," he says. A week before he had been upset, as he often was, by something Peterson had done. He went to commiserate with his good friend Bob Rubin and somehow, as he later told friends, "I got the feeling there was some hope."

Among those at the firm caught totally by surprise was James Hood, the Lehman spokesman. Tuesday, July 26, was to be a big day for Hood. After endless prodding by Peterson, of countless drafts and almost two years of effort by Hood and others, Lehman's first published annual report was due off the press this day. When Hood was summoned to Peterson's office at ten-thirty, he assumed the subject would be the report. Instead, Peterson told the bearded, mild-mannered Hood to prepare for a major announcement. Hood arranged for secretaries to type and collate the news releases and had messengers poised to deliver press releases that afternoon. But Hood was not let in on the nature of the announcement. He guessed it concerned a merger.

At noon, Glucksman came up to Peterson's corner office on the forty-third floor, and the co-CEO's met for the first time in thirteen days. They were joined by Ball, Rubin and Boshart. "The atmosphere was almost unreal. It was matter of fact," remembers Boshart. "Pete brought up some Lehman business." They agreed Jim Hood should be called in and told. When Hood arrived, Peterson handed him a six-page press release that had been typed by the lawyers, and said, "It would be simpler if you read this."

Hood was stupefied. Peterson, with Glucksman nodding approval, told him to be ready to issue it after the board met. Hood left, and Peterson, Glucksman and the three other men sat down to lunch in the chairman's private dining room, located between his corner office and the boardroom. Lehman waiters hovered over them, bringing a first course, then a second, then dessert, then cigars. Yet Glucksman did not feel the meeting was "tense"; he was grateful when Peterson offered, "Lew, we've always had an open relationship. I'm going to tell you what I'm going to tell the board." From handwritten notes, the chairman then read what.he intended to say.

When Peterson finished, he asked, "Do you have any objections, Lew?"

For once Lew Glucksman did not object to a speech by Peterson.

The directors gathered at two o'clock in the oak-paneled boardroom, a replica of the original boardroom at One William Street. A side door connected the boardroom to Peterson's dining room, where the two CEO's were finishing lunch. As nine of the twelve board members entered they filed around a thirty-foot-long mahogany table, centered under two brass chandeliers, and took their seats. The windows were blanketed by gold-and-cream Fortuny curtains. A dark mahogany breakfront stood alone against the north wall, containing books and board records. The sole art object in the room was a bust of Emanuel Lehman, a founding partner.

The board waited. Finally, Peterson and Glucksman entered, grim-faced, from Peterson's inner sanctum. They took their places at the head of the long table, flanked on either side by nine other directors: Robert Rubin, Richard Fuld, Harvey Krueger, Yves-André Istel, Sheldon Gordon, William Morris, William Welsh, Peter Solomon and Edmund Hajim. (Only Enrico Braggiotti, chairman of BCI, Lehman's one outside shareholder, was not in attendance.)*

Sipping some iced tea, Peterson looked down and began reading from his notes: "Thirteen days ago Lew said he wanted to run this business, and he wanted to run it soon—by September 30. Lew told me this firm has been his whole life, and he didn't have a lot of options. He felt I did." They had quickly agreed, Peterson said, "to bring in a trusted third party, and that was George Ball, who is outside now."

Board members were stunned and exchanged covert glances.

"My plan had been to remain as co-CEO for two to three years, and turn it over to Lew at the end of that time." But Lew wanted to run Lehman now. Over a two-week period, using George Ball as

---

*The account of this meeting is based on interviews with each of the twelve directors, and on Peterson's handwritten speech notes.

an intermediary, they had discussed several options, Peterson explained. "The theme of all of my options was a gradual transition." The chairman said he had even offered to step aside as co-CEO next May. But that was not satisfactory to Lew.

Peterson talked about why he decided not to fight: "What is an institution? It transcends individuals in the sense that it is more important. It is a corporation that goes on. A chairman perpetuates and thinks of the long-term interests of the firm. I had several choices. I could talk to a number of you and get your reaction. I could see if there were other alternatives. There was no way I could visualize this process without leaks, without divisiveness, without damaging this firm, without re-creating the very problems we had done so much to overcome.

"As for Lew, no one on Wall Street knows as much about so many aspects of this business—not just trading, not just money markets—but pricing and distribution and many broad aspects of finance." He is "a rare talent. I have concluded he is far more indispensable than many of us, and more indispensable than I am. Lew is fifty-seven, and every red-blooded American boy deserves the opportunity to run his own show at some point.

"As for myself, Lew said I had more options than he did. He's probably right." Peterson said he would remain at Lehman as chairman until the first of the year and assist in any way he could; after January 1 he said he would be starting a venture-capital firm with his friend Eli Jacobs. He concluded: "Paul Tillich once said, 'The challenge of Twentieth Century Man is to be comfortable with ambiguity.' I am comfortable with ambiguity. I see it as a challenge. What I want out of life is to see the firm flourish. And I want my reputation, to the maximum extent possible, protected." Peterson praised his partners and urged them "to unite behind Lew."

Peterson stood up to leave, saying there were "some retirement arrangements for me," which Bob Rubin would explain. If there were any questions about the press release, George Ball was outside and could answer them.

Peterson, trailed by Glucksman, turned to step outside, and as they left, the heavy silence was punctured by the booming voice of Peter Solomon, the curly-haired forty-four-year-old partner seated directly to Peterson's left. Solomon disdained Glucksman and was not close to Peterson, but he was enraged that the two men would make decisions without consulting the board and would expect the board to rubber stamp their wishes. "Have you resigned and are asking us to vote?" Solomon asked. "Or is this an issue open to discussion?"

"Among all the disagreeable alternatives, this one is in the best interests of Lehman Brothers," Peterson remembers saying. In effect, Peterson acknowledged that he had resigned.

PETER SOLOMON WAS IN THE HABIT OF SAYING WHATEVER WAS on his mind, and he did not like Pete Peterson's answer. Solomon, whose bright pink shirts matched his aggressive personality, had joined Lehman in 1963, became a partner in 1971, and came to be respected for his skills as a banker who specialized in the firm's retail industry efforts. Peter Solomon was a risk taker. In 1978 he left Lehman to become Deputy Mayor of New York City for Economic Policy and Development, a post that gave him the public exposure he enjoyed. In 1980 he joined the Carter Administration as counselor to the U.S. Treasury Department, though he knew that Carter was facing an uphill reelection. After Carter's thrashing, Solomon rejoined Lehman. While he liked to think of himself as a risk taker, many of his partners thought Solomon was aptly nicknamed "the brat." The plaque Solomon mounted on his office wall is revealing. A gift from the Student Loan Marketing Association, it contains this poem:

> There once was a young man from Lehman
> Who went rantin', ravin', and screamin'.
> He felt left out in spite of his clout
> Since he hadn't been part of the schemin'.

Peter Solomon remembered every slight, every wound, and was not shy about shouting his hurts to the world. He told near strangers that he had never received the credit he deserved for arranging the 1977 Kuhn Loeb merger by first suggesting it to Harvey Krueger.* He complained that he was ignored when he argued, beginning in 1982, that Lehman's capital was inadequate and that partners should explore the possibility of going public, as First Boston had done. At Lehman, Peter Solomon felt he was never given the title and recognition he deserved, and as a result some of his partners came to suspect

*Krueger concedes, "He's right."

that he let his resentments color his decisions. Nevertheless, for all his vanity, no one denied that Peter Solomon was a very independent man.

Peter Solomon had been taught the value of independence by his father, Sidney L. Solomon, who rose from clerk to chairman of Abraham & Straus, the New York department store. His mother's family once owned the Stop & Shop supermarket chain. Peter went to the right private schools, was the last member of his freshmen class to be accepted but nevertheless graduated cum laude from Harvard, received an M.B.A. from the Harvard Business School, and married Linda Newman, whose family were also successful retailers. Although his partners believed Solomon was far wealthier than he actually was, he did enjoy a degree of financial independence not shared by most partners, who did not think of themselves as wealthy despite annual earnings ranging from about $500,000 to more than $2 million, in addition to owning millions of dollars in Lehman stock.

As Peterson spoke, Solomon remembers thinking, If only I had known beforehand, I wouldn't have let it happen. He might have leaked it. He might have organized his partners in protest. He would have devised a strategy, because however unpopular he was within the firm, Peter Solomon was a superb strategist, a man experienced in handling the press, a rough in-fighter with a talent for "schemin."

With Peterson and Glucksman out of the room, Solomon glanced pleadingly around the table at each of his partners, hoping for some support. His eyes moved to banking partner William Morris, who looked older than his forty-five years, partly because of his straight gray hair and chalky skin, partly because of his I've-seen-it-all air of resignation, partly because he moves slowly and deliberately and speaks in a monosyllabic drawl acquired in Orange, Texas, where he was raised. Solomon knew that Morris found Peterson a callous man, and blamed Peterson for abruptly removing him as head of the banking division in 1982. Although Solomon knew that Morris also blamed Glucksman for his removal, he feared that Morris's hatred of Peterson and his intimate friendship with Bob Rubin might compel his silence. Solomon stared at Morris, who was not uncomfortable remaining mute.

Solomon then looked to Harvey Krueger, the former president of Kuhn Loeb, the partner who preceded Morris as head of banking and who, along with Morris and Solomon, were senior bankers who owned more stock than the troika then running the banking division.

Krueger, then fifty-four, was a solid banker and a solid citizen who spent his spare time raising funds for the State of Israel. A portly man, Krueger enjoyed his food and omnipresent pipe. But he had the reputation as someone who lacked the toughness to terminate employees at Kuhn Loeb and to control costs, or to take sides at Lehman. Krueger, who reveled in the affection of his partners, was wounded that at least one partner at Lehman—Bob Rubin—openly disliked him. As Solomon stared at Krueger he assumed that the banker would be a natural Peterson ally. In fact, Krueger was personally closer to Glucksman. As chairman of the audit committee, he and Glucksman worked together intimately. And although Krueger could not abide Rubin, who had opposed the Kuhn Loeb merger and whom Krueger replaced as head of banking after the merger, Connie and Harvey Krueger dined at least twice a year with Inez and Lew Glucksman. They had never dined alone with Joan and Pete Peterson. Krueger was not about to speak up.

Yves-André Istel, then forty-seven, who came over in the Kuhn Loeb merger with Krueger, also kept his silence. The international banker was a natural partisan of Peterson's. The French-born Istel came from a distinguished family and was a shrewd banker who could open doors around the globe. Istel was made nervous by the short-term, transactional environment that traders thrived in, and he knew his relationship with Glucksman was strained. Glucksman openly grumbled, as did some other partners, that Istel was coasting and getting by more on his agile brain than on hard work. That's why Glucksman had tried to reduce his stock ownership in 1982, and might do so again. Istel, therefore, was not about to risk alienating Glucksman further.

Also silent was another natural Peterson ally, Edmund Hajim, then forty-six, whom Glucksman had removed that May as chairman of Lemco, Lehman's investment management division. Hajim's position at Lehman was already precarious, and he wasn't about to speak up for a chairman who just weeks before had not spoken up for him. As George Ball had predicted, partners had more reason to fear Glucksman than Peterson.

Another potential Peterson supporter, William Welsh, fifty-two, was a popular figure around the firm, a short, roundish man with a ready smile. Welsh had reason to resent Glucksman because after he had succeeded in building Lehman's retail sales force, Glucksman shoved him aside to a lesser job as head of special projects. Instead of a line management function with hundreds of employees under his command, Welsh now performed a staff function with few employees reporting to him. Since he joined the board in 1977, no one could remember that Bill Welsh had ever said a word at a board meeting, and this day was no exception.

As he looked around the room, Solomon could see that the other board members were Glucksman partisans. Richard Fuld, then thirty-seven, who succeeded Glucksman as president of Lehman Commercial Paper, was a Glucksman disciple. He had worked as his clerk the summer after graduating from the University of Colorado; it was Glucksman who promoted Fuld to take over commercial paper, then all fixed-income trading, and had placed him on the board and the operating committee. To many of his banking partners the intense, dark-haired Fuld, who usually left the office during the day only to keep trim at squash or to play with the Lehman baseball team, epitomized the "digital mind" trader, someone who spent so much time in front of his green screen or making rat-tat-tat decisions that he was no longer quite human. Fuld did not see his partners socially. Rarely did he speak at board meetings, and when he did it was usually to express support for his mentor.

Solomon had a more complex view of Sheldon Gordon, who ran equity trading operations. But he knew that in a showdown Gordon would side with Glucksman. As, obviously, so would Rubin. That left only Enrico Braggiotti, whose bank owned just over 4 percent of Lehman, and who was absent today. Braggiotti had been informed in separate telephone calls by Ball and Glucksman of what was to happen this day.

As he looked around the table, Solomon noticed that most of his partners' heads were bowed. He could hardly contain himself. He declared that he was outraged that Glucksman and Peterson would take such a momentous step without first discussing it with their partners. What right did Glucksman and Rubin have to decide by themselves how much of the partners' money to award Peterson? Solomon waited for someone else to speak up. No one did.

Bob Rubin witnessed this scene with immense satisfaction, for he loathed Solomon, thought him a vain loudmouth; Rubin became enraged when Solomon called him "cousin" and boasted to partners that Rubin's "first cousin, Bunny Solomon, used to work for my father." Rubin could barely suppress a smile as he rose to discuss the proposed terms of Peterson's severance.

While the board met behind closed doors, Peterson and Glucksman were left to wait in Peterson's office. For the next two and a half hours, they engaged, with George Ball and Jim Boshart, in an almost surreal conversation. "We talked about the history of Lehman Brothers," says Boshart. "George Ball was telling me stories because I was the youngster of the group. It was open. I'd even describe it as friendly."

Back in the boardroom, Rubin explained the terms of Peterson's severance agreement: Peterson would be permitted to withdraw all of his almost $7 million in equity at once, rather than over the mandatory two-and-one-half- to five-year payout period; he would be entitled to a bonus as big as the one Glucksman would receive in September; he would continue to receive 1 percent of the firm's profits for the next five and a half years; he would receive $300,000 annually for five and a half years as "supplemental retirement benefits," which he could use as an office allowance; Lehman would invest, on terms comparable to those granted other investors, $5 million in Peterson & Jacobs,* his new venture capital firm; and if Lehman was sold anytime in the next five and a half years, Peterson, unlike other departing partners, would receive the same premium—the value offered shareholders above the worth of their stock—on the sale. Under the terms of the agreement, the size of his premium would decline after two and a half years, which gave Peterson a financial stake in a quick sale of Lehman. In exchange for this bountiful settlement, nothing was required of Peterson.

"You guys are nuts to allow this to happen!" shouted Peter Solomon when Rubin finished. "We represent an investment of forty million dollars, which dwarfs the investment of Peterson and Glucksman. We are allowing them to harm our investment." Solomon says he thought he was speaking for the institution, for tradition. Again, he looked about for support.

Silence.

"Come on, guys. That's our money!"

Silence.

Then, like clerks inspecting the details of a legal document, the board members began to quibble about the terms of Peterson's severance agreement, which they now say shocked them, the more so because they were paying for it. How could Peterson, who lectured federal employees on their "excessive" pension benefits, be so "greedy"? Why, partners asked, should Peterson be allowed to cash in all his partnership stock immediately, whereas if another partner

*Since changed to Peterson, Jacobs & Company.

left, he would have to wait years to withdraw all of his capital? They worried that Peterson would join a competitor. Yet, in the end they made only one amendment to the package—they asked Peterson to sign a clause, pledging he would not, over the next five and a half years, join one of Lehman's five principal competitors: Goldman, Sachs; Salomon Brothers; Morgan Stanley; Merrill Lynch or First Boston. Rubin paused to step outside and ask Ball to inquire whether this would be acceptable to the chairman. Ball reported back to Rubin that Peterson readily agreed.

Solomon again took the floor. If the board wouldn't discuss larger governance issues (What is a partnership? Who has the ability to make decisions for partners? Why weren't they consulted?), and if they wouldn't discuss money, then he was determined to frustrate the decision by focusing on the draft of the press release. Loudly, he demanded that George Ball come in to answer his questions. The draft, Solomon said, was so frank in revealing what really happened between Glucksman and Peterson that it would harm Lehman. He wanted a "limited hangout."

The six-page draft that Ball reviewed with them was unusually candid, though it did contain a few falsehoods—Peterson was quoted as saying, "In recent years, I have developed a very close working partnership with Lew Glucksman"; Glucksman was quoted as praising "Pete's generous encouragement," his "wisdom and understanding." However, the release laid bare the essential truth. "Just a few days ago," Peterson was quoted as saying, "Lew told me that after considerable thought he had concluded that this arrangement [co-CEO] fell short of permitting him the fulfillment of his larger goals and of realizing the full potential of his capabilities. He told me that he felt he could achieve that fulfillment only by assuming the sole direction of the firm."

Ball reassured Solomon and the board that based on his and Peterson's extensive experience with the press, such bold candor would disarm press skepticism.* With nothing hidden, there would be nothing to unearth and the story would eventually die.

Solomon was not appeased. He believed that his experience in public life, plus his friendships with reporters, gave him a sense of

---

*Solomon also remembers Ball or Peterson or Glucksman—he is not sure which—warning that the New York *Times* had gotten wind of the story and that unless the board acted quickly the firm would lose control of this story. Other board members do not remember this. Peterson says flatly, "It was never discussed." And Peterson's attorney, Mort Janklow, says, "I know for a fact that the New York *Times* did not have this story."

what made news. If Peter Solomon was not intimidated by swarms of honeybees, he was not about to be intimidated by George Ball or Pete Peterson's distinguished résumés. For years Solomon's private passion had been the 300,000 honeybees that he kept at his weekend house in Connecticut. "I always thought Lehman was like a beehive," he says. "In a beehive you need total control. Beekeeping teaches you to be extraordinarily calm in adversity. Your natural inclination is to get the hell out of there." Now, surrounded by adversity, Solomon refused to budge.

His instincts were shared by other members of the board. The candid release Ball was urging on them offended the partners' instinct for privacy. Lehman partners were not running for office, they were not part of a public corporation with thousands of shareholders. Why, some board members chimed in, did they have to display their dirty laundry? "Why not just announce that Peterson is leaving to pursue other interests," said Harvey Krueger. "Why create news in the newspapers?"

William Morris complained that it was typical of Peterson to be more concerned with his own image than with that of the firm. Morris said he wanted "less" in the press release. But Ball, speaking for Peterson, toughed it out, insisting that Peterson would not relent. Citing Watergate, he said Peterson would not "go the limited hangout route."

"This will pound on our shores like waves hitting the beach," Solomon exclaimed, in effect pleading for his partners to join him, to reject the press release, to refuse to accept as final a decision allowing Peterson to resign that he believed would devastate Lehman. "No one would talk," says Solomon. "They sat around looking at me."

Later, some board members would complain of the cavalier way Peterson and Glucksman treated them. Harvey Krueger, for instance, complained about how the decision was announced: "There were no options, no discussions of whether this was good for the firm. It was: 'Here's a press release.' In a strange sense they both showed contempt for the board."

Nevertheless, the board acquiesced in the press release without altering a comma. Peterson and Glucksman had correctly anticipated that the board would not resist decisions they made in the board's name. After the board affirmed the private agreement that Glucksman and Peterson had made, the co-CEO's returned together to the boardroom. Glucksman spoke briefly and without much emotion. Hurriedly, he thanked Peterson for his statesmanship, his good wishes and decade of service to Lehman. Glucksman made just one promise to his partners: In the future, he said, there would be "more participation in the management of Lehman."

The meeting broke at five o'clock, three hours after it began, and everyone rushed to attend a scheduled partners' meeting, in the meeting room on the forty-second floor. On his way, Peterson stopped by Jim Hood's office, giving him the signal to dispatch the messengers with the press releases five minutes after he entered the partners' meeting. Then Peterson started down the nearby staircase, only to reappear a moment later to snatch from Hood his sole copy of what he called Lehman's first glossy annual report. (Actually, as the annual report noted, it was the second.)

Most of the other seventy-six partners—all men—were waiting.* In recent years full partnership gatherings were held irregularly, but usually one was held in the fall. Most of the partners were puzzled as to why they had been summoned now in the midst of summer. Equally unusual was the way their co-CEO's seemed to slump, as if emotionally drained, at a rectangular table in the front of the meeting room. Then Peterson gravely rose to speak.

Partners sensed that something was wrong, and tensed. Trying to lighten the audience, Peterson held up the lone copy of Lehman's 1982–1983 annual report and joked about how, after all his harangues, it was finally done. He might have noted, but didn't, that the eighty-page report glowed with good news from Lehman Brothers. It began with a jointly signed statement from Peterson and Glucksman, who were photographed sitting side by side with tight smiles on their faces, and went on to say: "Our return on equity is at the very top of the industry and our capital is now in excess of $200 million . . . our organization has more than tripled in size since 1974 . . . In 1982, for the third year in a row, Lehman Brothers completed more mergers, acquisitions and divestitures than any other investment bank." The good news continued for four pages.

Then Peterson lavished praise on Lehman and his partners, singling out Jim Boshart. "He said I had done a terrific job and he hoped people would get to know me better," remembers Boshart. "I was really surprised by his comments. He was the ultimate statesman." More briefly than at the board meeting, Peterson then announced

---

*Lehman, like Goldman, Sachs; Salomon Brothers; and Morgan Stanley, had not up to this point had a female partner; such public firms as Merrill Lynch, Paine Webber, and Shearson/American Express had only a few women at a comparable level.

that he was leaving. He frankly explained why, and said an announcement was being delivered to the media at that moment. He thanked the partners and wished them well.

When Peterson finished, Lew Glucksman stood up, turned to his co-CEO, and said, "Would you now leave and let me be with my partners," words that would haunt the partnership for months to come.* Very little else of what Glucksman said in his brief remarks is remembered.

Peterson dutifully rose to leave the room, and the partners gave him a standing ovation. But they were even more stunned than the board had been. When the meeting broke, many wandered out of the auditorium singly and then gathered, like wounded birds, in the offices of colleagues. At a moment when the firm had just concluded the most successful nine-month period in its history, how could this happen? What would this mean for the firm? And what would it mean for them?

Many of the partners were distraught. One partner remembers wondering whether Glucksman was capable of "rising above his past, of becoming a statesman-leader." They knew Glucksman was smart, but many worried about his personality, about whether he was too much the inside rather than the outside person every firm needs to impress clients. Board member Enrico Braggiotti says, "Lew Glucksman was just a good trader. He was not a chairman of the board. He probably wasn't a president." It is difficult to gauge feelings accurately long after a moment has passed, for subsequent events can warp people's memory. However, one up-and-coming Lehman vice president, who worked closely with Glucksman and respected him, summarized the thinking of many Lehman employees this way: "What happened between Pete and Lew can be viewed as a profoundly selfish act by Lew. It can't be viewed as a fight between Glucksman and Peterson people, because not many people at Lehman were loyal to Peterson. He was not a personable individual. He was very self-centered. He had definite ideas. But Lew threw out of the firm his greatest investment-banking asset. No one in investment banking has Peterson's stature."

Some partners were openly pleased. Dick Fuld, who admired Glucksman and who speaks the way he acts—quickly—says, "It didn't bother me." Mergers and acquisitions specialist Eric

---

*Glucksman remembers dismissing Peterson, but adds, "If I did summarily dismiss him, it was in bad taste and inadvertent."

Gleacher, whom Peterson had removed as head of the M. & A. department in 1982, told colleagues at the time that he felt "like celebrating." As someone who befriended Glucksman when Glucksman was in trouble back in 1973–1974, Gleacher was one of the few allies Glucksman had in the banking department. He thought Peterson was too preoccupied with his own deals and had never paused to develop the kind of team culture Glucksman had forged in the commercial paper division. "A critical shortcoming of Peterson's years at the helm," Gleacher says, "was the failure to create a sense of teamwork across the firm—it was absent when he arrived, as well as when he departed . . . Lehman was held together strictly by money, blood money."

As stunned as most partners were at the time, they pliantly put on their public masks, professing pleasure that the firm was not put through a protracted succession struggle; they hailed Pete Peterson's majesty, and clapped Lew Glucksman on the back. "I heard very good things from people at Lehman Brothers after he took control," says Martin Lipton, a prominent attorney who works closely with many investment banks on mergers and acquisitions. "Everyone was enthusiastic."

With the passage of time, many Lehman partners and board members came to deplore what they call Glucksman's lust for power and his unwillingness to consult the board on an issue so vital to the future of the firm. They resented Glucksman for staging a coup that embarrassed Lehman and elbowed aside its foremost business getter, its most illustrious name, all at a time when the firm was thriving. "I thought it was catastrophic," says François de Saint Phalle. "Pete was one of the most significant forces ever to come out of Wall Street for corporate America, which is what we're all about . . . It was a tragedy. We were on our way to becoming one of the three or four crème de la crème investment banking firms."

But many partners were also outraged at Peterson. One partner, whom Peterson considers a friend, accuses both men of violating their fiduciary responsibility to the partnership. With the benefit of hindsight, he says Peterson should have insisted on taking the matter to the board when Glucksman first raised it or pushed harder for a longer transitional arrangement or taken the fight to the full partnership. "It was," he says, "a shameful episode which cast no glory on either individual. It should not have been allowed to happen . . . Pete's defense is that he held the interests of the institution uppermost. But you have to ask whether he exhibited good judgment. The fact is, he owed it to the board. In my mind the chief executive role implies custodiallike responsibility for the well-being of an institution. That responsibility was abdicated by both men."

Some of Peterson's supporters believe he had been afraid to risk a vote. "Peterson is not without fault, because he left as chairman under his own will," observes his friend Enrico Braggiotti. "He could have fought. When Ball told me the story of Glucksman before it was announced, I told him to fight, with the support of BCI. He had not the courage to fight. Pete had a very good golden shake of the hand, which I complained about. If Pete had not had all this money, perhaps he would have fought."

As time passed, partners speculated endlessly about whether Peterson could have won if he had fought, as Braggiotti wished he had. It is difficult to handicap such a vote, since board members would have had to gauge whether Glucksman or Peterson would leave if one of them had lost a showdown, and who would follow the loser out of the firm. That information could affect their judgment, as could calculations about who was likely to win. A board member who did not like Lew Glucksman might nevertheless cast a vote for him if he appeared a sure winner, especially because Glucksman was thought to be vindictive. Going into the board meeting, Peterson assumed he could get the votes of Solomon, Istel, Hajim, Welsh and Braggiotti. A poll of the board members reveals that two of these five men now say their vote would have been contingent on whom the likely victor would be. Peterson also assumed he had a sixth vote—Harvey Krueger's—which is unlikely, since Krueger felt closer to Glucksman. Of Glucksman, Krueger says, "I never had the problem other people had. Was he volatile? Yes. Was he a good manager? Absolutely." The only board member except Rubin to whom Glucksman even hinted that trouble was brewing with Peterson was Krueger.* Sometime before the July 13 confrontation with Peterson, Glucksman asked Krueger how he would feel if Peterson were to leave. "He indicated that he was going to talk to Peterson about resolving the management situation," recalls Krueger. "The firm would survive," Krueger reportedly answered. Nevertheless, Krueger—unlike Bill Morris, who was signaled by his friend Rubin—says he was truly surprised by the July 26 board meeting.

In addition to Krueger, Glucksman could count on the votes of Rubin, Fuld, Morris and Sheldon Gordon. That might have meant

*Glucksman also telephoned Braggiotti, but not until the morning of July 26.

a five to five split. But Glucksman believed, probably correctly, that since his trading divisions were then generating two-thirds of Lehman's profits, and since partners like Istel may have feared him more than they admired Peterson, he could pry one or two board votes from Peterson.

Peterson had another recourse, which was to take the issue to the full seventy-seven-man partnership. Here, since bankers outnumbered nonbankers, Peterson adherents can more assuredly, and probably more accurately, say that he would have won in a showdown.

However, this is idle speculation. Peterson chose not to fight, and the transaction was ratified at the time by a docile board of directors. Board members now defend their passivity by saying that they were merely complying with Peterson's wishes, affirming a *fait accompli.* "It was a trade that had been done, and we were there to bless it," explains William Welsh. Nevertheless, he concedes, board members feared retribution: "Those who rebelled might be remembered."

One person close to Peterson put it less gently: "It's a dirty little secret down there that a crime was committed in terms of corporate governance. Why permit Glucksman to do it? It was greed." The directors, this argument runs, were preoccupied with their bonuses and their shares, which were decided every September. "Because compensation at the firm has always been set by the top two executives," explains one partner, "a guy can throw you a tip of a half-million dollars! The chief executive is the Ayatollah." The CEO can sway the appointment or removal of partners from their perches on the board or a key committee, and is the major voice in the selection of division heads, in granting a partner special status at the firm, or in anointing new partners. The board was focused on the money the firm was gushing, not on its future or its traditions or the loyalty its members might have owed Peterson or Glucksman. Unlike the struggle that would be waged in the summer of 1984 between David Tendler and John H. Gutfreund (the victor), co-chairmen and co-CEO's of Phibro/Salomon, the parent company of Salomon Brothers, at Lehman the board did not weigh, over a period of time, the fateful options.

Instead, board members asked: Is it good for *me*? Is Glucksman the likely victor? Only Peter Solomon, who was accused of being selfish, dared ask whether the coup made sense for the *firm.* The board did not ask whether the coup violated the consensual traditions of a partnership, did not ask whether it was time for Peterson to move on, did not ask whether Glucksman possessed the qualities to lead Lehman. The momentous decision, which could profoundly

One William Street, 1929

Robert (''Bobbie'') Lehman

Mayor Fiorello La Guardia and Governor Herbert H. Lehman,
former Lehman Brothers partner

The entrance to 55 Water Street,
where Lehman Brothers moved in 1980

Lewis L. Glucksman

Peter G. Peterson

Robert S. Rubin whom Glucksman
called ''my consigliere''

Left to right:
Roger Altman, Stephen Schwarzman,
François de Saint Phalle

James S. Boshart III
(''the Boy Scout'')

Peter Cohen

The Trading Floor

Sheldon
("Leaves No Footprints")
Gordon

Peter (''the Brat'')
Solomon

Richard S. Fuld, Jr.

George W. Ball

Henry R. Breck ("the Spook")

Steven R. Fenster
("the Professor")

Harvey Krueger
("Uncle Harvey")

LAMOITTE TEUNISSEN

William E. Welsh, Jr.

The Trading Room

W. Richard Bingham

Eric Gleacher

William C. Morris
("the Cynic")

The Partners' Dining Room

Lewis L. Glucksman

Left to right:
Pete Peterson, Joan Ganz Cooney,
Melba Duncan

Saturday Night Live comes to Lehman Brothers

Sanford (''Sandy'') I. Weill

James D. Robinson III

affect the firm and all its members, was treated as just another transaction.

The partners, too, had an opportunity to say no, to rebel, to represent the broad interests of all shareholders, but they were passive. Today, partners ask: What were we supposed to do? How does a partnership order two men to get along? What if Glucksman refused? All fair questions. But these were not the questions asked then. Back in July 1983, no one invoked the memory of the Lehman family or the tradition of the firm, of a common interest or common memory. "Everyone enjoyed being raped," says one former partner embarrassed by his own passivity. "We were making money. All the people cared about was their money. Greed. The place had no tradition, no culture . . . Read *In Search of Excellence,* and look at the qualities the excellent companies have. None of these factors were present at Lehman. Every time there was a business presentation, or in the annual report Peterson did, the customer was never mentioned. We only mentioned what a great year Lehman had had."

Looking back on his own ten-year stewardship, Peterson concedes, "I lived under the illusion I had built some kind of a corporate ethic there, some kind of governance and sense of belonging to an institution."

With the exception of Solomon's outburst at the board meeting, and a few stray dissents from partners and Peterson allies like Stephen Schwarzman and Mario d'Urso, most partners remained silent. They vied to toast Lew Glucksman, to tell him they wished to be a member of his "team." Only later did many come to agree with Peter Solomon's immediate assessment: "Attila the Hun has just arrived."

T HE OUSTER OF PETERSON WAS TREATED AS A MAJOR NEWS story, one in which Glucksman was usually depicted as a pirate. However, because the press release was relatively candid, there was little else the media could uncover. To probe

Glucksman's thirst for power, his psyche or Peterson's surrender when the bottom-line numbers at Lehman glittered, and when Peterson had publicly praised Glucksman, would put the press in the uncomfortable position of an agitator seeming to foment trouble if it pursued the story more deeply. The prevailing attitude outside Lehman, and probably inside as well, was: *Give the man time!*

Pleased to be navigating Lehman alone, Glucksman moved swiftly to seize command. He brought to this task a sense of mission. Lew Glucksman was determined to break up Lehman's independent baronies; to impose rigorous, centralized management, a chain of command. He would supplant the independent princes who jealously guarded their prerogatives as if they were national borders. He would not allow trading and banking to operate as separate duchies, as he believed Peterson did. He would not permit internal squabbling, as Peterson did. He would not spend hours at lunch with prospective clients, call endless marketing meetings, seek public acclaim, as Peterson did. Lew Glucksman prided himself on being Mr. Inside. He assumed that the same tight, hierarchical structure typical of trading —partners arriving early, huddling, agreeing to a course of action, and plunging ahead—could profitably be imposed on the banking division. He assumed that the team spirit he had engendered in the commercial paper division could be spread to the entire House of Lehman. He rejected the notion that he had been selfish in supplanting Peterson, and jarred many bankers with this argument, which he made often: "At the margin no one investment banker is as important as a good manager who is running the business well." He spoke of how, from the day he had joined the Navy as a teenager, he always admired the military, and now, he enthused, perhaps a dose of spit, polish and discipline might alter Lehman's culture, generate a team spirit, induce the independent baronies to pull together as one.

The new chairman's first management decision involved Robert Rubin. Glucksman says that he first talked with Rubin about assuming the presidency of Lehman after his initial confrontation with Peterson but before the climactic board meeting and that although Rubin at first resisted, he finally agreed to accept.*

One of the first to learn of this decision was Enrico Braggiotti. Glucksman knew that Braggiotti was unhappy that Peterson, who had induced him to invest in Lehman nine years earlier, had been

---

*Questions were later raised about this, since Rubin negotiated Peterson's severance agreement on behalf of the board at a time when he had an "interest" in the outcome.

deposed; he also knew that Braggiotti was displeased to see so much money shoveled to Peterson, which Braggiotti likened to "a bribe"; he could sense that Braggiotti was worried about BCI's more than 4 percent ownership of Lehman. In fact, Braggiotti was appalled by what had happened and feared that Glucksman, though he considered him an astute trader and an able manager, had neither the stature nor the statesmanship to serve as chairman. Sensing this, Glucksman took care to phone the Italian banker on the morning of the July 26 board meeting.

In early August, he invited Braggiotti to visit him at Lehman Brothers. The regal, usually impeccably polite Braggiotti got down to business at once. Distressed that he could not be present and was not represented at the meeting, Braggiotti asked to have an observer sit in for him at those meetings he could not attend. Glucksman readily agreed. Then, much as a bank loan officer probes an applicant, he asked a series of questions, including: "Who will you put in as president?"

"I will put in Rubin," he recalls Glucksman responding.

"I cannot agree. He is totally unable to become president." Braggiotti protested that he was never satisfied with his own tense relations with Rubin, who made no secret of his opposition to bringing in BCI as a shareholder. Braggiotti complained, he recalls, that Rubin was too taciturn, too private, too much an insider; in other words, too much like Glucksman himself. What was needed, he said, was the blend of talents displayed by Peterson and Glucksman, Mr. Outside and Mr. Inside.

Glucksman was unfailingly polite to his business partner, trying to soothe him by saying, recalls Braggiotti, that Rubin would be president only a short while, to be succeeded by Sheldon Gordon, a smooth, outgoing professional much admired by the smooth, outgoing Italian. What Glucksman didn't say was that he fundamentally disagreed that he and Rubin were alike. Lew Glucksman thought of himself as a superb public speaker, an adroit salesman, a far more likable person than Peterson, as a man whose natural public flair had been stifled by Peterson and by those who tried to pigeonhole him as "a trader." Now, he was convinced, the true Lew Glucksman would emerge.

That summer Glucksman moved slowly, first paving the way toward Rubin's presidency by placing him on the seven-member operating committee, the firm's day-to-day management body, which usually met every Tuesday and Thursday. "Talk to Rubin if I'm not here," Glucksman began to tell select partners. Jim Hood remembers getting calls from the press early in September asking who was to be selected as Glucksman's heir apparent. Glucksman told Hood to answer, "No comment." Then, when questions persisted, Glucksman instructed him to say, "No president has been named, nor do we anticipate naming one. But Bob Rubin is the chief operating officer."

Stalling the appointment of Rubin was one of the few cautious steps Glucksman took that summer. Over the next two months he announced that Shel Gordon, whose career had been in sales and trading, would be shifted as head of the nine-hundred-employee equity division (which covered all common stock trading, all retail and institutional distribution, and all of Lehman's proprietary trading, including risk arbitrage) to run the banking department, displacing the troika of Roger Altman, François de Saint Phalle and Vincent Mai. Although banking partners were not happy with the unwieldy, relatively inexperienced troika, to impose someone from trading on the forty-fourth-floor banking department—no matter how personally agreeable Shel Gordon was—made many bankers queasy. "Lew's idea of breaking down the barrier between traders and bankers was for a trader to come up here," says one longtime Lehman banker.

Glucksman merged the equity division with the fixed-income division, which included all commercial paper and all trading in government securities. To manage the merged department, he elevated his thirty-seven-year-old protégé, Richard Fuld, who had been running fixed income alone. This move, in particular, made partners uneasy. Fuld was a man who, for all his abilities as a trader, was almost defiantly antisocial toward bankers; he avoided the partners' dining room and complained openly about those "fucking bankers" who hogged Lehman's shares. Some bankers referred to Fuld as "the gorilla," in part because he spoke in monosyllabic grunts. He was a stranger to most of his partners. And what especially jarred them was that although Fuld had limited managerial experience, he now had twenty-two departments reporting to him and supervised one of the three principal divisions of the firm (banking and money management being the other two). Fuld's new division at the time accounted for two-thirds of Lehman's profits.

Personnel decisions came rapidly. This confirmed the partners' suspicions that Glucksman was hopelessly mired in the mind-set of a trader, making rat-tat-tat intuitive judgments. Dissatisfied with

Lehman's rank in the second tier of public finance, Glucksman removed the head of the public finance department and replaced him with Peter M. Dawkins, a retired Army brigadier general, Heisman Trophy winner and Rhodes Scholar. Dawkins was an attractive man with no public finance or investment banking experience whatsoever. Glucksman knew that public finance—advising state and local governments and authorities on how to raise money from investors—hinged on personal relationships at least as much as technical skills, since each investment bank recruited technically proficient people and had roughly the same fee structure. He knew that Lehman, like other firms, had volunteered to do pro bono work for government and maintained a political action committee (PAC) to funnel campaign funds to candidates, all in the hope of massaging relationships with elected officials. Surely a forty-five-year-old "golden boy" like Dawkins could open doors to city halls and state capitols. Who wouldn't want to meet Pete Dawkins? Besides, there were internal reasons. "I've always loved basketball and football players," explains Glucksman. "A guy who's been a basketball or football player—his success depends on interaction with other people. For the same reason, I also did well over the years by hiring a lot of ex-service academy people." When he was recruited that summer, Dawkins remembers Glucksman's bluntness: "He talked about the fact that Lehman had a history of people behaving principally on the basis of selfish self-interest rather than the interest of the firm as a whole . . . he really wanted to correct that."

On the recommendation of his friend, banker Eric Gleacher, Glucksman met and offered Cravath, Swaine & Moore partner Allen Finkelson, an able lawyer who had worked on various Lehman deals, a partnership as a banker. This offer shocked people at Lehman because, like the Dawkins appointment, it had not been taken first to the board, as was customary.

That summer there was also grumbling among bankers who assumed that Gleacher would eventually return as head of the mergers and acquisition department, a speculation fanned by Gleacher himself, who pressed Glucksman for the job. Glucksman tried to do the noble thing, telling Gleacher that the decision would rest with the management of the banking division. He sent him to Shel Gordon, and Gleacher told partners that Gordon had "committed to do it." (Gordon says they spoke of it, but no committments were made.) There was also a major blowup when Peter Solomon learned that Gordon was to move from trading to banking. Solomon offered to run the banking department until Gordon had completed the management task he wanted to finish downstairs and Dick Fuld could surround himself with more executive talent. "I'll run it for a year, and then Shel can come up to banking," Solomon volunteered in a meeting with Glucksman and Rubin.

"You'll never run anything here!" shouted Bob Rubin, outraged by the suggestion. Glucksman said nothing.*

Counting the management changes he had engineered in the previous twelve months—including the removal of the well-regarded William Welsh as head of retail sales, bringing in John Levy from the outside to oversee institutional equities, installing young Michael Schmertzler as the chief financial officer, replacing Ed Hajim with Henry Breck as the head of Lemco—by the fall of 1983, Glucksman had installed his own men at the head of most departments in the firm.

Even Glucksman's allies worried that he was moving too fast. His closest adviser, Bob Rubin, says of the management upheaval that summer: "The speed was too fast. We didn't give enough thought. Frankly, that was supposed to be part of my role." Rubin was supposed to have served, he says, "as a moderating influence on Lew. I think Lew needs that."

M EANWHILE, PETE PETERSON LICKED HIS WOUNDS BY spending more time than usual that summer in East Hampton, improving his tennis, relaxing with Joan and his visiting children, and talking incessantly about what had happened at Lehman. He received warm, testimonial letters of praise from competitors, clients, friends and Lehman colleagues.

John C. Whitehead, co-chairman of Goldman, Sachs, wrote, in part:

*The three men confirm the conversation.

"This is an unabashed fan letter . . . You've done a wonderful job in bringing Lehman Brothers from the brink of disorganized chaos to the highly profitable, distinguished organization it is today. Your partners will miss you—more than they know."

Barbara Walters wrote: "You have made success out of failure, respectability out of chaos. You are admired within your industry and, even more important, loved by all of us who are fortunate enough to have you as a friend."

Peterson's behavior at Lehman during his remaining months was magisterial. So as not to embarrass Glucksman, he stopped attending board meetings. He agreed to call and reassure clients of Lew Glucksman's virtues, calls that also conveyed the impression that Pete Peterson was standing tall. He drafted three different form letters and dispatched literally thousands of them to corporate clients, to Wall Street competitors, to the five-hundred members of the Bi-Partisan Budget Appeal, to acquaintances in Washington and New York. The *A* list—consisting of his most important friends and clients, of movers and shakers and people in the media—received a telegram on July 26, followed later that evening by a hand-delivered packet containing the press release. In each of the four versions one paragraph was the same:

> I am personally excited at the prospect of going into the classical merchant banking business of special investments in promising businesses and corporate restructuring, a line of activity in which I have long had an intense interest. I would not feel free to leave, however, were I not so confident of Lew's ability to manage the firm successfully.

Torn between wanting to tell the truth and wanting to retain his dignity, Peterson and George Ball finally adopted the "limited hang-out route." When the July 30 issue of the *Economist* reported that Glucksman gave Peterson "a polite, but firm shove out of the door," Ball shot back a two-page letter, insisting the parting was done "in a friendly spirit." (Later asked to explain "friendly," Ball, who was not a diplomat for nothing, said, " 'Friendly' is a word of art in that situation." By that definition, so is *war*.) Ball wrote to *Fortune* denying its assertion that both men knew that in a board showdown Glucksman would win, the opposite of what he told Peterson. And Peterson granted interviews in which he flatly denied that an ultimatum had been given or implied. Glucksman wore a similar mask. The August 8 issue of *Time* magazine quoted Glucksman as saying of

Peterson: "We've been good friends, and we will always be good friends. In fact, I do not have many friends besides Peter."

What Glucksman's "good friend" didn't know was that the new CEO of Lehman was seething inside, angered that Peterson still came to the office, still served as a counterpoint to Lew Glucksman. What Peterson thought was noble, Glucksman thought demeaning, another example of noblesse oblige. "Pete was just hanging on," says Glucksman. "It created dissension."

B EFORE THE SUMMER ENDED THREE OTHER PARTNERS HAD left or announced their intention to: Edmund Hajim, who had been demoted to the banking division in May, announced plans to leave and become chairman of Furman, Selz, Mager, Dietz & Birney; international banker Mario d'Urso, a social friend of Peterson's, was squeezed out by Glucksman and left to run for the Italian Parliament; and banker George Wiegers went to Dillon, Read, late that spring, before Glucksman had ousted Peterson. When partners leave they withdraw, over a period of time, the cash value of the stock they own, thus depleting the immediate net worth of the firm, and the long-term capital of the partnership. Coupled with everything else that had transpired, these costly departures further unsettled the partnership.

Insecurity mounted at Lehman, particularly among bankers, who feared that Glucksman was incapable of understanding what they did. Glucksman told associates that he wished to meet more current and prospective clients, to perform more as Mr. Outside. Yet former banking associate Steven Rattner remembers the day he brought a client to Glucksman's office for a previously scheduled courtesy call. After they had waited awhile, the secretary came out and said, " 'Sorry, he can't see these people.' There was no explanation. Nothing. I later made a point of checking what was going on. He was just sitting there with his cronies." A senior banker offered this explanation of Glucksman's curious behavior: "Lew paid lip service to relationships, but in his heart he only believed in marketing the products. He didn't really believe in long-term relationships. He believed that the real market was the product, not the client. Meaning that if you price the product right, the client would buy it. He didn't understand that in a competitive world all the top people price it right. So you've got to price it right *and* develop relationships."

In contrast to Peterson—who continued to appear in the office and who played the role of august if fallen leader, conversing with partners he had long ignored—tales of Glucksman's arbitrary or capricious behavior multiplied. One of his first decisions was particularly unpopular; a recommendation, approved by the operating committee, to cease volunteering free cigars in the Lehman dining room. No longer would the tuxedoed waiters routinely offer a large polished box brimming with a variety of expensive cigars. No longer would partners be permitted to reach in and pull out a fistful, using Lehman as their no-cost supplier. No longer, Glucksman hoped, would the annual Lehman cigar bill approach $30,000. Glucksman thought he could cut that bill by a third. Free cigars would still be available, but now partners would have to ask for them.

The decision stood—for one day. "We rescinded it the next morning," says Glucksman. "Everyone became so upset." Not surprisingly, partners aware of Glucksman's aversion to Peterson's cost-control efforts saw this decision as vindictive, especially since it was the bankers who necessarily used the dining rooms to conduct business. Glucksman's effort to police cigars invited jokes comparing him to Captain Queeg. "Who ate the strawberries?"

As Glucksman's professional behavior aroused questions, so did his personal actions. Lew Glucksman had always been fat and slovenly; now he had—seemingly overnight—shed about seventy pounds from his five-foot-nine-inch frame, though he remained a heavy man. For those who had not seen him in years, the effect was startling. Former partner and then Deputy Mayor Kenneth Lipper had not seen him since he left Lehman in 1975. "I always thought of him as a big man," says Lipper, who saw Glucksman that summer. Lipper remembers thinking, My God, he's just a little man!*

By that summer, Glucksman had shed not only a quarter of his

---

*Lipper sought, and lost, the Democratic nomination for New York City Council President in September 1985.

body weight and his co-CEO but his wife of twenty-six years. Partners say he shed his old tailor as well, in order to improve his wardrobe. He purchased an elegant five-room apartment in Manhattan's luxurious Museum Towers, straddling the Museum of Modern Art, a place where Rockefellers lived and where apartments were priced from $500,000 to $5 million. Now he drove a new, sporty brown Chrysler convertible. Gossip spread about whom he was dating, much of it ugly and untrue.

There was, of course, another side to many of these tales. Glucksman, for example, says he began losing weight in late 1982, long before he challenged Peterson. His marriage had waned years before. And the Chrysler convertible, he says, was the result of a chance conversation with Lee Iacocca at a Catholic Charities dinner. He needed a new car, and seated beside the Chrysler chairman, Glucksman blurted, "Let's see how good a salesman you are. Sell me a car!" Iacocca convinced him, he says, to purchase a $13,500 convertible with a special package, including power windows. "I think you should patronize your own clients," says Glucksman. "For me to buy a Japanese or a GM car would be wrong." In this case, Glucksman was a traditionalist, for it has sometimes been a source of pride among investment bankers to purchase the products of clients.

The legendary Sidney J. Weinberg, who managed Goldman, Sachs for many years, made a fetish of using the products of the fourteen corporations on whose boards he sat. When he shifted from the General Motors to the Ford Motor Company board, he traded in his Cadillac and Oldsmobile for a Lincoln and a Mercury. When he rode the train to Chicago, he argued with the dining-car steward when there was no Kraft cheese, a National Diary Products offering, on the menu. Often, Weinberg went sailing with his friend Paul C. Cabot. "When he learned at the start of one voyage aboard a forty-foot sloop belonging to Cabot that the galley was stocked with Borden's instant coffee, he threatened to jump ship," wrote E. J. Kahn, Jr., in a *New Yorker* profile.* "Reminding Cabot of their joint allegiance to National Dairy Products, Weinberg accused him of treason. He couldn't face his associates on the General Foods board, he said, if word got around that he had been faithless to Maxwell House, even on vacation. Anyway, he was sure that Borden's tasted awful. At the next port, Cabot bought a jar of Maxwell House instant coffee, and after its contents were exhausted, he refilled it periodically from his supply of Borden's. Weinberg ecstatically made him-

*The New Yorker, September 8 and September 15, 1956.

self several cups a day, and kept asking his crewmates if they had ever tasted anything so delicious."

Client loyalty was good business practice. Once, Joseph Cullman, then the chairman of Philip Morris, lunched at Lehman Brothers, his bankers. At the end of the meal the waiters came by carrying a sterling silver cigarette box. Cullman reached in and was shocked to pull out a Camel. "We damn near lost Philip Morris's business because we had some other brand in the dining room," recalls former Lehman president Warren Hellman. Despite this history, many partners who heard about Glucksman's convertible saw not client loyalty but personal impulsiveness.

Nevertheless, the majority of Lehman partners were in Glucksman's corner. Business was good. And there were those who saw little change in Glucksman. Harvey Krueger thought Glucksman had behaved well through much of that summer. Says Enrico Braggiotti of that first summer, "He was not Napoleonic. He was very humble. And he was listening." Braggiotti believes that Peterson is partially responsible for exaggerated tales of Glucksman's manic behavior: "Pete is so much upset by the fact that he left—that he had to leave Lehman Brothers—that Glucksman has become his only enemy. He is paranoiac about Glucksman."

Many partners, however, were rattled. They found Glucksman too quick, for example, to boast that he was "a street fighter." Observes one former board member, "His only real rudder was Peterson. He had no ability to govern his excesses." One corporate executive who had done business over the years with Lehman Brothers, describes an appointment that summer with Glucksman. The executive was ushered into Glucksman's chart room office where "he told us what a terrific appraiser of horse flesh he was." After some chitchat, Glucksman grabbed a small silver mountain climber's ax, a gift from Bill Welsh. "I'll tell you what kind of a company we are!" he shouted. "We're going right to the top!," and he slammed the ax into the plaster wall. The executive chuckled nervously, eyeing other marks in the wall. "He was well practiced at it," he says. "I definitely thought he was a little nuts."

At a publication party for Cary Reich, author of *Financier: The Biography of Andre Meyer,* given by *Institutional Investor* editor Gilbert Kaplan, guests came up to Glucksman and said, "I was anxious to meet you. I've heard a lot about you."

"Yep. I'm the toughest guy on Wall Street. And proud of it."*

---

*Several guests confirm this exchange.

At the same publication party, Michael Thomas, the former partner who became a successful author, shouted across the room to him, "Lew, you out-survived them all!"

Glucksman yelled back, "Did you ever doubt it? You know how I do it, Michael? I always keep my back to the wall of the latrine."

Thomas remembers one other conversation at Kaplan's home, which was witnessed by no one else. Huddling privately, he said to his former partner, "Are you going to do the South American thing? Grant general amnesty and then line 'em up in front of a wall?"

"Something like that," said Glucksman, half smiling.

These tales quickly circulated among partners, filling them with trepidation. The press got a whiff of what was going on. In September, *Newsweek* wrote of the "Lehman circus," asserting that "the tension at Lehman has become even worse since the midsummer coup . . ." A more comprehensive September cover story in *Institutional Investor* by Lenny Glynn, "The Big Power Play at Lehman," hinted of partners who would be chased out. It captured Glucksman's belligerent mood with this quote: "My object in life is to be respected, not liked."

However, none of these stories prompted the kind of reaction among the partners unleashed by stories of Glucksman's generosity with their money. Partners fumed when they learned that Glucksman, in order to recruit Dawkins and Finkelson, had circumvented the operating committee and had not first consulted the board before lavishing an offer on them. They learned that Glucksman had made Dawkins a low-interest loan of about $1 million to buy an East Side Manhattan apartment; that Finkelson was promised a minimum annual compensation of $750,000, plus an initial 1,000 shares and a jump to 2,000 shares within two years "if things worked out," recalls Finkelson. The number of shares given Finkelson particularly galled people at the firm, since a new partner—like Dawkins—usually started with just 500 shares, rising gradually to average about 1,300 shares; only about a fifth of the seventy-seven partners had 2,000 shares or more. In a partnership, in which all the partners own a piece of the firm, the awarding of shares is supposed to be consensual.

While partners stewed over their new chief executive officer's management techniques and personality, and the board fretted that Glucksman ignored the rules and etiquette of corporate governance, nothing so focused the attention of the firm as the annual September decisions regarding bonuses and stock. To Lehman partners, these ranked as the most fateful decisions made each year.

B EGINNING IN JULY THE OPERATING COMMITTEE, UNDER Glucksman's direction, met to recommend that year's bonuses. The six members of the operating committee, in addition to Glucksman, were Bob Rubin; Jim Boshart; Shel Gordon; Dick Fuld; and bankers François de Saint Phalle and Roger Altman. In turn, operating committee bonuses were determined by Glucksman, Rubin, Harvey Krueger, William Morris and Peter Solomon —members of the now defunct executive committee. Traditionally, the CEO at Lehman had the power, if there were disagreements, to make final decisions about the size of a partner's bonus, including the size of the bonus of all seven members of the operating committee; in consultation with the board, he decided what percentage of the firm's common shares (then showing a book value of $640.19 per share) each partner was entitled to.

Dividing into subcommittees, the operating committee that summer interviewed individual partners, allowing each to make a case for how much business he had brought to Lehman that year; the full committee, after receiving the recommendations of department heads, reviewed these recommendations with the CEO, and then gave its sanction to the board.

By mid-September, bonus decisions were set. Division chiefs would meet individually with their employees to relay the verdict. Despite the style of living many partners enjoyed and the ample fees Lehman was billing (merger and acquisition fees alone totaled $56 million for the fiscal year ending September 30, 1983) partners' salaries were relatively modest, ranging at the time from $75,000 to $125,000 annually for all but Glucksman, who received $225,000, and board members, who received $150,000. Bonuses were not modest. Whereas salary and bonuses totaled an average of $166,000 in 1974 and $196,000 the next year, at least half of which was salary, by the 1980's bonuses ranged from two to ten times salary. In 1982, to take an extreme example, Dick Fuld, then thirty-six, received a bonus of $1.6 million. Not surprisingly, partners did not take bonus or stock decisions lightly.

Bonus expectations were high among the partners, and not without reason. It had been a good year on Wall Street, with bullish trading activity swelling profits. At rival Salomon Brothers, John H. Gutfreund, the managing partner, earned $2.08 million in 1983. Lehman partners knew that executive compensation was up throughout the nation. That year, for example, the president of Apple Computer, John Sculley, earned $1.8 million; the CEO of Paramount Studios,

Barry Diller, received $1.7 million. And Lehman partners knew this had been another spectacular year at Lehman, with profits climbing to $147.7 million (before taxes and bonuses). The pool of money set aside for bonuses jumped from $20.6 million in 1982 to $27 million in 1983. Most divisions, including banking, bettered their budgeted projections for the year.

Therefore, when word of the final bonus and stock decisions rumbled through Lehman's corridors, banking partners wailed. For years they had been told that the traders were upset that their bonus and stock participation was eclipsed by the bankers'. Glucksman had warned during the 1982 bonus and stock deliberations that he believed a fundamental redistribution of the firm's income and ownership was in order. Dick Fuld, in the time he served on the board and operating committee, had often growled about the need to redistribute the firm's wealth to those traders who produced most of the profits. To Glucksman, and traders he had worked beside for years, this was simply a matter of justice. Between 1980 and 1983 the fixed income, or trading, divisions produced $4 of profit for every $3 brought in by banking—$210.8 million against $165 million. This reasoning, however, didn't convince the bankers, since they knew that fee-related banking entailed low overheads and little risk or capital, unlike trading. They considered banking profits "higher-quality earnings," and thus believed they deserved more generous bonuses than Glucksman's mathematical formula apportioned. To alter past formulas dramatically, they warned, would leave deep scars.

Now alone at the helm, Glucksman was determined to right past wrongs; no longer would bonuses and shares be allocated according to what partners had traditionally received or to their status within the firm; rather, he strove to make decisions on what he said were "the merits" of each partner's performance. Glucksman thought he was being objective. In fact, many banking partners believed his decisions were too personal, meant to settle old scores. They feared Glucksman was not controlling his demons.

When the tentative bonus schedule was reviewed by bankers Peter Solomon, Harvey Krueger and William Morris—who as members of the former executive committee had traditionally reviewed bonuses —they were outraged. Solomon, who had had what he considered a very good year—what he considered a $500,000-bonus year—was the firm's premier retail-industry investment banker, and he was scheduled to get $375,000, a miserly $25,000 raise over 1982. Krueger's bonus would drop $25,000, from $325,000. And Morris's was scheduled to plunge from $400,000 to $300,000. On top of this, they learned that Glucksman and Rubin planned to expropriate 500 shares of Lehman stock from each of them, reducing their ownership from 2,500 to 2,000 shares apiece.

At lunch in the forty-first-floor executive dining room off the trading floor, the three banking partners expressed to Glucksman and Rubin their outrage. "This will tear the firm apart!" exclaimed Solomon. There was some shouting, and the meeting ended inconclusively. The five men agreed to meet again with Glucksman the next morning.

Working feverishly through the night, Solomon came to the meeting the next day armed with a proposed new bonus schedule. Glucksman and Rubin summarily rejected it. Their strategy was to try to break Morris and Krueger away from Solomon. Morris was Rubin's good friend, and Krueger was Glucksman's. In the meeting, as Glucksman and Rubin offered personal cajolery, as well as amendments to the bonus schedule, they asked repeatedly, looking only at the two bankers, "Is this okay with you guys?"

Morris and Krueger sat there tight-lipped, their expressions frozen. They said nothing.

It was not unlike an auction, in which each gesture drives the bid up. Eager to gain support, or at least acquiescence for the overall bonus package, Glucksman finally relented, agreeing to fatten each of their bonuses. Solomon got an additional $25,000, a "tip," as he disparagingly called it; Krueger and Morris each got $100,000 more than originally offered. Glucksman also agreed to leave their stock intact, justifying their 2,500 shares—more than other bankers received—by naming them "senior bankers." In a protest, Krueger says that he and Solomon sold back 100 shares of stock, and gave the proceeds to Jewish charities. Solomon's stock was worth approximately $100,000. Krueger, who also sold and donated the proceeds from some of his more valuable preferred shares, says his donation to Hebrew University was worth about $200,000. Bob Rubin offers a less charitable interpretation: "The cheapest way to give to charity is to give away appreciated stock. It's like buying something for one dollar and seeing its worth climb to a hundred dollars. The value of your gift is a hundred dollars and you don't pay a capital gains tax."

Solomon, outraged by the bonus schedule, gave key partners a peek, hoping to fan opposition; he warned that if the plan passed, it would "blow apart the firm." Solomon insists that he, joined by

Krueger and Morris, opposed the entire bonus and stock plan. Their opposition, he says, came in private conversations among the five men. His recollection is shared by Krueger, who insists, "I raised hell about the bonuses." Their recollection does not square with that of the three other witnesses. "I'm not saying they were ecstatic. But they went along," says Rubin. Morris agrees, and says of himself: "I went along. As I went along with all others." At the September 21 board meeting, where the allocation of bonuses and shares was endorsed, neither Solomon, Morris nor Krueger dissented. Although these five partners deny that they had been given what some partners came to call "hush money," a member of the operating committee says, "They got bought off. Lew came to the operating committee and told us, 'These guys are bitching and moaning. I got to give them more to shut them up.' "

The September 21 board meeting featured a slide presentation by Bob Rubin. He explained that under this plan the banking division, which produced one-third of the firm's profits, would still receive 60 percent of the bonus money (down from 67 percent the year before); and the number of nonbanking partners would rise from twenty-eight to just thirty-five, still less than half. Banking partners seemed not to hear this; instead they seized on other things, such as the fact that Lew Glucksman and a coterie of four other senior executives received 25 percent of the total bonus pool. Glucksman's bonus jumped from $1.25 million in 1982 to $1.5 million (and since Peterson's severance agreement guaranteed him the same bonus as his former co-CEO, that was his bonus as well); Richard Fuld, whose trading operations attained record profits, also received $1.5 million, down from $1.6 million the previous year. (Glucksman thought it would look unseemly if his protégé received more than he did.) Shel Gordon went from $400,000 to $1 million (according to Bob Rubin, Gordon complained when his bonus did not match Fuld's); Bob Rubin's rose from $700,000 to $900,000; Jim Boshart's went from $300,000 to $400,000; and Henry Breck's from $250,000 to $325,000.

The bonuses of several bankers were also sweetened. Operating committee members Roger Altman and François de Saint Phalle climbed from $350,000 to $450,000 and $500,000, respectively. Generally, however, the bonuses of various banking partners did not conform to this pattern. For example, Yves-André Istel dropped from $250,000 to $200,000; and most stunning of all, Glucksman's ally Eric Gleacher, after a robust year of orchestrating mergers, including Allied's merger with Bendix, was raised a mere $25,000 to

$400,000—less than other M. & A. partners, particularly rival Steve Schwarzman. The recommendations were made by the banking division's management, Rubin explained, and Lew Glucksman refused to overrule his managers. In the case of Eric Gleacher, he says, "Mr. Schwarzman's revenues were approximately 20 percent higher than Mr. Gleacher's in 1982 and 1983."

These arguments did not stem the rising tide of anger. What appeared to be favoritism toward trading and sales—and "cronies" —was also noted in the way the partners' stock was distributed. Each September, the board decided how to redivide a fixed pool of approximately 100,000 shares. The shifts in stock were usually incremental; rarely did senior partners find their shares sharply reduced or augmented. But in September 1983, past patterns were shattered. Glucksman's shares jumped from 3,500 to 4,500; although he had once owned 4,300 shares, this move reeked of the same greed Glucksman laid at Peterson's doorstep—"He's the greediest man I've ever known," says Glucksman. Yet Glucksman, like Peterson, had been granted, starting in 1982, 1 percent of Lehman's profits, after both men protested that their ownership shares were puny. Now, two months on the job, Glucksman appeared to feather his own nest and the nests of his friends. Rubin went from 2,500 to 2,750 shares; Shel Gordon and Dick Fuld each rose from 2,000 to 2,750 shares—250 more shares than Solomon, Krueger or Morris. And the disparity between them would have been greater had Glucksman succeeded in reducing the three bankers' shares by 500 each. Jim Boshart jumped from 1,500 to 2,000 shares.

It seemed that a disproportionately large number of bankers had their shares shaved and reapportioned to the trading department— including Yves-André Istel (down from 2,250 to 1,700 shares), James H. Manges (down from 1,500 to 1,000 shares), Raymond A. Charles (down from 1,000 to 500 shares) and Robert McCabe (down from 1,325 to 1,000 shares). Even popular William Welsh from the sales side relinquished 300 shares. While it is true that some bankers' shares rose—M. & A. head Richard Bingham went from 1,800 to 2,000 shares, Roger Altman and François de Saint Phalle rose from 2,000 to 2,250 and Steve Schwarzman advanced from 1,700 to 2,000 —the overall message telegraphed by Glucksman to the bankers was clear, and terrifying.

To Richard Bingham, whose compensation climbed and who tended not to get involved in Lehman's internal feuds, the details were less important than the signal: "Glucksman had just taken control of the firm, and instead of moving to consolidate the firm and bring people together, he took steps which exaggerated that division and created more division. It didn't matter whether he was paying me more or less. I felt he was making improper management decisions. It indicated to me that there was some question whether Lew had the ability to manage the place."

Glucksman's decisions jarred even some members of his own management team. Jim Boshart, who remains loyal to Glucksman, nevertheless says the stock decisions were "stupid"—too dramatic. Pete Dawkins, the new partner, was struck by how Glucksman's actions clashed with the aims he professed when he had recruited him: "One of the ironies of all this is that what Lew said he was trying to do, and what I believe he meant, was different than what his actions led to."

Glucksman defended his actions. The basic problem, he believes, was the greed of his partners. He says of the bankers: "Their idea was for me to lean over backward to screw the trading side . . . We used to joke that there was no way of making people happy who were making so much money. People were making a million and a half!" —including salary, bonus, dividends and annual appreciation of the worth of their stock.

Glucksman was reassured by Bob Rubin, who says he told Glucksman the ownership changes were, in fact, "gradual."* If Glucksman & Company were practicing cronyism, they say, why would they hold down Gleacher's bonus? And why would they reward Schwarzman, whom Rubin and Glucksman disliked? And, says Rubin, the 25 percent of the total bonus pool earmarked for five executives "was the same percentage paid to the five men in 1982."

Glucksman may have failed to appreciate the anger his actions aroused because he received support from some prominent bankers, including operating-committee member Roger Altman, a former Peterson protégé eager to work closely with the new chairman. Altman cast his vote for the bonus package, describing the bonus and stock distribution plan as both "fair" and "consistent" with the changes made in prior years. The jump in Glucksman's stock ownership was applauded by operating-committee member François de Saint Phalle, who headed a study committee that found that the CEO's of their competitors owned 4 percent to 5 percent of the stock,

---

*Boshart contradicts Rubin, saying, "Bob Rubin fought Lew Glucksman tooth and nail on the stock issue, saying it was too dramatic."

not the less than 4 percent owned by Glucksman. "Compare his ownership as chief executive with other chief executives, and he was light. There was plenty of justification for his increase in stock," says de Saint Phalle.

These views were not widely shared, certainly not within banking. Partners noted, for instance, that with 4,500 shares and 1 percent of Lehman's profits, Glucksman's effective ownership was between 5 and 6 percent, not the 4 to 5 percent industry standard. "It was a lost opportunity," says Harvey Krueger, who rarely criticized Glucksman. "Everybody had a good year. It was no time to be niggardly. If that opportunity couldn't be seized, then I had fears for the status of the banking division within the firm." Peter Solomon, who groused openly about Glucksman, says, "My God, the first year Glucksman was in charge he should have taken less. Instead, he pigged out."

The question of fairness that Glucksman had championed in prior years was now being asked of him. Glucksman had succeeded in creating a spirit of teamwork within the commercial paper division; now, when granted the opportunity he had craved, he was failing to extend that spirit throughout the firm. In a partnership, where the rewards are to be shared, a loss of trust can be devastating. And in his first two months at the helm of his own ship, Lew Glucksman began to lose that trust. "If you were Machiavelli, you would have hired people to do Peterson's job," observes one former partner. "You would have been modest in your own bonus and stock. You would have shored up your weakness in banking . . . Since he's smart, my theory is that something tripped in Lew."

B Y THE END OF SEPTEMBER THE WHISPERS ABOUT GLUCKS-man grew louder, though he was not hearing them. Partners compared him to Ahab, to Captain Queeg, to Richard Nixon, to protagonists whose real enemy was within, men who succumbed to what Melville called Ahab's "fatal pride."

Peter Solomon was openly morose. "I actually then decided to leave the firm in December," he says. "I was a voice in the wilderness." Solomon was distressed by the decisions about bonuses and shares, by Glucksman's behavior in general, by the failure of Glucksman and the board to take him seriously on any number of issues, including his warning that Lehman lacked sufficient capital to compete with the giant full-service investment banking houses and should consider going public, as First Boston and E. F. Hutton had done. His growing fury was shared by other partners, but rarely would they betray their private feelings, certainly not to a "big mouth" like Peter Solomon. Besides, Glucksman was still much respected for his golden business touch, and much feared. September, the end of fiscal 1983, would show another record-busting year of profitability. With business booming, partners were busy and had less time to gossip or grouse.

Partners went along with the bonuses and the stock plans, as they had gone along when Glucksman toppled Peterson. They were carrying on in the Lehman tradition, going it alone, celebrating what they referred to as their "entreprenuerial culture." The emphasis at Lehman was on the individual rather than on the firm. Such an emphasis was hard to quarrel with, for Lehman's profits had ballooned over the years, and Lehman had attracted stupendously gifted individuals. But such a go-it-alone culture offered no common shelter, no common purpose other than making money. Since Money mattered more than the Firm, even the most individualistic partners usually marched in step with Glucksman & Company when their own money was at stake. Partners "were scared," explains one banking partner. "These guys can fire you. It's as if you had five guys in leather jackets in the schoolyard. You don't want to enrage them because they can hurt you."

After these pocketbook decisions, Glucksman began to sense unhappiness within the firm. And in October he sought, in the words of Shel Gordon, to "bring a feeling of cohesion and peace." At a partners' meeting in October, Glucksman announced a five-point program, approved by the board, that he thought would please his partners. He knew that despite the hefty sums each received, many partners complained of being cash poor; they could not afford expensive Manhattan co-ops or second homes in the Hamptons. So Glucksman told his partners he planned to raise their salaries by

$25,000. Starting salaries would now be pegged at $100,000, not $75,000, and would rise to $150,000 rather than $125,000. (Board members had their salaries rise to $175,000.) Second, Glucksman said the annual dividend paid partners on their preferred stock would triple from 1 to 3 percent, and would henceforth be paid quarterly rather than yearly. This meant that a partner who owned 2,000 shares, assuming he held about $4 million worth of preferred stock, would now receive annual dividend payments of $120,000 rather than $40,000. Furthermore, Glucksman announced that bonuses would now be paid quarterly instead of once a year. Additionally, a $250,-000 line of credit from the Marine Midland Bank would now be available to each partner. And, finally, partners who wished to take sabbaticals for a year or less—to teach, to travel—would be encouraged to do so. The extra after-tax cost to the firm of the new salary structure and the dividend payment boost amounted to about $5 million.

In isolation, these peace offerings might have had a more salutary effect. But to a partner a quarterly versus an annual bonus payment matters far less than whether his bonus has been raised or lowered. More than money was involved. On Wall Street, where bankers have become highly visible gladiators, vanity is also at stake. "The money is a point system," observes one Lehman banker. "Ego counts more. Arguments here always revolved around what the other guy got, not on what you needed to live on."

Other events conspired to sour the atmosphere at Lehman. Before October ended, additional partners announced their departure. What came to be seen as a caravan was led by board member Yves-André Istel, whose shares and bonus had just been cut and whom Glucksman intended to remove from the board. Istel, whose native talent as an international banker was acknowledged even by critics who thought he was coasting, believed the firm was shifting its emphasis from high-fee investment banking to high-risk trading, and lacked the reservoir of capital possessed by such giants as Merrill Lynch, Shearson/American Express, Prudential-Bache, Dean Witter Reynolds (owned by Sears, Roebuck) or Salomon Brothers. He told partners that profit margins were too low and too volatile in trading. Istel believed that Lehman was heading for trouble. And since Istel knew he was in trouble himself at Glucksman's Lehman Brothers, he had conversations with competitors and ultimately decided to jump and become co-chairman of the international banking division of the First Boston Corporation. His Lehman clients—Saint-Gobain, Henkel and Olivetti—soon joined him.

Thus, in just a few brief months, five partners had resigned—Istel, Hajim, Peterson, Weigers and d'Urso.

And then came a sixth: Eric Gleacher. "What they did when they paid out the bonuses in September was the primary reason I left," says Gleacher. "The fact that Lew and Rubin allocated 25 percent of the bonuses to themselves and three other guys" (Gordon, Fuld and Peterson) "was unfair. I thought this was such a sign of real trouble. Anybody with common sense would not be so greedy. And not pay off three guys to get the bonuses passed. Something in me went off. Life is too short." Gleacher assured his partners that he did not leave because his bonus was relatively modest or because no movement was afoot to make him head of the M. & A. department. Another reason for Gleacher's departure, and his estrangement from Glucksman and Rubin, would not surface until November. In the meantime, partners were left with the knowledge that the banker closest to Glucksman was bailing out, withdrawing his $5 million in stock—a sum representing about 2 percent of Lehman's equity—and moving laterally to become a partner at Morgan Stanley, where he was to receive new stock and where, in January 1985, he would become director of their mergers and acquisitions department.

The tremor from Gleacher's decision shook the entire firm. "Eric was the best of the M. & A. partners," observes one Lehman associate. "He had just come off doing the Allied/Bendix deal. We were the bankers for Allied, which won. Eric was king. It was an enormous blow." Historically, partners didn't defect to another firm, certainly not to one of their principal rivals, says board member William Welsh. Today, says Welsh, the ties of tradition or memory no longer bind. Gleacher's departure was a reminder that free agents existed on Wall Street as well as in major league baseball. Weigers had gone to Dillon, Read and Istel to First Boston, but to Welsh these moves were not comparable to going to Morgan Stanley or to Goldman, Sachs, Lehman's longtime competitors.* "After Gleacher left I thought the company would eventually be sold," Welsh says. Why? "It said a partner could have a life after Lehman Brothers . . . If you can go from Lehman to Morgan, it means there is transportability. What does it say to people? It says there is an

*Many investment bankers group First Boston with Morgan Stanley, just a rung below Goldman, Sachs.

opportunity to transfer this team to another team. To me it meant other players would be doing the same thing." What unsettled partners was that Gleacher, unlike Istel or Weigers, had been an intimate of Glucksman's. Partners began to wonder, recalls banking partner Steven Fenster, "What has he thought of that we haven't thought of?"

The six partners who left provoked more than a psychological crisis; their exit prompted partners to contemplate not only their own, but the firm's pocketbook, to raise what came to be called "the capital issue." Unlike the procedure in many firms, when a partner departed Lehman there was a relatively short payout period. For equity in the firm owned prior to 1979, the payout period was two and a half years; for stock acquired after 1979, the payout period was extended to five years. (When a partner leaves, his equity is converted to subordinated debt, which means that the size of the firm's overall equity is reduced and that, among all debtors, departing partners stand last in line.) The six who left would eventually take with them almost $30 million in capital, representing about 17 percent of Lehman's total capital. An additional drain on the firm's capital was caused by the redistribution of stock; those partners compelled to give up shares sold them at their current value, which was six times the $110 per-share purchase price paid by partners for new stock. Should other partners follow, the drain might prompt a panic.

In addition, the departure of the six came at a time when Lehman's "gray books," the monthly performance reports sandwiched between gray covers and circulated to all partners, made clear that business was declining, a decline that reflected a drop in trading activity, Glucksman's source of power. Partners also worried that with Peterson gone they might lose some blue-chip clients, which inevitably led them to wonder whether they would be able to withdraw the enormous wealth they had accumulated, all in Lehman stock. Even though they knew Glucksman was an implacable foe of selling the firm, partners who had stopped talking about a possible sale now began to think about it and about the premium—the bonus paid by the buyer that might run to three times the worth of their stock. In countless huddles commencing that fall, partners recalled the situation at Salomon Brothers, when seven senior partners owned 35 percent of that firm's capital. By merging with Phibro in 1981, recalls one senior executive at Salomon, "we replaced our capital with public capital." Phibro, a publicly held company, paid partners for their stock, replacing it with shares sold to the public.

True, partners became employees, rather than owners. But as an added inducement, each partner received a premium worth one and a half times more than the worth of his stock. Managing partner John Gutfreund, alone, was said to have made $40 million on the merger. Within months of the Phibro-Salomon merger, Dean Witter Reynolds partners cashed in on a piece of the $800 million offer from Sears, Roebuck & Company, and Shearson Loeb Rhoades partners collected part of the $930 million from American Express. By selling or merging Lehman, the firm's capital would be replenished, and partners would get rich—quick.

"The Gleacher thing scared me," admits Glucksman. "I was concerned that too many partners had near-term needs for cash. The Gleacher move was made out of *greed.* We were paying 1 percent on the equity partners had in the business." Their equity appreciated with each year's rise in profits, but aside from their annual 1 percent dividend, which Glucksman had just raised to 3 percent, this wealth was untouchable unless they sold their shares. Glucksman continued, "If they could pull their money out and get maybe 10 percent from a money fund and they had $2 million in equity, they could increase their income by $200,000." Partners could cash in their stock, invest this lump sum, and be awarded new equity as a partner in another firm.

Greed was the word that hovered over the troubled partnership. To their faces, Glucksman accused Gleacher and the senior bankers of *greed* for money. Behind his back, senior bankers accused Glucksman of *greed* for power. Traders said the bankers were *greedy* because they were privately angling to sell the firm. Bankers said the traders were *greedy* to steal their shares and to take such fat bonuses.

G REED WAS A MELODY RUNNING THROUGH THE DEBATE that autumn about "capital adequacy." There was no debate, however, that capital does in fact matter to an investment bank. Nor was there disagreement that there is no objective right or wrong answer to the question: What is an adequate level of capital? "It depends on what you want to do with the capital," says Peterson. Clearly, certain activities require more capital than others. A full-service financial supermarket like Merrill Lynch, for example, has a higher overhead than a banking boutique like Dillon, Read, which concentrates on traditional banking services. To maintain a distribution and sales force or offices overseas demands a reservoir of capital. Similarly, as a firm moves away from a fee-related business to gambling its own money on companies and products it believes in—the way Lehman and the merchant banks of another era did, or firms like Allen & Company, Oppenheimer or Bear Stearns do today—it needs added capital.

Traders, who daily wager on the direction the market or interest rates will bounce, need capital to risk, as do the arbitrageurs, who speculate in rising and falling markets. To satisfy the institutions—pension funds, mutual funds, banks, insurance companies—that now control more than $1 trillion in savings and an estimated 60 percent of corporate stocks and bonds, requires capital. For these giant institutions want to deal with giant investment banks that can buy or sell huge blocs of stock, which requires a bank to have sufficient capital to bid for their business.

The movement toward investment banks that possess vast pools of capital was also spurred by deregulation. Once, investment banking had been a predictable business. Bankers obeyed strict regulations dating back to the New Deal. But by 1983, the Securities & Exchange Commission, which regulates the securities business, had already shed scores of strictures, a process begun in the mid-seventies. In the face of fierce opposition from Wall Street firms that would, ironically, later benefit from this decision, the SEC in 1982 imposed Rule 415, which now permitted companies to register in one filing all the securities they planned to issue over the next two years and then to sell these in whole or in part "off the shelf." This move, which suspended the requirement to file formal applications for each underwriting, was designed to grant corporations speedier access to capital markets. One result of this measure was to relax corporate loyalties to bankers. Because companies could now register without listing their underwriters, they were free to shop for the best price, unleashing intense and often ungentlemanly competition among bankers. By 1983, of the $97 billion underwritten by Wall Street, almost two-fifths was "off the shelf."* And to capture this business, an investment bank had to set a price, and be prepared to swallow a loss if the bond was sold for less. That takes capital.

Capital was also required as protection against a more volatile economic climate. Inflation and interest rates, which had once been relatively steady and predictable, now rose and crashed like ocean waves; Wall Street reeled from boom to bust to boom cycles. By 1983, Lehman's fixed-income division alone was trading up to $15 billion a day; share volume on the Amex, the Big Board, the regional exchanges and the over-the-counter market jumped 50 percent that year. The gentlemen's world of investment banking had become what Lehman vice president Jeffrey Garten calls "an Arab bazaar."

The advance of technology also had capital consequences, for the planet is now joined in one global financial market. In 1980, U.S. investors traded $18 billion in foreign stocks; by 1988 they were projected to trade about $63 billion. By September 1983, Lehman had a hundred employees in their London office, and would shortly send Garten to open a Tokyo office with twenty employees.

In addition to meeting the minimum capital requirements imposed on investment banks by the New York Stock Exchange, capital also serves as insurance should the firm suffer a sudden loss, guaranteeing that there will still be funds to carry on and to pay bonuses and salaries to the 2,985 people Lehman employed in September 1983.

All of these forces mesh with what was happening at Lehman. Following Glucksman's success in building a trading and sales operation, and prodded by Peterson's commitment to develop "new products" and to nudge the firm into "the special bracket" group of the five top investment banks, Lehman was committed to becoming a full-service bank, on a par with Goldman, Sachs and Salomon Brothers. Retail, institutional, corporate and governmental customers could already come to Lehman if they were shopping to merge, to divest, to undertake a leveraged buyout, to swap debt for equity, to have bonds underwritten, to trade stocks, to purchase zero coupon bonds or Treasury notes or municipal bonds, to invest in a money fund or real estate. Lehman provided one-stop service, which, in turn, required capital.

Against this backdrop, it is not surprising that partners in the fall of 1983 began to discuss "the capital issue"; that they began to worry

*Paul Ferris, *Gentlemen of Fortune: The World's Merchant and Investment Bankers,* Weidenfeld and Nicolson, p. 83.

aloud that Lehman's capital base as of October 1983 ($254.7 million) was fragile. This had certainly become Pete Peterson's view, for as he observed in a speech he made in London in September, "Two large organizations, Sears and American Express, have more equity than all of 'Wall Street' firms in the entire U.S. I believe we will see Wall Street firms doing all sorts of things to get a broader capital base . . ."

Lehman's competitors were now giants like Merrill Lynch ($2 billion in capital at the end of 1983); Shearson/American Express ($1,056 billion in capital); Phibro/Salomon ($1.3 billion in capital); Dean Witter Financial Services Group ($964.5 million in capital); E. F. Hutton ($746.5 million in capital); and Prudential-Bache Securities ($493.7 million in capital).

These behemoths, which have risen over the past decade primarily through access to rich parent companies or to the public markets, are rivaled by the giant banks, including Bankers Trust and Citicorp, which are pressing for further relaxation of laws that for decades have maintained a wall between deposit and investment banking. Similarly, giants like American Express have pushed into the commercial banking business.

Lehman partners were of course aware of the trend on Wall Street for investment banking houses to merge into larger firms—Hayden Stone into Shearson, Hammill; Shearson, Hammill into American Express; White Weld into Merrill Lynch; Bache into Prudential; J. Aron & Company into Goldman, Sachs; Dean Witter Reynolds into Sears; Salomon Brothers into Phibro; Kuhn Loeb into Lehman Brothers. To some Lehman partners the future began to look bleak for private partnerships like Goldman, Sachs, Morgan Stanley, and Lehman. They worried that Lehman was neither fish nor fowl. Too small to compete with the giants and too big to specialize.

"The face of Wall Street is changing," observes John Whitehead, who recently retired as co-CEO of Goldman, Sachs. "Our clients no longer look to us as wise advisers, as they once did. Now the emphasis is on transactional business rather than advisory business."

An important aspect of this transactional environment was captured in *Business Week* (August 13, 1984): "Within minutes of ITT Corp's announcement on July 11 that it was cutting its dividend by nearly two-thirds so it could afford heavy investments in the U.S. telecommunications business, money managers stampeded to dump their shares. By day's end, the price of the stock had dropped by roughly a third, in response to the cut and an announcement of lower earnings. In effect, institutional investors knocked the price down until ITT's new $1 dividend once more yielded the minimum 5% return that most institutions demand. And now the low price of ITT's stock makes it a potential takeover candidate . . . The ITT incident is the clearest evidence of the broad—almost dictatorial—power that money managers wield today over corporate destinies . . . they can virtually set the price of any company's stock through the impact of their massive purchases or sales. By comparing equity investments with alternate opportunities such as short-term debt instruments, they keep prices low. They can, at will, sell shares in their portfolios to an arbitrageur—a trader who thrives on rumors, buying up shares quickly on hints of a raider's interest, in the hope of reselling them to anyone willing to pay a premium for control of a company. And the institutions base their decisions not on the underlying worth of a company or on its long-term prospects but on whether the arbitrageur will give them a quick profit on their investment."*

The consequences for business of a preoccupation with short-term considerations have been much remarked upon: chief executives often sacrifice long-range growth plans in order to boost present earnings; they cannot turn to the depressed equity markets to raise funds, so they borrow, often saddling the company with massive debt and menacing its very life if a recession hits; managers become risk avoiders rather than risk takers. The entrepreneurial spirit that drives capitalism and that has produced so many economic miracles calcifies. The by-word—caution—often becomes the product.

The consequences for investment banking are also profound. Too many investment bankers, says Herbert Allen, Jr., president and CEO of Allen & Company, act like bureaucrats. "How much do they own of the companies they advise? If you're an entrepreneur, you've got to own. One of the great weaknesses of the Street is that firms are rendering opinions in the best interest of shareholders and yet they don't invest any of their massive capital to become shareholders." Inevitably, many investment bankers come to see their role much as lawyers do, as advocates. They don't own or produce a product; they are a service business that generates fees and profits. The surge, for example, in hostile corporate takeovers (from 1981 to

---

*An alternative explanation for the sharp drop in the price of ITT's stock is that their reduced dividend was taken by investors as a signal that the top management of ITT was deeply worried about the long-term viability of their main lines of business, in particular the telecommunications business, which the chairman of ITT had trumpeted for years.

1984 there were forty-five $1 billion-plus mergers, compared to only a dozen in the previous 12 years)* has at least in part been provoked by investment bankers, who are paid handsomely to perform such services.

In any case, the crush of supermarket activity generates elephantine investment banking fees, but also requires a larger capital base. It is this capital question that for the past few years had attracted the attention of Steven R. Fenster, forty-two, Lehman's resident thinker—the "professor," as partners sometimes called him, a former Fulbright Scholar and "whiz kid" systems analyst in Robert McNamara's Defense Department. Fenster became convinced that Lehman needed more capital. Without it, Fenster's nightmare was that the firm would be squeezed between low-cost giants like Shearson or Merrill Lynch and specialty boutiques like Lazard Frères, which concentrated on banking services, or Drexel Burnham Lambert, which has cornered the market on issuing higher yield and higher risk "junk bonds." Lehman, Fenster feared, would try to provide full services yet lack the capital to do so. This was the fate of A. G. Becker, which catapulted toward bankruptcy and was finally gobbled up at a bargain price by Merrill Lynch in 1984.

Fenster did not believe the business could continue to expand the way it had. A downturn was in order. And when it came he feared that Lehman could not easily shrink its $437 million overhead, as the firm was able to do when it was much smaller in 1973. "We had an enormous investment in trading and distribution," he says. "We had leasehold improvements and real estate leases and back office arrangements. We had an extraordinary investment in communications, including an expensive telephone complex and a branch office network. We had people who, if released, would receive substantial severance pay. Second, with the elimination of these activities it would be like running a movie backward. Some of our banking activities would become uneconomic. There would have to be adjustments there. Thirdly, there were fewer and weaker competitors in 1973, fewer predatory animals. If we went through a retrenchment in 1983 similar to what we did in 1973, we would have lost considerable business."

*Time, March 4, 1985.

S TEVEN FENSTER'S NIGHTMARES CAME ALIVE IN THE FALL OF 1983. In the capricious world of trading, the market suddenly turned bearish. Lehman's profits began to shrivel, and analysts agreed: the trading engine, which had been driving Lehman's profits, was stalling all over Wall Street. The dreary business outlook produced new converts to the belief that Lehman's capital was inadequate. Among them was Roger Altman, who all that summer had been whispering to Glucksman that he was an ally in opposition to the sale of the firm. "I only came to the conclusion we were seriously undercapitalized during the budget process of October," says Altman. "Because we had had five consecutive years of record growth and had been retaining 80 percent of earnings, our capital went up each year. We had been generating enough capital to finance the growth we were experiencing. I was of the view we could continue —until October 1983. Many people came to this conclusion earlier," Steven Fenster and Peter Solomon among them. "What changed in 1983," Altman continued, "was the business outlook. The business turned down all over Wall Street in the last quarter of 1983. I realized that whatever we would earn in fiscal 1984 was modest. Therefore, our retained earnings would be modest. Therefore, we wouldn't increase our capital very much. At the same time, I was listening to our managers tell us of their plans to grow and the opportunities to grow if they had capital."

But Roger Altman was not the type to lead a parade. Nor, as a former associate of Peterson's, was Altman the right leader. Arrayed against the view that Lehman's capital was inadequate were some internally powerful forces, including Bob Rubin, Dick Fuld, Jim Boshart and, at first, Lew Glucksman. The man who on October 1 officially became Lehman's sole CEO, worried that an infusion of substantial outside capital would come about only through one of three means: merging the company into a larger entity, as Kuhn Loeb did when it married Lehman or Shearson when it linked with American Express; recruiting an outside investor to purchase some of Lehman's stock, as Dillon Read had done when it recruited Bechtel; or taking Lehman public, as Merrill Lynch, Dean Witter and First Boston had done. Each of these options was unattractive to Glucksman, because each threatened Lehman's traditional independence as well as Glucksman's own newly acquired power base. Joining Glucksman's core group in opposition to those who said Lehman's capital was inadequate were two longtime members of the banking department, William Morris and Henry Breck (who had recently been placed in charge of money management). They believed the "capital issue" was really a subterfuge for partners who were either panicky about getting their own money out, or simply wanted to cash in and sell the firm at a premium.

The intellectual leader of those proclaiming the adequacy of Lehman's capital was Bob Rubin. In late September, Glucksman and Rubin had arranged a $50 million loan from Prudential, which was added to Lehman's subordinated debt, and thus became part of its capital base. "I don't believe that we had a capital shortage," says Rubin. "I believe partners were concerned about a lack of significant earnings. We augmented our capital by $50 million from Prudential in September. So if they were concerned about capital, they didn't understand the numbers. We had more capital in September after Peterson was paid off than we ever had in our history."

Rubin's close friend Bill Morris made the same point another way: The only reason a firm requires capital, he says, is "to survive a one-hundred-year storm" of losses, to "satisfy the New York Stock Exchange's capital requirements," or as insurance. When a firm needs capital it borrows it, just as a homeowner does. So the question, he argued, was not whether Lehman's capital was adequate but: "What was it the partners desired to get done? I don't think getting more capital into the business was uppermost in their minds. Getting their capital out of the business to reduce their risk was."

This group began to advance the argument that if partners were truly concerned about capital, there was a fourth alternative in addition to standing pat, selling the firm, or bringing in outside capital, and that choice was to shrink. Lehman didn't have to be a supermarket, they said. Nor did it need an infusion of three times its current capital, as some partners argued. Instead of compromising the private partnership, they believed Lehman should concentrate on banking services and on those products—perhaps commercial paper, perhaps money management, perhaps M. & A.—where it was strong.

In the capital debate that raged in the fall of 1983, Lew Glucksman was indecisive. In his heart, he was with Rubin and Fuld and Boshart, who sensed that now that the traders enjoyed their place in the sun the bankers were greedily maneuvering to dilute their power. But Glucksman's head told him something else. That is why he was the prime force behind the $50 million loan from Prudential. Nor did Glucksman believe Lehman could shrink without paying a terrible price, including revenues that might plunge faster than costs. Caught between his heart and his head, Glucksman was uncharacteristically ambivalent.

Into this vacuum stepped Shel Gordon, gingerly. "Shel Gordon could tiptoe through a beach and not leave a footprint," says former Lehman associate Steven Rattner, who admires him. Gordon, the new head of the banking division, believed that Lehman had made the correct decision in the mid- to late seventies to become a full-service firm. He supported Peterson's efforts over the last several years to nudge Lehman into more venture capital, leveraged buyouts, real estate deals and other activities where the risks—and the rewards—were vast. Because of the volatility of trading, Gordon also believed that partners would rest easier with a more ample capital cushion. As a manager, he saw new opportunities beckoning in Europe and Japan that required investment. "I always felt the size of our capital base was probably half of what it would have to be over a two to three year time period," explains Gordon. "We faced the prospect of having a half dozen of our good clients—Chase Manhattan Bank, Philip Morris, D.E.C., Westinghouse, Caterpillar Tractor —wanting to come to market at the same time."

Shel Gordon gently coaxed his partners. Those, like Solomon and Schwarzman, who felt estranged from Glucksman, were seduced by the open door they always found to Gordon's office. Since Gordon was trusted by Glucksman, he was the perfect umbrella under which various factions could gather. Mergers and acquisitions specialist Eric Gleacher recalls how Gordon would instruct him in how "to maneuver Lew." Gordon "does not recall" those words to Gleacher, but he does acknowledge the delicate diplomatic role he performed: "I was more concerned with getting people to focus on that issue than on the outcome of that issue. Not having the issue focused on risked destroying the firm in the long run."

The ferment at Lehman was growing, as was the level of anxiety. From the day he arrived at Lehman that fall, Pete Dawkins put his back into the grind, as if he were back in boot camp. He was intent on mastering a new field, public finance. He didn't partake in the capital debate or in the firm's internal politics. Yet the erect former West Pointer remembers that from October 1, the day he arrived, there was the sense that he had been parachuted into a minefield. "Sitting around the partners' dining table," he says, "you picked up part of this. But a lot of it was taking place in private meetings."

I N NOVEMBER, OTHER BATTLES DEBILITATED THE PARTNER-
ship. On November 8, Glucksman formally told the six other
members of the operating committee that he intended to appoint
Robert Rubin president. This was not a new idea to Glucksman. He
had planned it around the time he confronted Peterson in July. That
fall Glucksman had sounded out a few senior partners about it. It
is unclear whether those he approached were genuinely enthusiastic,
in which case he was talking to too few partners, or whether those
he approached were too timid to share their true opinions. What is
clear is that Glucksman was as oblivious to the anger this move
would arouse as Peterson had been to the fury smoldering within
Lew Glucksman.

When Glucksman told the operating committee of his decision, he
immediately encountered some resistance. Three committee members—Roger Altman, François de Saint Phalle and Shel Gordon—
told him they were troubled by the way he had anointed Rubin.
"Roger, Shel and I felt there hadn't been a formal process to decide
how to choose the next president," says de Saint Phalle. Glucksman
countered by saying that he wanted a united operating committee to
recommend Rubin to the board, which was scheduled to meet on
November 10. Although they did not then share with Glucksman
their substantive concerns about Rubin's managerial abilities, like
many partners the three men worried about Rubin's leadership skills,
about whether he was too much like Glucksman, a Mr. Inside. No
one questioned Rubin's brainpower, his ability to size up a financial
deal or spot risks. He was, by most accounts, the most brilliant
banker at Lehman, but he was a private, prickly personality.

With Glucksman the three confined their objections to procedure,
not substance. Gordon wanted to give the board more time to deliberate and, some said, to maneuver for the position himself. Altman
and de Saint Phalle agreed that more time was needed, and emphasized an additional concern: They did not want to take responsibility
for recommending a president unless they had the authority to vote
for a president. Since they were not members of the board, they said
this authority was denied them. For months, members of the operating committee had complained that they should also sit as members
of the board. They were already meeting twice weekly to ponder
major operational and strategic decisions. Of the seven members,
only three—Altman, de Saint Phalle and administrative partner
James Boshart—were not board members.

Glucksman asked Altman, Gordon and de Saint Phalle to meet

privately with Rubin to ventilate these concerns. They met the next day in Rubin's small office on the forty-first floor. The taciturn Rubin sat there, quietly drawing on one of his long, thin Schimmelpenninck cigars, and listened as his three partners told him they questioned the process Glucksman had followed in arriving at this decision.

"Fine. I'm not a candidate for this position," Rubin remembers saying. "I have no burning desire for this job. I'm willing to do it. If more than one person on the board votes against me, I won't take the job and I'll decide what I have to do." The operating committee delegation took this as a threat.

That night, on the eve of the board meeting, the committee was summoned to a meeting. Glucksman knew he had the votes to make Rubin president. He had met alone with Shel Gordon and came away satisfied that he had a committment from Shel for Rubin. In an act Glucksman thought would be perceived as ecumenical, he announced that he wanted to nominate de Saint Phalle and Altman to the board. He also planned, he announced, to nominate Jim Boshart and Henry Breck. Glucksman said it was good management for members of the operating committee to serve on the board, which set broad policy. Since Breck was responsible for managing one of the three major divisions of the firm, Glucksman said he belonged on the board as well. Some members of the committee interpreted Glucksman's action as a bribe. "Lew bought us off by putting us on the board," one of the four men shamefully admits.

For three hours the next morning, November 10, the four waited outside the boardroom on the forty-third floor, sipping coffee, pacing, making phone calls. Inside, the board argued, often vehemently, about the merits of expanding, about the demerits of the four candidates, about whether new board members should be permitted to vote for president. Solomon, as usual, led the charge, comparing Glucksman's proposal to Franklin Delano Roosevelt's scheme to pack the Supreme Court. He got a silent nod of approval from a Rubin ally, Bill Morris, who was a strict traditionalist. Morris later told friends he believed Glucksman was in fact trying to "pack the board."

Analogies with FDR were not the fulcrum of this debate, however. The focus was on personalities and on balancing internal interests. There was no opposition to adding Breck or Boshart, says Glucksman. But there was intense resistance to adding Altman, who as head of new business development was thought not to have the internal clout and to be "too political"; there was lesser but real resistance to de Saint Phalle, since he, like Altman, no longer headed the banking department. Resistance to de Saint Phalle evaporated relatively quickly; to gain support for Altman, Glucksman recalls importuning the board: "I never thought of Roger Altman as my man. But I always thought we needed a new business program. He did a good job at it. It's vital that you support your chairman. It's vital to have in this body someone who represents the new direction we're talking about—the development of new products and new accounts."

The other major debate, recalls senior banker Harvey Krueger, was "an argument about balance—bankers versus nonbankers, managers versus nonmanagers. And someone had to say something about each person." Even though three of the four candidates had their roots in the banking department, bankers on the board were either so paranoid or so preoccupied with maintaining their own status within the firm that they once again felt their power was being diluted.

The meeting went on so long that Glucksman had to cancel a previously scheduled luncheon with the editors of *Newsweek* magazine.* Finally, after three hours, a compromise was reached: the four new members were approved; and the bankers on the board were appeased by the addition of a fifth member—Richard Bingham, then forty-seven, the head of the M. & A. department, who, it would soon be announced, was going to run Lehman's San Francisco corporate finance office. Bingham was nominated by banker William Morris, and encountered no opposition. "I didn't know Bingham well. But I knew he was a professional," says Glucksman.

"For at least ten minutes peace reigned," says Glucksman. The five new board members filed into the meeting. Everyone knew what Glucksman proposed to do this day, and now he did it. He nominated Rubin as a candidate for president. But before Rubin could speak, Peter Solomon had something to say. Tension filled the boardroom, for as one board member says, "Solomon and Glucksman hate each other with enough electricity to light half the United States." And the hatred between Solomon and Rubin might light the rest.

---

*The luncheon idea was triggered by Richard Holbrooke, who had invited a friend, *Newsweek* editor Maynard Parker, to dine at Lehman with visiting Chinese officials. At this dinner, Glucksman, who was upset by a recent *Newsweek* story, "The Lehman Circus," suggested the lunch. It was canceled, then rescheduled and held at Lehman Brothers. According to William Broyles, former *Newsweek* editor-in-chief, the article that provoked the invitation was never discussed.

Pausing for effect, Solomon turned to Rubin and asked, "What are the talents you have to be president of the firm?"

Rubin answered the question head-on, between puffs of his Schimmelpenninck. "I made it clear to the board," recalls Rubin, "that I am a private person. I do not like meeting new people. I probably don't like the normal social amenities that people from all walks of life like. I don't go out for three-hour dinners. I'm not going to change." He didn't have to, he said, because "Lew is not like that. He acted like that while Pete was chairman, because Pete was the consummate outside person. If only you would look at Lew's diary from last July to now, you'd see what functions he went to, what clients he visited. I think you'd see by the record that he was happy, and doing well as an 'outside person.' " Rubin told the partners he believed Lehman's capital was adequate, and flatly stated his opposition to going public or to selling all or part of Lehman Brothers. He also promised that Lehman would be more open, and embraced Glucksman's plan to inaugurate regular Monday board luncheons.

Still, Bob Rubin was not a man to grovel. He wanted to satisfy his partners, but he did not see himself as a seeker of this office; he was responding to a request from his friend Lew Glucksman. He said he wanted the job and was qualified to hold it. He repeated what he had said the day before about how he would decline the job if the vote was not nearly unanimous.* Rubin simply concluded his remarks by expressing the belief that he could do a good job.

"You are the only one who feels that way," shot back Solomon, who was incensed at Rubin's remarks. He believed that Rubin was dead wrong about the adequacy of the firm's capital, and thought he was obstinately and wrongly opposed to taking the firm public or bringing in a minority investor to shore up Lehman's capital base (and, not incidentally, provide partners with a considerable amount of cash, while diluting Glucksman and Rubin's power base).

Rubin left the room to allow the board to deliberate. Those, like Glucksman, Morris, Boshart, Fuld and Breck, who believed Rubin was the most intellectually impressive banker they knew, a man of principle and character, were pleased by his presentation. But many were astonished. Did Rubin, and for that matter Glucksman, really believe Glucksman could be Mr. Outside, like Peterson? How could Rubin believe Lehman had adequate capital? Was Lehman electing

---

*Memories differ on whether Rubin issued a threat or merely said the next president would need broad board support to function properly.

a president or a hermit? Would he be a hands-on manager, more
open than he had been in the past? Why would a private man, who
said he did not seek the job, subject himself to such public abuse?

Such were the private reservations of many board members, but
only Peter Solomon uttered his misgivings publicly. Seizing center
stage, Solomon fulminated against Rubin. At one point he recalls
saying, "Rubin is qualified. But he doesn't complement you, Lew.
He's an inside guy. Why not leave the spot open so a Shel Gordon
or a Dick Fuld can think they can be president?"

"Because I want him," snapped Glucksman, his Russian general's
face reddening.

Harvey Krueger, the genial fifty-four-year-old chairman of the
audit committee, spoke next. Of all his partners, Bob Rubin was the
only one Krueger could not get along with. He had disliked Rubin
from the first, feeling he was negative about the Kuhn Loeb merger
and much else. In his avuncular way, Krueger asked whether
Rubin's talents complemented Glucksman's. With Peterson gone, he
wondered, did Lehman need a salesman, a visible rainmaker? Bill
Welsh, as usual, said nothing. Mario M. Arcari, president of the
Long Island Trust Company, who was representing BCI and Enrico
Braggiotti as an observer, also said nothing.

But Shel Gordon stunned Glucksman by saying that a decision
should be delayed to allow more time to make a considered management judgment. Glucksman glared at Gordon. For the first time,
Glucksman sensed that Gordon, his handpicked choice to head
banking, was no longer his agent. "The real break with Shel began
when he backed down on voting for Rubin," recalls Glucksman. "He
wanted to delay. He was trying to marshal support for himself."

Glucksman summarily dismissed Gordon's effort to stall a vote.
Joining Glucksman in advancing Rubin's candidacy were William
Morris, Richard Fuld, Henry Breck and James Boshart. To them,
Rubin was a counterweight to Glucksman, a man who stood up to
Lew and could slow him down, a man who made them feel secure.
They personally admired Rubin. To most trading partners and associates, Rubin was perceived as the one person whose roots were in
banking but who, nevertheless, understood their grievances. Among
this group of employees, few admired Rubin more than Jim Boshart.
"Bob Rubin is the most unfairly maligned person in this organization," Boshart recalls saying. "He is the single person I met here in
fourteen and a half years that I respect the most. He is the most
intelligent person I have met here. He is the most decent person I

have met here. Bob Rubin is always concerned with the pay of all employees here, not just the best-paid employees. I'm astonished by the negative comments made about Bob. When many of us started with the firm, Bob Rubin was the person many of us aspired to be."

The other new board members had said little, so Harvey Krueger solicited their opinion, inviting them to speak. They wobbled, like yearlings. Bingham asked who would be responsible for controlling costs. (Rubin, answered Glucksman.) De Saint Phalle opined that the main objective of the president should be to instill confidence and to facilitate communication, and he wondered whether Rubin would communicate. Altman spoke, somewhat vaguely, of the need to fashion future procedures to identify and select top managers. Breck unhesitatingly defended Rubin, the partner who first hired him at Lehman.

The arguments flared for an hour and a half, with people sometimes repeating themselves. Then Glucksman, impatient for a decision, started to poll the partners. The tide turned when he called on Harvey Krueger, who said, "You're entitled to pick your own chief operating officer." Others chimed their agreement. Krueger moved for the unanimous confirmation of Rubin as president. Peter Solomon shrugged and went along. The vote was unanimous.

The reaction inside the firm was hardly unanimous. "It did not make good management sense," says James Hood, the former head of marketing and public relations, who is today director of marketing at First Boston. "You heard all the jokes about Mr. Inside and Mr. Inside. Deserved or not, there was a great concern that with Peterson gone, Lew was not willing to assume the mantle of Mr. Outside. That is an accurate criticism. There appeared to be either a total lack of awareness or sensitivity to how people felt. Like Lew, Bob was a guy who had little client contact. Perhaps he made a substantial contribution to the firm, but those he made were very much inside. We plugged into the president's slot a man who never indicated an interest in management. Who spent time sitting in his own office doing things no one understood. People didn't know what Bob Rubin did. He was resistant to new business and marketing. If you have those personal beliefs and biases, how can you be president?"

T HE FIRST OF THE PROMISED MONDAY BOARD LUNCHES WAS scheduled for November 14, in the unadorned, windowless dining room off the trading floor, where meals were kept in a food warmer in a small adjoining kitchenette. This informal lunch turned out to be harmonious.

But the harmony was short-lived. Before the month was out another bomb went off at Lehman. And its fuse was lit by former Lehman partner Eric Gleacher when Gleacher's friend Peter Solomon told him that Pete Peterson had some nice things to say about "the graceful way" Gleacher had left the firm. Gleacher was taken aback, for he and Peterson had never gotten along. But Peterson, Gleacher observed before he left on November 1, was in a melancholy mood, finding time for daily chats with partners he once treated frostily, including Solomon. So Gleacher telephoned Peterson to thank him. One thing led to another and they agreed to meet for coffee in the Hamptons. On Sunday morning, November 6, the two former adversaries sat reminiscing and sipping coffee at Gleacher's weekend home not far from the beach.

"He was telling me how bad it was, how teams of people were leaving," recalls Gleacher.

"It's a shame, Pete," said Gleacher. "It didn't have to be this way. There were opportunities. When they turned down the ConAgra offer I knew they would never sell the firm," Gleacher said.

"What?" said Peterson, genuinely puzzled.

"You mean they didn't tell you of the ConAgra offer?"

"What offer?"

Gleacher, who was settled now at Morgan Stanley, then told Peterson of a conversation he had had with Bob Rubin in May 1983. Bill Morris and Gleacher had just lunched in the partners' dining room and were chatting in Morris's office when Rubin happened by. The three partners lapsed into a conversation about the firm. What Gleacher did not tell Peterson is that they had also discussed their common dislike for him. But Gleacher did tell Peterson that Con-Agra, one of his regular clients, a large agriculture and food company based in Omaha, Nebraska, was prepared to pay $600 million to acquire Lehman. This was more than three times Lehman's worth at the time. ConAgra, Gleacher told Rubin and Morris, would structure a deal in the following way: $300 million would be in cash; $100 million would come to the partners through the sale of new ConAgra common stock; and $200 million would go to the partners in the form of convertible preferred ConAgra stock.

Rubin contemplated the offer overnight, then telephoned Gleacher the next day. ConAgra was too small to digest Lehman, he said. It didn't have sufficient capital to launch Lehman as a full-service rival to, say, Salomon Brothers. Therefore, he concluded, the deal wasn't "do-able."

Peterson couldn't believe what he was hearing, and there was more. Gleacher said that the next afternoon he went to see his friend Glucksman in the "chart room" where he laid out the deal to him. He recalled that Glucksman said, "It's the wrong time. Look, I could pick up the phone now and sell for $900 million. The bankers own too much of the equity of the firm compared to the traders, and it would be unfair to sell now because the bankers would get too much of the profits." Gleacher countered by urging Glucksman to meet with Charles M. Harper, the chairman and CEO of ConAgra. "Now's a bad time," said Glucksman. "I'll do it, but let's wait a few months."*

Gleacher never thought of bringing the ConAgra matter to Peterson because at the time they were estranged and because ConAgra was interested in expanding its trading operations, which meant that Glucksman was the key to any deal.

Gleacher was flabbergasted that Peterson, who was chairman and co-CEO at the time, knew nothing of this. Peterson was mortified, believing that Glucksman and Robin had violated a basic rule of corporate governance by not telling him, and had, perhaps, violated their fiduciary responsibility to their partners as well. Although Peterson (and Glucksman) did not share the events of the previous July with his partners before deciding to leave Lehman, he perceived no irony now in accusing Glucksman and Rubin of violating their responsibility to the partnership. A major difference, Peterson would correctly say, was that at least he took his agreement with Glucksman to the board for their approval, while Glucksman and Rubin did not take the ConAgra offer to the board. Gleacher, who says Lehman was a "blood money" partnership, too much concerned with money and too little concerned with tradition, also perceives no irony in the fact that he was pressing to sell, at considerable profit to himself, Wall Street's oldest continuing partnership.

Peterson related to Gleacher how, when he received a purported feeler from American Express to acquire Lehman in 1982, he told the

*In the June 18, 1984, *Forbes* magazine, Glucksman flatly denied a ConAgra offer—"that offer was not communicated to me." Yet Glucksman now says, "I would not repudiate what Gleacher says. But any $900 million figure I used is too high."

intermediary, Salim (Sandy) Lewis, "I won't meet with you alone. I'll only meet with Glucksman there." They met in Peterson's apartment, and because no concrete proposal followed this meeting—unlike ConAgra, which put a dollar figure on the table through its banker—he says the matter was not brought to Lehman's board, although he did insist that Bob Rubin be briefed.

The conversation between Peterson and Gleacher stretched beyond breakfast, with Gleacher going on to tell Peterson that "ConAgra is still interested in having discussions with the firm." Soon after this breakfast, Peterson consulted with his counsel Morton Janklow and Janklow's partner, Jerome Traum. Janklow and Traum advised Peterson that Glucksman's and Rubin's behavior might be actionable. "Any lawyer will tell you that when a serious offer is made to the CEO of a company, he's got to go to his board with it," Janklow says. "My judgment is that it's almost actionable. If Pete calls me and says, 'I just got this proposal from ConAgra, what do I do?,' I'd tell him to convene a meeting of the board right away. My God, it's a partnership! Partners have the right to consider the sale of their company."

On November 17, Peterson addressed a five-page memorandum to Glucksman and Rubin, relating his understanding of the facts. He expressed displeasure with their behavior and demanded that they disclose this matter to the board. Peterson further demanded a piece of paper certifying that he had not been privy to information about ConAgra's interest in Lehman, and thus could not be a target of potential lawsuits from partners who might claim they were deprived of the opportunity to sell their stock, worth $175 million at the time, at more than three times its stated value. Finally, Peterson asked for a meeting with Glucksman and Rubin.

They breakfasted at Lehman on November 21. Glucksman remembers being annoyed, perhaps because once again Peterson was lording something over him. He remembered the Gleacher conversation, but he was not about to give Peterson the satisfaction of admitting it. So he told Peterson he had only a vague recollection of his May conversation with Gleacher. He dismissed it as a totally improbable deal: "Show me how these guys can finance such a transaction!"

Glucksman took the offensive. How could Peterson say the ConAgra discussion was less serious than the Sandy Lewis feeler from American Express? Why didn't Peterson share that with the board? Sharp words were exchanged between them. Bob Rubin avoided the cross fire by affecting boredom. He acknowledged the discussions and added, "So what?" He explained why the deal wasn't "do-able." The meeting concluded with Glucksman and Peterson agreeing that their lawyers should confer.

Peterson returned to his office and telephoned Gleacher, who emphasized how serious the original proposal from ConAgra had been. He noted that Touche Ross, ConAgra's accountants, at the time had prepared computer studies testifying to the feasibility of the deal; in addition, he shared part of the analysis with Rubin, handing him papers to study overnight. Back in May, Gleacher had also shared the information with his immediate superior, Richard Bingham, head of the M. & A. department. Peterson and Gleacher commiserated, agreeing that it had been outrageous, a violation of fiduciary responsibility, for Rubin and Glucksman not to have at least shared this information with the chairman of Lehman Brothers.

The board was told at lunch that day, November 21. Rubin reported matter-of-factly that "Peterson was annoyed" about something, and then briefly recounted the May feeler from ConAgra, and explained why he dismissed this feeler as "a nonstarter." At the time, the board seemed to agree with Rubin, for there were no explosions. Some board members said they thought there should be further discussions with ConAgra, and encouraged Glucksman and Rubin to pursue this.

The anger the ConAgra issue would arouse took a while to build. "Board meetings were sometimes stilted," explains one board member, who acknowledged that the board feared Glucksman. "They were awkward because Lew was not an easy, relaxed guy. So sometimes people didn't say what they thought." Many members of the board sided with Rubin that the deal was not do-able, including at least five bankers—Shel Gordon, Bill Morris, Roger Altman, Harvey Krueger and François de Saint Phalle; they thought that even if ConAgra could raise the money, it was too small to digest Lehman. Others, particularly Peter Solomon, dissented. "Rubin is a terrific analyst," he says. "But he's not a deal-doer." Eric Gleacher was a deal-doer.

Whatever the differences within the board over the do-ability of the ConAgra deal, most board members were privately aghast at the unilateral process Glucksman and Rubin followed in reaching this decision. And those who knew were chagrined by a falsehood spread by Rubin's allies that François de Saint Phalle, head of the underwriting syndicate department, had confirmed Rubin's judgment that the deal was not do-able. Not so, bristles de Saint Phalle: "I was approached by Gleacher that spring and asked how much money could ConAgra raise in the markets. I was not told it was because they wanted to buy Lehman Brothers. If someone had come to me and said, 'ConAgra wants to buy Lehman Brothers. Can they finance it?,' there might very well have been a way to finance that transaction."

Like so much else that had happened in Glucksman's reign, ConAgra became a corporate governance issue. It was, partners thought, high-handed and, ultimately, selfish; it also signaled that there was no way Glucksman or Rubin would contemplate the sale of Lehman now that they captained the ship.

"I was disappointed but not surprised," says Bill Welsh, who said nothing at the board meeting. "I thought they should have brought it forward. But I know where they stood. They were not sellers. They did a disservice to the firm." The ConAgra incident ignited talk of selling Lehman Brothers, which many—Pete Peterson says most—partners favored doing long before business soured. ConAgra legitimized and spurred these desires. "ConAgra opened Pandora's box; it opened discussions about the sale of the firm," admits Jim Boshart. "Lew and Bob were genuinely puzzled why this was made a big deal of." But they knew partners were upset.

Glucksman and Rubin were put on the defensive, again. To appease Peterson, Rubin signed a piece of paper certifying that Peterson "was not informed of the ConAgra proposal" prior to November 1983. The paper was dated December 4. Three days later, Glucksman received a letter from Charles M. Harper of ConAgra. After congratulating Glucksman on becoming chairman and praising the work Eric Gleacher had done for his company, Harper wrote:

I understand that there were some misunderstandings relating to my initiative this past May with regard to the possibility of ConAgra acquiring Lehman Brothers. It is important that I convey to you the seriousness of that approach and my disappointment when Eric informed me that you had no interest in pursuing the possibility. I also asked Eric at that time to arrange a meeting between us. He told me that you would be willing to meet with me, but you said the timing was not opportune last summer. I am still interested in meeting with you. Possibly if you learn more about ConAgra and its rationale for the development of its international grain trading business, you may see the fit which could exist between our two firms.*

*Harper, like Glucksman, would later deny to *Forbes* magazine—June 18, 1984—that he ever made an offer to purchase Lehman. Technically, of course, he did not make a formal offer; but his letter makes clear that Gleacher spoke for ConAgra when he offered $600 million for Lehman Brothers in May.

Clearly, Glucksman could see the fine hand of Gleacher lurking behind this letter, and, he suspected, that of Peterson as well. "There was no question Peterson wanted to see the thing sold," says Gleacher, who received regular phone calls in November from his former adversary. "The guy wanted to do anything to make himself look good, and to make himself rich."

Glucksman felt compelled to respond to Harper's letter. He felt chastised, pressured. "It was clear the business was being aggressively shopped," he says. On December 13, Peggy Krieger, Glucksman's secretary, read to Harper's secretary on the phone his dictated response. It read, in part: "While I am not optimistic that pursuing the matter will yield any results, I would be willing to meet with you at a mutually convenient time and place early next year."

But Glucksman had second thoughts. He was aware that a growing number of board members were interested, and says, "I agreed it was my responsibility to come back and review with the board all conversations with the outside." That same afternoon he dictated and signed his formal letter to Harper. It was the same letter, except this time he dropped the line about his lack of optimism.

Neither this letter nor Glucksman's more conciliatory tone restored peace. Within weeks another bomb would go off. The setting was yet another Monday board lunch. The prime focus of the meeting was capital. Board members were reviewing their needs and their fears. Glucksman called on his protégé Dick Fuld to make a business presentation. The tightly coiled chief of all trading operations at Lehman explained his five-year plan for the trading departments, mentioning that he had just hired William L. Silber, a professor of economics and finance at New York University's Graduate School of Business, to study trading operations at the firm. A simple query from M. & A. chief Dick Bingham lit the fuse.

"How did you make money in your trading operations over the last five years, and how are you planning to make money over the next several years," Bingham recalls asking, innocently.

"I don't know how I made it over the last five years," answered the thirty-seven-year-old Fuld, a man of few words. "We have hired some people, including Bill Silber, to study how we're going to do it over the next several years."

"How long will the study take," asked Bingham.

"Two years."

Bingham, who was not belligerent, was appalled that the man responsible for what had been two-thirds of Lehman's business couldn't explain how he made money. He was not alone. "It was disconcerting to everyone," says Welsh. "It seemed that Dick did not respond to the question, and maybe didn't have a handle on the business." Said one mortified banker on the board: "Fuld is a very good trader, but he was thrust into a management position earlier in his career than he should have been."

The incident may be symbolic of the increasing polarization at the firm, of the communications chasm. Fuld, for example, remembers the meeting and the incident, and offers this explanation: Silber was to look at "options and futures. Maybe that was taken out of context because we had not done that much on options and futures." In other words, perhaps Fuld had, in fact, said something similar to what many board members remember, but that's because he thought he was answering another question. "So maybe I could have said, 'Since we are not in the options and futures business, I don't know about them,'" Fuld later explained. Lew Glucksman concurs, but offers another context: "Dick had a problem communicating with other members of the board. Dick tends to be fast-thinking and somewhat impatient. He talks a lot in shorthand. He did not communicate well what he did. Very few board members could understand Dick when he was talking."

Whatever the context, most board members walked away from this meeting shaken. They wondered whether Fuld, who they knew was a superb fixed-income trader but who had been given responsibility for the equity division when Shel Gordon moved to banking in September, was in over his head as a manager, a worry that Fuld seems privately to have shared. "I had all of the business other than investment banking and money management reporting to me," he now says. "And having had no background in equities, I found it difficult to accomplish what I wanted to in a day's time."

The hard line taken over the months by outspoken Peter Solomon appeared more and more reasonable. "That was a crucial meeting," says Solomon. "Here we are arguing about capital adequacy and here is the fella who should have thought this out. If he can't do it, Rubin should have. They're supposed to have a strategy." Instead of a strategy, what some board members saw, fairly or not, was cronyism. Again, the governance issue.

R UMORS BEGAN TO ENGULF LEHMAN BROTHERS. BANKING partners buzzed about new trading losses, provoking fears that Dick Fuld would take even greater trading risks in hopes of making a financial killing to strengthen Glucksman & Company. Word of a mass exodus of partners was in the air—Dick Fuld heard that five partners planned to leave; François de Saint Phalle pegged the number as closer to ten. There were whispers about a move to bring Peterson back as chairman; about how Solomon and Schwarzman were aggressively shopping and trying to sell the firm; about how Peterson was slyly maneuvering to locate a buyer because if the firm were sold in the next two years, he would still receive a premium.

Business went on, deals were closed, trades made, clients advised. Partners continued to devote most of their day to clients, not internal politics. But, increasingly, the inflamed internal politics of the firm intruded. There was upheaval in the banking department when it was announced that M. & A. chief Richard Bingham, for family reasons, was moving to San Francisco. Various M. & A. partners clamored for the post he was vacating. They lobbied Shel Gordon, a man of caution, a consensus builder, who moved slowly. Gordon looked first to a former Peterson protégé Stephen Schwarzman, then thirty-six, as a possible successor, but the talented Schwarzman was about as popular as Peter Solomon, and for some of the same reasons. Glucksman and Rubin were not displeased with the opposition to Schwarzman, who made no secret of his disdain for them. The post went unfilled. To end the management impasse, a makeshift solution was devised that in many ways typified both Gordon's craftiness and Lehman's internal bickering—a five-member committee was named to run M. & A., chaired by Schwarzman. The committee, however, proved unworkable.

About this time word leaked of a scheme, crafted by Bob Rubin and his friend Bill Morris, and endorsed by Glucksman, to lengthen the payout period from two and a half or five years, as then was the case, to ten years. In other words, if a partner wished to leave, he would be permitted to collect each year only 10 percent of the money due him. The plan was designed to shore up Lehman's capital base by stanching the outflow of partners' dollars. Instead, it fueled protests from many quarters, including those who said they worried most about the adequacy of capital. Partners bantered about becoming "indentured servants" and "Glucksman slaves." Rubin says he tried to explain that for anyone who wished to leave, the plan would still pay them over two and a half or five years, not ten. But those who agreed to stay would have to accept a ten-year payout plan. The timing of the plan could not have been worse. "You can only do that in good times. If not, you panic guys. It's like yelling fire in a theater," says Peter Solomon, who loudly opposed it. Glucksman was forced to scuttle the plan before it was even presented to the board.

These events took their toll on Lew Glucksman. Partners noticed that he seemed depressed and wore a perpetual scowl on his face. Pete Dawkins saw the change in the man who recruited him: "As tensions grew, Lew withdrew from involvement with the banking side of the firm. Physically, he was on the trading floor more—an environment he was more comfortable with." By December, says one banker who thoroughly disliked Glucksman, "It became clear that we were dealing with an unstable personality. It was clear the firm was in jeopardy. The markets were starting to change. We weren't making as much money. Everybody was saying, 'I'm going to leave before this thing sinks.' Individual partners were talking to people on the outside to see if they could sell the firm. The place was like Russia. You couldn't trust anyone; they might be a spy for Lew."

The impending departure of Peterson made partners feel less secure. Although Peterson was no longer immersed in Lehman business, he retained the title of chairman until December 31; he still helped partners with clients; he was much more available to chat now than he had ever been. "He called me every day," says one former partner. "I talked to him more in one month than I did in six years." The worse Glucksman looked, the better Peterson appeared. The anger many partners harbored toward Peterson receded, replaced by sentimentality for the good old days, and perhaps a bit of self-pity.

Bankers found a release for their emotions at a joyous December 17 farewell party Peterson threw for himself at River House. Peterson paid because Glucksman & Company did not offer to, a decision that annoyed many banking partners. "It was humiliating to the firm not to pay for a dinner for a man who saved the firm," says banking partner Stephen Bershad. In all, forty-three present or former partners and such Lehman advisory directors as George Ball, former Defense Secretary James R. Schlesinger, and former Assistant Secretary of State Richard C. Holbrooke (with his regular date, Diane Sawyer of CBS) attended, accompanied by their spouses. Joan and three of Peterson's children from his second marriage—Holly, Michael and David—came, as did a cousin, Anatasia Vournas; his new partner, Eli Jacobs; and executive assistant Melba Duncan, who smoothly organized this event, as she did most others.

It probably says something about the polarization at the firm that only one partner with a trading background, Shel Gordon, was invited.* Partners noticed that Gordon came for cocktails but left before dinner, thus paying homage to one faction without alienating the other. Gordon says he had "a longstanding commitment" to attend the annual Kindergarten Society Dinner at the Heights Casino, in Brooklyn.

The Peterson dinner was held in a private dining room at the River Club. At the end of dinner, several partners rose to speak. Peter Solomon, an accomplished mimic with a Don Rickles sense of humor, was first to jump up. Roger Altman presented Peterson, on behalf of the firm, with an untitled Willem de Kooning drawing, and a word of thanks. The back of the gold-framed drawing was inscribed: WITH THE ADMIRATION AND AFFECTION OF HIS MANY FRIENDS AT LEHMAN BROTHERS.†

Peterson, who could be very witty when he put his mind to it, spoke from handwritten notes. "Only at Lehman would a chairman have to give himself a going-away party!" he said. He jokingly referred to Lehman as "a mental health ward," populated by "subnormal professionals." "I once made the mistake of asking each partner how much of the fees were attributed to them. The total added up to a thousand percent of revenues!" He affectionately singled out each business associate in attendance, including several wives, for insult and good-natured ribbing, and concluded with a quote from Nietzsche and a tribute to his partners.

Then everyone went to an adjoining room to witness a hilarious roast of the outgoing chairman. Billed as "A Day in the Life of Pete Peterson," it starred Lehman partners. Those in the room were not surprised to see Steve Schwarzman play Pete Peterson, because he was close to the outgoing chairman, suitably irreverent and an accomplished mimic. They were pleasantly surprised to see Roger Altman play Lew Glucksman, for Roger was not thought to be

---

*One other trader, Jim Boshart, was offered an opportunity to attend. Boshart says Peterson telephoned and said, "I just want you to know we're having a party and it will be in good humor, and given your relationship with Lew, you might be uncomfortable." Boshart agreed, and was not invited.

†Partners had planned to chip in to cover the approximately $15,000 cost of the De Kooning, but Glucksman, after consulting with Altman, decided the firm should pay.

daring—and Glucksman's nerves at this point were raw. "No one wanted to portray Lew Glucksman for fear that he would take it personally," recalls Altman. Altman organized two rehearsals for the several partners who would participate, and on the night of the dinner he arrived carrying cone heads, a steering wheel, a telephone and a bathrobe.

In the opening scene Schwarzman (Peterson) is in his bathrobe ordering a partner to appear at the River House at six o'clock in the morning to review a memo. The partner arrives in scene two and finds the lobby crawling with Lehman partners. Peterson comes down the stairs with a cup of coffee, which he spills; he bumps into a wall while walking and reading. In scene three, four partners are sandwiched in Peterson's car. Each is speaking, while Peterson is paying no attention, signing papers and throwing them over his shoulder. He barks to his driver (played by Altman), "Frank, get me the 'Big Man' in Chicago." Then, to no one in particular, he announces, "God, it's so wonderful to be important!"

Scene four is in the office. "You remember Mr. Goldfedder, the chairman of Federated Department Stores," says one partner to Peterson.

A distracted Peterson then introduces the visitor as "the chairman of Goldfedder's." At that point, Glucksman (Altman) enters, scowling. Like the actor in the Federal Express TV ads, Glucksman speaks in machine-gun fashion: *"Interest-rates-are-going-up. Interest-rates-are-going-down. Better-finance-now."* Glucksman exits. They go to the Lehman dining room for lunch, where Peterson, who was always trying to resist sugar and who was constantly ordering raspberries, lunges for the sugar bowl and absent-mindedly pours it over his salad.

Scene five is set in the boardroom. Peterson and Glucksman are there when the servile board members file in, wearing their white *(Saturday Night Live)* cone hats. The phone rings, and someone announces: "It's Golda Meir!"

"Tell her I'll call back," says Peterson.

Brusquely turning to Glucksman, Peterson says, "We've got a problem with our overhead. We've got to get rid of cigars."

Glucksman's leg twitched violently. "You can't get rid of my cigars," he says, almost choking on the fat cigar in his mouth. As an alternative, Glucksman shoots back: "We'll get rid of raspberries!" The coneheads say nothing, just sitting there, their names draped over their chests.

People left the River Club as if floating on air, feeling they had taken part in a magical evening. Walking toward First Avenue, Linda and Peter Solomon were joined by Holbrooke and Diane Sawyer. They walked silently, savoring the jokes, the comradeship, the memories.

"If Pete had done this a year ago," blurted Solomon, wistfully, "none of this would have happened." Holbrooke sadly agreed.

L EW GLUCKSMAN WAS FEELING ANGRY ABOUT THE PETER-son dinner, and much else. "The dinner was very significant," he says. "It says something about the schisms in the organization he did nothing to heal. The farewell party, by just inviting bankers, could only create divisions here, which it did."

Yet such was his sense of vulnerability at the time that Glucksman controlled his anger, struggled to ignore the rumors, the unhappiness among partners, the sense of betrayal he felt. Lew Glucksman was determined to be a statesman, and this urge led him to make a fateful decision. The only way to keep partners from fleeing, he said, was to have some means of "liquifying their capital." To placate what he believed was an emerging majority who wanted to cash in, or were unhappy with Lehman's management, while at the same time preserving a measure of Lehman's independence (and, not incidentally, his own control), he decided Lehman would need an outside investor to purchase, at a premium, something less than 50 percent of Lehman's stock. In making this judgment, he parted company with Rubin, as well as Boshart and Fuld, who preferred to shrink the firm.

But events were racing ahead of Lew Glucksman's ability to control them. He believed he had come to the correct business decision about capital, though he hated agreeing with Solomon, among others. He believed he had arrived at this decision on its merits, because the firm needed more liquidity, while his partners, he thought, had raised the capital issue as a cover for their avarice, for their hunger to humble Lew Glucksman.

Nevertheless, Glucksman tried to reach out, to heal the wounds at Lehman. In what he thought was a magnanimous gesture, he suggested, at a mid-December board luncheon, that to avoid even a hint of unfairness in awarding future bonuses and shares the board should select a compensation committee to make recommendations. He said Gordon and Fuld, as the managers of the two largest divisions, should be members. He wanted the board to select the others. As an added gesture, Henry Breck recalls, Glucksman said, "Look, I think this should be a committee of the board on which Bob Rubin and I don't serve. I think you should select some more members of the board so there is fair representation." He wanted them to reach beyond members of the operating committee, who already had a hand in bonus decisions. Glucksman said that neither he nor Rubin would attend the selection meeting.

The meeting convened one afternoon right before Christmas in the forty-fourth-floor corner conference room (later, Bill Morris's office). And without Glucksman and Rubin there, the dynamics were altered. François de Saint Phalle describes the mood this way: "We were all very goosey about the outlook for our business. There was an enormous amount of disgruntlement. A real sense of impending disaster was lurking in the wings."

Partners were worried about the downturn in business at Lehman and all over the Street. The October and November monthly operating results, the so-called gray books circulated to each partner, showed that trading revenues were plunging, as were profits. In addition, by December, because of the capital withdrawn by the six partners who had left, Lehman's equity had dropped from $176 million in September to about $150 million in December.

Partners worried that with business and capital down, Lehman might not survive the next storm, as they had survived the storm of 1973. Trends were against them. Financial supermarkets now dominated Wall Street. In 1982 the top ten Wall Street firms possessed 54.4 percent of the capital of all investment banks, and these chosen ten, reported the Securities Industry Association, earned almost "two-thirds of the industry's pre-tax profits." Consolidation was now the norm on Wall Street, and in commercial banking, where a recent industry report forecast that the number of banks would decline from 15,000 in 1980 to 9,600 by 1990; newspapers were being swallowed by giant chains; publishing houses, law and accounting firms, department stores and supermarkets were consolidating. Was Lehman Brothers, they wondered, trapped in an updraft of historical forces beyond its control? How could they shrink the firm, as they had done in 1973, without irreparably damaging the franchise?

Partners were now more apprehensive of their business, and their own wealth, than they were of Lew Glucksman. "We were prepared like the proverbial poker player who starts out with $100," says Breck. "You're playing seven card high/low and betting gets out of control. You suddenly realize you're in for $150 and you have three kings. You can put a lot of dollars in to draw a few more cards and see if you can get a full boat. But that's risky. So you fold with three kings and go home."

The formal business of the meeting—selecting three compensation committee members—was concluded speedily. Several board members vied for a spot, and Peter Solomon actually lobbied for it. Paper ballots were distributed, and the winners were announced—Morris, Krueger and Bingham. Then the conversation veered to the forbidden subject.

"Okay, how do you feel about selling the firm?" Henry Breck asked each partner, one by one. Some members of the board were absent. In addition to Glucksman and Rubin, Shel Gordon and Dick Fuld were missing. But nine of the remaining ten board members were present (Braggiotti was absent). As Breck went around the room and partners spoke up, the realization dawned that what they had been thinking and whispering but never daring to say in a group, certainly not in a group containing Lew Glucksman or Bob Rubin, was almost universally shared. Many of them had talked privately with Shel Gordon about their fears, and their hopes, of selling the firm. Shel was their captain, the trusted partner, the dexterous Howard Baker of Lehman Brothers, who could gain the confidence, as the former Senate Majority Leader did, of senators as diverse as Jesse Helms and Bob Packwood. At Lehman, Shel Gordon commanded respect from Lew Glucksman and Peter Solomon, two partners who couldn't stand to be in the same room together.

The smokescreen behind which the board cloaked its desire to sell the firm or to get rid of Glucksman & Company was "the capital issue." This became the dominant subject of the meeting in the conference room. Peter Solomon, who had advocated that Lehman go public back in 1982, and was not shy about reminding his partners of his prescience, spoke of the firm's skimpy capital base and how it could never do the kind of merchant banking he favored without an infusion of fresh funds. Harvey Krueger and Dick Bingham remembered the last days of Kuhn Loeb before it merged with Lehman, and how they feared for the firm's survival. Today, for the first time, every board member save one said he either worried about the adequacy of the firm's capital or wanted to sell. Today, for the first time, Henry Breck and Bill Morris publicly sided with those pushing for a sale. Bill Morris later explained: "As one wag said, 'We had to choose between our money and our lives.' " And today, for the first time, four of the five new board members asserted themselves. With business slumping, eight of the nine men said they favored the sale of the company.

For these men, and other partners, talk of selling the firm was motivated by many factors, including: greed; a lack of confidence in Glucksman & Company; personal unhappiness; genuine worries about the adequacy of the firm's capital; partners concerned about whether, with business slipping, they could get their own capital out; and sheer fatigue. What weight one gives to each of these factors has much to do with whether one was a Glucksman partisan or foe. "For those who opposed Glucksman and Rubin, greed was 60 percent of it and lack of confidence was 40 percent of it," says their ally, Henry Breck. Glucksman's foes argue that greed played a minor role.

For Peter Solomon, several factors may have converged. His relations with Glucksman and Rubin were malignant; he felt like a pariah—unrecognized within the firm, rejected for the compensation committee, rejected as interim head of the banking division, his counsel spurned in July when Peterson left, and in November when Rubin was made president. In 1982, Solomon stood almost alone in raising the capital issue. "Peter was like the fella who cries wolf all the time and no one any longer listens," observes one of his banking partners. Solomon was wealthier than most of his partners, and had enjoyed himself when he had left Lehman to serve first as Deputy Mayor of New York and later as counselor to the Secretary of the Treasury. He knew there was life after Lehman Brothers. It was time to do something else. For Peter Solomon, it was time to sell.

Harvey Krueger, the former president of Kuhn Loeb, was haunted by the memories of that crippled firm. Although Krueger played an important role at Lehman, he had been bumped as head of the banking division in 1980 and removed from the executive committee when Peterson and Glucksman placed that group in limbo. Krueger was not likely to resume an important management position and may not have wanted one. He was a solid banker, who serviced a core group of clients, including Automatic Data Processing, the Rockefeller Group, Supermarkets General, and the Scoa Corporation. Krueger was a man respected for his kindness. But partners thought he lacked the killer instinct. "Krueger is like your uncle Ben," says one banking partner, summing up a common perception. "He's a nice guy. But he's not an operator. He's a philanthropist. He raises enormous funds for Israel. But he can't run anything. He's not tough enough." Harvey Krueger now thought often of his own retirement, just a few years away, and of the freedom a sale would bring; he could travel to Israel more frequently as president of American Friends of Hebrew University in Jerusalem, bearing larger gifts. For Harvey Krueger it was time to sell.

Bill Morris, forty-five, who succeeded Krueger as head of banking, had also been supplanted, in 1982. While Morris was an intimate of Bob Rubin's, he knew that Lew Glucksman, as well as Pete Peterson, was responsible for that decision. Besides, Morris had an I've-seen-it-all air of resignation about him, which is why some partners referred to him as "the cynic"; if selling the firm is what the partners wanted, so be it. He had tried to convince partners to shrink the firm, tried to work with Rubin on a plan to lengthen the payout period when partners left, thus providing more insurance. To no avail. Bill Morris was a capable banker, yet a passive one. "He tends to be negative," admits a friend. At the firm Morris was negative about new marketing plans, about aggressive efforts to promote new business, or publishing brochures, or the firing of partners except in extreme circumstances. And so now, after at first dissenting from the view that Lehman's capital was inadequate, he became resigned. For Bill Morris it was time to sell.

Henry Breck, forty-six, shared Morris's cyncism. They were, in fact, best friends. Breck, however, was more cosmopolitan than Morris, who was reared in rural Texas. Breck had gone to the right schools—Buckley, Groton, Harvard, and Oxford for a law degree. He then spent seven mysterious years in "the Agency," as he calls it, and a year in Rhodesia supposedly writing a book. Henry Breck was a loner, a man who sealed his past from his partners and who viewed life as if it were a movie about others. He was thought of, by some partners, as a bloodless "mercenary" who had somehow transformed Glucksman from an antagonist three or four years before into an ally. "The important thing in this business is to always appear definite," Breck would often say. "You can call your client back the next day and say you had reflected on your initial advice overnight.

This way you get credit for being decisive—and thoughtful." If the firm were sold, Breck knew he could strive to improve his professional-level seven-handicap golf game. For Breck, the fratricide at Lehman was becoming a hassle. It was time to sell.

Dick Bingham, forty-seven, whose influence was rising at Lehman, was about to move to San Francisco, unavoidably distancing himself from the firm. Because Bingham was little involved in Lehman infighting, this too distanced him from Lehman. Nor could he shake memories of the final days of Kuhn Loeb, sweating to see whether it would be rescued by a sale. Kuhn Loeb was both too small to compete with the giants and too big to be as agile, say, as Lazard Frères. If Lehman wanted to be a full-service firm, and he believed that decision had already been made and could be undone only at great peril, then it needed capital. For Bingham, too, it was time to sell.

Roger Altman, thirty-seven, lost his mentor when Peterson left, then lost his job as part of the troika running banking. He was just now getting deeply involved again in his first love, politics and government, as an adviser to Walter Mondale in his bid for the 1984 presidential nomination. The sale of Lehman would give him the financial independence coveted by those who wish to serve in government but can't afford it. Altman's antennae were too sensitive for him not to pick up the whispers that he had damaged himself by tacking with the prevailing winds when Glucksman assumed command. Although he now began to impress his partners by showing more spine, for Roger Altman it was time to sell.

Like Altman, François de Saint Phalle, thirty-seven, lost his elevated position as one of three men running banking. For him it was an even ruder shock, since he had once been considered a member of Glucksman's "team." Unlike Breck, who seemed fatigued with life, de Saint Phalle was fatigued with Lehman Brothers. He didn't talk much, he didn't scheme and involve himself in the firm's internal politics; he kept his head down and did his job as chief of all corporate underwriting activities. And although he could be gruff, he was widely respected: "France is as good as anybody at what he does," says a partner who became an adversary. But he feared for the firm, and for his own investment, under Glucksman. Selling Lehman became a way to remove Glucksman & Company. For de Saint Phalle it was time to sell.

Bill Welsh was a sweet, happy-go-lucky man, both liked and respected. He would walk the trading floor and people would look up from their green screens and yell, "Hiya, Bill." Yet after building up the retail sales division, in late 1982 Welsh was shifted by Glucksman to a staff job as head of special projects. Welsh was such a serene man that it took him some time to realize that he had been demoted and that as long as Glucksman was at the helm his past was his future. Now fifty-two, his children grown, Bill Welsh dreamed of traveling and learning foreign languages. For him it was time to sell.

For Jim Boshart, thirty-eight, it was not time to sell. He was an idealist who believed in the simple verities, which is why some partners called him "the Boy Scout." To sell, Boshart believed, would not be fair to traders, who did not yet own their fair share of the firm. Boshart and his best friend, Dick Fuld, had spent many hours recruiting M.B.A.'s, holding out to these young men and women the promise of one day becoming partners in a private banking house. To sell the firm would be to brand as a lie all the dreams he had dangled before eager recruits. And so Jim Boshart registered the lone dissent at this meeting. Normally a polite, open man, Boshart grew extremely agitated as the meeting wore on. He sat and listened quietly as his partners spoke of attempts to sell the firm, of sharing private financial data with prospective buyers. The boyish-looking former basketball star could take it no more, and jumped up and exclaimed, "This is a rump board meeting! This is a rump meeting! We shouldn't be having this meeting without the other members of the board!"

"I agree with you," Bingham recalls saying. "But this is just a bunch of guys sitting around talking."

Boshart stalked from the room.*

The meeting ended soon thereafter, but its effect lingered. "At the time, the meeting didn't seem terribly significant," says Harvey Krueger. "But in retrospect it was the first articulation of a consensus view about the possible sale of the firm." Shel Gordon, who could not be there but who was quietly calling many signals, says, "It did move forward the crystalization of the capital issue." Peter Solomon put it less neutrally: "It was maybe the first time these guys on the board expressed worry publicly. Any meeting where partners could talk and not worry about Lew was significant."

Glucksman's decision to expand the board had backfired. He had inadvertently granted a working majority to those favoring a sale, since four of the five new recruits now joined Shel Gordon, Bill

---

*Boshart agrees with this account.

Morris, Harvey Krueger, Bill Welsh and Peter Solomon. After months of ranting alone, of being considered an Enemy of the People, Peter Solomon realized that the board was now hastening toward his position, toward the sale of Lehman Brothers.

With this meeting, the board effectively seized control of Lehman from Lew Glucksman, Glucksman having seized control himself a mere five months earlier. "What Glucksman had done is allow the board meeting to take place without his being there," says Henry Breck. "It was a classic management error. An error we never allow our corporate clients to make."

Glucksman's error was inadvertent; much of the activity leading to the sale of Lehman was deliberate. "By December we were conducting a destabilization campaign, the way they do in the Kremlin," says one leading conspirator from the banking department. "By Christmas we had the votes. Shel would never play a card he can't win. He knew he had the votes."

O N JANUARY 1, 1984, LEW GLUCKSMAN ACHIEVED HIS American dream: he became chairman of Lehman Brothers Kuhn Loeb. He moved into Peterson's suite of offices, claiming the corner office with its panoramic view of New York Harbor. Up on the walls and bookshelves went the bright red fire chief's hat, the pictures of clipper ships and fish, the tool catalogues, the books on maritime warfare and marine life.

Yet Lew Glucksman felt no joy. He was worried about the weakened business climate, about liquidity, his partners' unhappiness with how he was managing the firm, the personal insecurity of partners, their desire to participate in a single transaction that would net each a handsome premium. All of these factors came together at the same time that he realized his life's dream of becoming chairman of Lehman Brothers.

Something else seemed to be gnawing at Lew Glucksman, and it was observed by former partner and then Deputy Mayor Kenneth Lipper, who was invited back to smoke the peace pipe with Glucksman, with whom he had often feuded. Over lunch, Lipper remembers Glucksman saying, "We're both from the streets. You know how hard it is to make it. I just wanted to square things. We've both made it, and I know you can appreciate it."

Lipper felt sympathetic toward his former partner. He looked at Lew and said, "Lew, you've got it all. But do you really feel you've got it all?"

"I don't know what I've gotten from it," answered Glucksman, sadly shaking his head.

Lipper thought Glucksman was surprised to feel no joy after finally getting to the top. "When I walked out," Lipper says, "I thought, Here's a man who went to Brooks Brothers and bought a suit to go to Harvard. For thirty years he had gone on a quest. He believed that once he opened the door, there would be sun. When he finally got there and opened the door, all he saw was darkness. He didn't get invited on any more boards. He found that you don't get to be one of *them* just by taking over the company."

AT THE NEXT MONDAY BOARD LUNCH, ON JANUARY 9, IT WAS immediately clear that power had shifted from Glucksman to the board. New board members became more assertive, as did Shel Gordon. Before the meeting, Gordon, who was installed next door, in the office that once served as Peterson's conference and dining room, met privately with Glucksman and urged him to appoint a committee to probe the "capital question," which Glucksman knew was a euphemism for *sale.*

Gordon's footprints were beginning to show. He had left marks when he tried to stall Rubin's appointment as president, a maneuver that had displeased Glucksman. And now it was obvious to Glucksman, as well as to the other leading partners, that Shel was not only becoming more assertive on the capital issue but that he was speaking for the partnership. He had emerged as the one person in the firm who commanded the respect of a broad cross section of traders and bankers. "He had the broadest functional experience of anyone on that board, including Lew Glucksman," says Richard Bingham. "He had worked in all areas of trading. And for four to five months he had been running investment banking. He's a balanced individual.

He was someone who was respected by a number of people." Shel Gordon, clearly, was the rising star at Lehman.

By January 1984, most members of the board wanted out from under Glucksman's rule. They wanted the opportunity, which some feared Glucksman would deny them, to receive a lucrative premium on the sale of their stock. If, for instance, Lehman had been sold to ConAgra for more than three times its book value, the average partner would have received about $8 million. A partner who owned 2,000 shares, as almost one-fifth of the partners did, would have received about $12 million.

At this board luncheon partners discussed the capital issue more frontally than they had before. They talked about inviting an outside investor to purchase shares, about how much capital was needed to expand the business, about merging with a larger firm, about what kind of sale would be acceptable to the partnership and how it might change the nature of the partnership. The debate had shifted. No longer were they debating *whether* it was necessary to seek outside capital; now they focused on *how* to do it.

Bill Morris suggested a two-man committee, he recalls, composed of Bob Rubin and a partner who was not a board member. There was no way partners who wanted to sell would entrust their fate to Rubin, who did not. So that proposal was quickly scratched and was followed by a lengthy discussion. Finally, with Glucksman's reluctant approval—"I responded to what the board wanted," admits Glucksman—he recommended and the board passed a resolution to appoint a three-member committee (Glucksman, Rubin and Shel Gordon) "to examine capital alternatives, including the adequacy, permanency and liquidity" of Lehman's capital.

There were no dissents about appointing a committee, in part because board members were voting for different things. To most of Glucksman's allies, the vote served two purposes: to appease a potential runaway board, and to forestall the outright sale of the firm by bringing in an outside minority investor, thus strengthening Glucksman's rule. Dick Fuld walked away from the meeting believing they were resolved to look for additional capital, perhaps from an insurance company, as they had done in September with Prudential. "I was not thinking along the lines of a partner or a merger," he says. To the emergent majority of the board, however, the committee was meant to lead to the partial or total sale of the firm, to the weakening of Glucksman & Company.* "There was a feeling—a consensus view—that the vote meant we would sell a substantial portion of the firm or all of the firm," says Harvey Krueger. "If the committee had come back with a 60 percent deal, I don't know that it would have been agreed to. People wanted to get their capital out."

In adopting a posture to sell part or all of Lehman, the board may have spoken for a majority of the partners. It certainly spoke for the overwelming majority of banking partners, says partner Stephen W. Bershad, who he says by this time were motivated by equal parts of both fear and greed: "Fear in the sense that if we didn't sell, what little we have here would evaporate or we would get pushed out. Greed in the sense that you might wind up with zero and someone might offer you two times the value of your stock." Peter Solomon summarizes the view of the board and the partnership starkly: "Anxiety about the future at that moment overwhelmed their fear of Glucksman."

To underscore its new strength and courage the board set a March 19 deadline for the committee to report on its "capital search." The board also insisted on adding a fourth member to the committee— Peter Solomon. Suddenly, Solomon was no longer a pariah. In fact, it was his thorny independence that made him so attractive to the board. "A number of us felt there should be someone on the committee who brought balance to the discussion," says one board member. "Rubin was against it. Glucksman didn't know what he should do. And Gordon was trying to hold the whole thing together. It made sense to have Peter Solomon on to give it push."

Solomon knew that Shel Gordon was responsible for his emergence, and why. "I have a lot of admiration for how Shel handled himself," he says. "He was fortunate to have me on the left, or the right, of him. He needed someone to establish the poles." Board members believed that Solomon would never permit Glucksman or Rubin to maneuver to avoid the sale of the firm. And they knew that of the four members, Peter Solomon might have the most valuable business contacts.

Glucksman also knew who was responsible for Solomon's emergence. "I think Shel and Peter Solomon made a deal a long time

---

*Recollections of what was actually voted on vary dramatically. François de Saint Phalle came away thinking the board left "unclear" how much it would sell; Bob Rubin and Roger Altman say they resolved to try and sell "at least" majority control—Rubin says "at least 80 percent," though Rubin continued to act as if the firm need not be sold; Lew Glucksman says they "did not vote to sell a majority" interest.

ago," he told intimates. It could not have been pleasant to accede to placing their number-one adversary on this critical committee, but Glucksman and Rubin went along. "I was in favor of adding Solomon on the theory that it's always good to see where people are who are antagonistic to you," says Glucksman.

One other matter was resolved this day, and it was partly inspired by Jim Boshart. In the weeks prior to this lunch, Glucksman and Rubin had heard Boshart's laments about partners who were trying to sell the firm and swapping secret data with others, had heard him speak eloquently about how selling the firm would constitute a betrayal of all those associates who were reaching for the brass ring that would make them partners at Lehman Brothers. Boshart, who had been well-liked as a person but dismissed as a "staff man," neither a tough administrator nor a premier financial analyst, was becoming increasingly alienated from banking partners; instead of serving as a bridge, as he had been to Peterson, now Boshart fed Glucksman's sense of betrayal. He honestly did not understand the hatred or terror Glucksman and Rubin inspired in some partners, and why this might drive them to drastic measures, which Boshart deemed immoral and they deemed necessary. "He became bitter," recalls Dick Bingham. "Beginning around January 1984, Boshart was unable to communicate with certain board members on even the most superficial matters. He was developing hostility that became quite emotional." Boshart concedes that his personality changed and that he stopped speaking to certain partners. "I've never seen such greed and absolute lack of concern for people we had responsibility to," he says.

Goaded by Boshart, and mindful of the damage a press leak could cause, before the meeting concluded Glucksman proposed the following resolution: "Anyone who divulges what we are talking about at these meetings will be asked to resign." It passed unanimously.

The board approved the secrecy resolution, agreed that premature disclosure would weaken Lehman's bargaining position; but typical of the Rashomon-like quality of communications at the firm, different partners heard different things. Glucksman allies thought the secrecy resolution was in the best interests of the partners; other members of the board heard something else: another blustery threat from Lew Glucksman.

This meeting, and the turn of events, left Glucksman depressed. He blamed Lehman's poisoned culture, and blamed himself for failing to change this culture, not for failing as a leader/statesman. "We did a lousy job of changing the culture of Lehman to a better culture," he says. "A culture where people work cooperatively. God, we had guys running around this place—Solomon, Schwarzman—and talking about the firm on the outside.* We never made a culture where people were concerned with the firm and not just each other. We had a level of greed here and personal selfishness that was disgraceful."

Glucksman thought he had dealt with the concerns of partners for more personal liquidity in October, when he agreed to boost the annual dividend on their preferred stock from 1 to 3 percent, when he announced the $25,000 hike in salary for each partner, the new personal loan program, and agreed to advance three small quarterly bonus payments during the year so partners might have more liquidity to purchase their $2 million Manhattan co-ops or their weekend retreats in the Hamptons. Glucksman had parted company with Rubin in coming to believe a minority investor was necessary to shore up Lehman's capital. But he says, "the last thing they [the board] wanted was a minority shareholder and not being able to sell their stock at a premium. I wanted the money to go into the business." Like partner pressure to increase the dividend, he believed they wanted the money to swell their pockets.

Lew Glucksman saw support slipping away. He sensed that Shel Gordon was using Peter Solomon as his battering ram, and no longer counted on Shel's certain support in a showdown. He believed Harvey Krueger—who like most partners had his wealth tied up at Lehman—was determined to sell because, nearing sixty, Lehman policy required him to begin selling back his stock at book value. Glucksman also knew that Krueger wanted to spend more time raising money for Israel. Although Glucksman got along with Krueger, to friends he lumped together Krueger and Solomon: "The only thing they have in common is *Our Crowd*," he said. He felt William Welsh, who was then fifty-two and had been shunted aside by Glucksman in the Lehman management structure and who had spoken often of learning foreign languages and traveling, was also inclined to sell. He knew that Bill Morris and Henry Breck, though dependable allies in a corporate power struggle, were now resigned to selling the firm; they were hard-edged cynics. He complained that three of the newer board members—Altman, de Saint Phalle and Bingham—probably thought more of the cash than the independent

---

*Schwarzman concedes he actively sought a buyer; Solomon acknowledges that he had discussions with Shearson/American Express in late 1982, but "to the best of my knowledge" had no other unauthorized conversations.

Lehman tradition. No one had to tell Lew Glucksman that the stock market was not then on his side. Stable interest rates had slashed profits; a slowed stock market meant less volume and fewer commissions; and the business outlook was dim at Lehman as it was all over the Street, particularly in trading and sales.

Glucksman felt secure that in any showdown he could count on the loyal support of Rubin, Boshart and Fuld. But he also knew they preferred to shrink the firm rather than seek more capital. "My allies were not my allies," he says, ruefully. "I was caught between two groups . . . It was clear to me the board wanted to sell the company. That's where I disagreed with Dick and Bob and Jim Boshart. I felt it was difficult to oppose the board and a clear mandate of what the partners wanted. So I became an advocate of a position I didn't want."

O VER THE NEXT TWO MONTHS THE FOUR-MAN COMMITTEE deliberated in secret. Numerous potential buyers were approached, and in some cases the talks inched toward a successful conclusion. In late January, Glucksman lunched alone in a private Lehman dining room with Charles M. Harper of ConAgra. They hit it off, and it was agreed that Glucksman, accompanied by Bob Rubin, would fly to Omaha to spend time with ConAgra's CEO and his people. In mid-February, Harper's plane flew them to Omaha. After Glucksman and Rubin returned to New York, Eric Gleacher, who remained ConAgra's investment banker, flew to Nebraska and spent the better part of three days structuring a potential deal. Harper, Glucksman and Rubin met again in New York on February 27 and talked about a deal that would have given Lehman partners $300 million in cash and $150 million in convertible debentures; Glucksman would be made co-chairman of the entire company, a power-sharing arrangement similar to that reached by John

Gutfreund when Salomon Brothers merged with Phibro. Glucksman could not fail to note that the $450 million offer was appreciably less than the $600 million dangled in May 1983 and that he would not be co-CEO, as Gleacher had said the May offer had provided. But Glucksman knew that times had changed. Lehman's net worth and profits were down. He was not dealing from strength, as he would have been in the spring of 1983. According to Eric Gleacher, "They made a deal"—subject first to a "due diligence" check by ConAgra's accountants, Touche Ross, and then to approval by their respective boards.

The "deal" fell apart in the first week of March. Touche Ross came back to Harper, who was holed up at the Helmsley Palace Hotel, and reported, says Gleacher, that "overheads have gone completely out of whack. They are putting on people, new phones—and at the same time their business was going down." Glucksman's aversion to cost-cutting, which constantly frustrated Peterson, now scared Harper. And not without reason. Lehman's March 1984 gray books, for example, showed that net pre-tax income for the first six months of the fiscal 1984 year was down by $75 million compared to the same period in 1983; at the same time, expenses rose by $13 million. Harper tried to structure another deal, but the momentum was lost.

Glucksman liked the idea of a nonindustry partner, one who might leave the investment-banking side of their business to the experts. Such a merger promised more freedom for the partners and enhanced the chances that Lew Glucksman would remain as chairman. This desire led to discussions with Laurence and Robert Tisch of the Loews Corporation. Glucksman felt comfortable with Larry and Bob Tisch. They were all alumni of New York University and had undertaken to raise funds for the university. Each man sat on N.Y.U.'s board. Larry Tisch liked Lew Glucksman, and fondly remembered the dinner they once shared at N.Y.U. when these two millionaires mourned the death of the five-cent hotdog, and Glucksman told him that he still did his own laundry rather than send it out and pay "ridiculous" prices. They talked about Loews putting up between $150 and $200 million to purchase a 50 percent interest in Lehman's stock. A deal with the Tisches would mean that Glucksman would probably remain as chairman and CEO, but partners would not receive a premium above the book value of stock that the firm would redeem with part of the Tisch investment, although they would remain a private partnership. "Our idea was to maintain it as a private partnership," says Larry Tisch. "I think Lew liked the idea.

I don't think it gave the partners what they wanted, which was a premium." Lehman board member Harvey Krueger, who says he suggested the Tisches to Glucksman, puts it another way: "The principal reason the Tisch transaction didn't go through was that they only wanted to purchase 50 percent."

Initially, all conversations for Lehman were usually conducted by Glucksman and Rubin. "They were chairman and president," says Solomon. "That was dead-solid proper." Glucksman and Rubin also talked with Martin Davis, who had just stepped into the CEO slot at Gulf & Western. These were just discussions, not negotiations, says Glucksman. They spoke of selling 100 percent of Lehman's stock for $350 or so million. "I was very enthusiastic. I like Martin Davis. I thought it would be a great fit. His problem was that he was concerned about the general reputation for divisiveness that Lehman had. And as a relatively new executive officer, I think he was wary of controversy and wary that the brokerage business had turned sour. He was right."

There were conversations with Prudential, where Glucksman returned to talk about adding more capital. Prudential was interested, says Glucksman, but they had their hands full at that time with Bache, which they had acquired. "The Pru," Glucksman says, offered to purchase a 50 percent interest in Lehman, at a lower price than the Tisches had bid. This was not acceptable to Lehman. According to members of the four-man Lehman committee, there was one discussion each with Chicago businessman/investor Jay Pritzker, who was not interested in paying a steep price; with an intermediary of Merrill Lynch; and with a medium-size insurance company.

There were no discussions with Enrico Braggiotti of BCI, Lehman's sole outside shareholder, though he says he would have invested more, but only after "restructuring the firm—a new chairman, a new president, a new board." There were no serious discussions with Stephen Bershad, who headed Lehman's London office, and who says, "If it were just capital we needed, there were plenty of foreign firms that would put in capital. I suggested early on that people in Europe would be interested in this. It was never pursued." These were not pursued because Glucksman and a majority of the board, and perhaps a majority of the partners, embraced contradictory goals. Glucksman's primary interest was in preserving Lehman's independence and his own position of power, which he might best achieve by selling 50 percent or less of the business, or by selling to a nonindustry partner. A majority of the board, on the other hand, had as its primary interest collecting a premium for their stock, and displacing Glucksman.

With these conflicting aims, not surprisingly the committee failed to locate a buyer. The chemistry among committee members did not help. Once in a meeting in Glucksman's office, recalls Peter Solomon, Bob Rubin jumped up and shouted at him: "You're the cause of all this!" Glucksman, who shared Rubin's contempt for Solomon, tried to play peacemaker. "Lew once thanked me for not reacting," says Solomon. One day Glucksman was restrained, tolerant, the next he was an open wound. "Lew and Shel were hardly speaking," recalls France de Saint Phalle. "Lew saw Shel becoming a rallying point against him."

For two months, January and February, the four-man committee met and came up empty-handed. And in those two months, dreading leaks, they said little to their fellow board members or to their partners, many of whom did not know of the existence of the committee.

Rumors feast in a vacuum and the news blackout fanned the paranoia at Lehman. Partners, including a few outside the board who had gotten wind of the panel, wondered why there was no news from January through February. Why were they so passive? How had Glucksman tamed ferocious Peter Solomon? "In two and one-half months I don't think they did anything," observes one banking partner. "They didn't make calls. They didn't do up professional memorandums. They received people who made calls." Says board member Dick Bingham, "They probably could have been a lot more aggressive. There were pressures, however, pressures of other business and at least two of them were fundamentally reluctant to pursue the sale alternative."

The mood at Lehman Brothers that winter was "uncomfortable," remembers Dick Fuld. "It was very antagonistic. When you went to meetings people's paranoia began to manifest itself in antagonistic remarks." Partners were further antagonized by reports that Henry Breck, without authorization from the board, tried to peddle Lemco, the $10 billion money management arm of the business that he ran. They were outraged to hear that Breck offered the business for $60 million, far less than the $75 million once discussed at operating committee meetings when they debated shrinking the business. Breck explained to his partners that the vice chairman of the Continental Group was in his office on another matter. After talking to him about the inherent problems of running a financial business, Breck recalls the following exchange:

"What a wonderful business we have at Lemco," he said, walking out with the vice chairman.

"Henry, if I hear you right, you're asking me to be a partner in Lehman management?" said the vice chairman.

"Don, you may be right," answered Breck, who says he never mentioned $60 million or any other figure, but immediately reported the discussion to Glucksman and Rubin. From his contacts at the Continental Group, Pete Peterson heard something else; he heard that Breck had offered "one of the crown jewels of Lehman for a bargain price"—$60 million. He says Lemco was then worth $75 to $120 million. Shocked, the former chairman says he called a director and asked, "What's going on here?" The board member called back to confirm the substance, and to say that this, like ConAgra, was not first presented to the board.

Between January and March, recalls François de Saint Phalle, "A lot of partners came to me and said, 'Look, you get us out of this. You're on the board.'" What they wanted to get out of, he explains, was "the management crisis. The capital crisis. The business crisis. People were sitting there looking at their investment and seeing the high probability, over the next three to six months, that Lehman could lose considerable money. For it was a straight investment decision. We had made a lot of money in the last four years, and it was time to sell."

The partners were depressed, and frightened, by Lehman's internal earnings reports. From October 1983 through February 1984, income totaled just $7.1 million before taxes and bonuses, compared with $87.3 million a year earlier. Since the banking and money management divisions were still thriving, partners understood that buried in these figures were substantial trading losses, though they did not know how large these would eventually be. And the future looked even more bleak than the immediate past. In early March, chief financial officer Michael Schmertzler drafted a somber report for the four-man committee, warning: "Management does not anticipate that the environment in which it is operating will necessarily improve this fiscal year. Indeed, trading and distribution losses could lead to consolidated losses in net income in certain months." Primarily because of money siphoned from the firm by the six partners who had left, the equity capital or book value of the Lehman holding company had plunged by $31 million between October 1, the day

Glucksman became sole CEO, and the end of March, when Lehman's equity value was $145.1 million. And that number would shrink still further if more partners escaped with their capital.

Rising interest rates, coupled with a weak stock market and high overheads resulting from the 1982–1983 boom, were depressing earnings all over Wall Street. The quarterly profits of the brokerage houses that relied on trading were down, and several posted losses. Merrill Lynch lost $32.8 million in this, the second quarter of the 1984 fiscal year; Dean Witter lost $25.8 million; E. F. Hutton lost $7.8 million. Perrin H. Long, Jr., a Wall Street analyst with Lipper Analytical Services Inc., calculated that pre-tax profits for the investment banking and brokerage community totaled just $150 million in the second quarter, down from $497 million in the first quarter of 1984 and $1.46 billion in the second quarter of 1983.

Board members despaired on March 12, when the "capital committee" reported back to them. The committee sketched the various conversations they had had with potential suitors, without naming them. Some board members found the four men strangely vague, eerily calm. "They came up empty-handed," recalls William Welsh. "That stirred up the troops, who were waiting around for something good to happen." The board admonished the committee to be more vigorous in seeking suitors.

The committee vowed to become more aggressive. "I decided we would initiate some conversations," says Glucksman. They knew this might make them appear eager to sell, which would lower the price. But the alternative was worse. Glucksman and Rubin visited Equitable, the insurance giant whose chairman had hosted the July 1983 lunch that precipitated Glucksman's challenge to Peterson. Glucksman also went back to Martin Davis. He talked to Prudential and to General Electric. This time Glucksman was outlining propositions. And the fish were not biting.

B Y LATE MARCH THE BOARD'S SKEPTICISM HAD HARDENED into cynicism. The climate inside Lehman was fractious and unpleasant. Yet the internal battles, the hatreds, were still, essentially, a private matter. As long as those outside knew nothing of this, there was hope that Lehman could command a generous sales price. In February bits and pieces of Lehman's dirty laundry began to show. Banking partners were unnerved by a February cover story in *Business Week,* featuring a glowering Lew Glucksman, under this headline: THE TRADERS TAKE CHARGE. Partners were appalled by a February story in *Institutional Investor,* titled: IS LEW GLUCKS-MAN CLEANING HOUSE? Page one of the story contained a carica-ture of Captain Glucksman, astride his ship, with partners diving off the sides. The article reported that several Lehman partners were peddling their résumés and described the anger aroused by the Sep-tember bonuses; it went on to mention that there were also "signs of a Stalin-style purge, with Glucksman methodically uprooting Pe-terson supporters."

But as unsettling as these stories were to partners, they were mere pistol pops compared to the mushroom cloud detonated by *Fortune* magazine. The four-paragraph piece, written by Monci Jo Williams, first appeared on newsstands on March 28, and began this way: "In Lewis L. Glucksman's first six months as head of Lehman Brothers Kuhn Loeb, the firm became so deeply split that the board has decided to sell it." Ms. Williams noted that in March "Lehman suffered a loss in trading"—without citing a figure (she could not, since the March results were not circulated until April); that a "committee of Lehman partners" was "busily peddling the firm"; and concluded: "But several potential buyers have already decided to pass on Lehman, saying that the personality of the firm and its politics may make Lehman more trouble than it's worth."

"I remember standing outside my office with Lew and Jim Bo-shart," recalls James Hood, who was responsible for marketing and public relations. "Jim Boshart said, 'Oh boy, this is really going to cause problems.' It was a devastating article. As that article moved around the firm, it only took reality a few days to catch up with the perception *Fortune* painted. At that point, the paralysis was full. People stopped working."

The article infuriated as well as terrified partners. To many part-ners the *Fortune* piece was a reminder of a new and sometimes seamy fact of life on Wall Street: Now the well-placed leak or other aggres-sive public relations moves are weapons in corporate combat. In a world of instant communication, perceptions are all. Rumors concerning the activities of T. Boone Pickens, Jr., or the Bass brothers can overnight inflate or depress a company's stock price; word that First Boston was "hot" in the M. & A. field attracted business to the firm; publicity has fattened the client list of corporate lawyers like Joseph Flom of Skadden, Arps, Slate, Meagher & Flom, or Martin Lipton of Wachtell, Lipton, Rosen & Katz. Public revelations that Lehman was for sale were bound to depress the sale price.

Was this part of the "destabilizing campaign" one banker had boasted of? Partners assumed the story had been leaked, and speculated endlessly about who might have leaked it, with four theories vying. The first held that a potential buyer, desirous of reducing Lehman's asking price, was responsible. The second held that the leak came from inside Lehman. For a partner to leak such a story seemed so senseless, so self-destructive, so . . . venomous. Unless—and this was the third theory—those who leaked it believed there was no other escape; that Glucksman & Company would never relinquish control until the ship sank.

Finally, there were also those who believed the "leak" was cleverly orchestrated by Peterson. "Follow the money," Deep Throat advised Woodward and Bernstein when they were investigating Watergate. Following the money, Peter Solomon and Bob Rubin, who agreed on little else, believed—without proof—that Peterson was out hawking the firm. Why? Because if Lehman were sold anytime within two years, Peterson's severance agreement entitled him to receive a full premium. John Gutfreund of Salomon Brothers also believes this, and says he heard that Peterson was shopping Lehman. Peterson responds, "I did not at any time approach anyone about the sale of Lehman; not Equitable, not American Express, not anyone. I was, however, approached on three occasions by others": by the investment banker of a "modest-sized insurance firm," and by "two very wealthy individuals who offered me a major piece of the firm if I would go back as CEO." He says he declined. Peterson does not deny speaking to *Fortune.* He says, "It is entirely possible someone from *Fortune* called . . . I know the people at *Fortune.*"

The prevalent view within the firm was that the presumed leak came from inside. It had to come from inside, says Jim Hood. "It was too accurate. *Fortune* may have started with some information, but the details about the four-member committee and other facts could only have come from inside." But this is not necessarily true, since the existence of the group was known to those outside companies with whom the committee met.

Some partners took the "leak" in stride. "I wasn't angry," says Bill Morris, fatalistic as usual. "You don't get angry at a carrot because it's red. I wasn't angry because I wasn't surprised."

But Jim Boshart did not take the presumed leak in stride: "There was such a lack of dignity—people going around on their knees saying, 'Buy us for any price!' I thought that made it unsalable, shopworn." Boshart could hardly contain himself. He had become increasingly indignant at the activities of his partners, blaming Schwarzman especially for leaks, blaming Solomon for trying to sell the firm and bad-mouthing Glucksman on the outside, blaming Altman for being two-faced, blaming Gordon for betraying Glucksman. By this time, Boshart had undergone something of a personality transformation. His Jimmy Stewart wholesomeness had given way to truculence. Instead of being Glucksman's conciliatory dove, he was now hawkish. No longer was Boshart the "Boy Scout." He wanted to trace the leakers and fire them. He wanted Lew Glucksman to be tough. Jim Boshart's view mirrored that of many of his adversaries. Both had come to believe they were at war with evil.

When the *Fortune* piece exploded, Glucksman, a man who instinctively shied from the press, followed the advice of Boshart and instructed Hood to issue a "no comment" to all press queries. Appalled, Hood appealed to Shel Gordon and Bob Rubin. Together they persuaded Glucksman that a "no comment" would be taken as a confirmation of the story. The problem was how to walk the tightrope between lying and telling the awful truth. The next day, March 29, Glucksman convened a meeting of the Lehman board in his forty-third-floor corner office. He was smoking mad. "I think the story was planted by a partner here," he charged. Though he did not make this allegation to the full board, his suspicions were directed upstairs, to the banking partners on the forty-fourth floor. He had two chief culprits in mind—Peter Solomon and Steve Schwarzman —and two lesser suspects, former partners Pete Peterson and Eric Gleacher. Each of the four denies having been the source of the story; Schwarzman and Gleacher, however, concede they did return the reporter's phone calls. "The *Fortune* reporter got it from the outside and read it to me," says Schwarzman. He told her, he remembers, "You don't need my confirmation. You've got it cold." Gleacher says he spoke once to the reporter, but did not know such vital facts as the existence of the four-man committee. Ms. Williams, the reporter, says the assumption that "someone there leaked it to us is not correct."*

The board talked about what to do. The feeling in the room, recalls de Saint Phalle, was that the *Fortune* story "killed the firm's ability to negotiate from a position of strength." Boshart remembers that it was the consensus of the board that the *Fortune* story killed a sale. He reported to the board that Lehman employees were edgy, and deserved to be told something. "They told us," he recalls, "to tell the people who work for us that the firm was not going to be sold and that they could take our word for it."

The board debated what to say to reporters, who were calling, and to partners, who were agitated. For the press, they decided to issue a carefully hedged statement crafted by Hood and Altman that was designed, says Hood, "to say something truthful and informative, and yet at the same time say something whose net affect would be to calm employees and the rumor mill."

Hood and Glucksman read this statement over the phone to reporters: "We have no plans to transfer ownership of the majority of the capital, nor will the firm initiate such a plan. Nothing has been done or consummated, nor are we in serious negotiations to that end." Literally, this was true—there were no concrete "plans" or "serious negotiations"; but it was hardly an accurate statement of the facts. Hood was quoted by Leslie Wayne of the *Times* as saying that Lehman was "absolutely" not searching for a buyer and that the board did not vote in January to locate a buyer, which was simply untrue. To reassure the partners, the board decided to summon a rare meeting of the full partnership the next day.

The next morning's newspapers rudely greeted partners with these headlines: LEHMAN MAY SELL A STAKE, announced the New York *Times.* The *Wall Street Journal* blared: LEHMAN BROTHERS WANTS TO INCREASE CAPITAL BASE BY SELLING MINORITY STAKE. The stories were advertisements for Lehman's internal bloodletting. The second paragraph of the *Journal* story, for instance, reported: "The firm's management said it intends to retain a controlling interest, but sources close to Lehman Brothers main-

---

*At first I accepted the common assumption at Lehman that the story had been leaked. For the pieces that appeared in the New York *Times,* I was reluctant to call the *Fortune* reporter —or any reporter—and quiz her as to her sources. As I delved deeper into this matter for the book, I nervously telephoned Monci Jo Williams. She was upset that I had accepted the "leak" theory without checking with her. While refusing to discuss her sources, Williams noted that the "leak" could have come from any one of the outside investors the committee met with and with those they consulted.

tained that its ultimate goal is to find a buyer for the entire firm willing to pay as much as $400 million."

The partners' meeting on Friday, March 30, the first since October, was abrupt—lasting just fifteen minutes. As partners filed into the boardroom, Glucksman sat erect at the end of the mahogany table, glaring; he was flanked on either side by Rubin, Boshart and Fuld, who slumped in their chairs. Glucksman opened the meeting by saying, "I am going to read you a press release already released" —and then read the brief, misleading statement issued by the board earlier. Glucksman refused to discuss the substance of any rumors about the sale of the firm or the trading losses or questions of capital adequacy. No one else was encouraged to speak or to ask questions. Glucksman had hunkered down; he was visibly angry, and warned that anyone who spoke with the press should—many partners heard *would*—be fired.

The meeting was terminated.

The partners were more unsettled at the end than at the beginning of the brief encounter. They wandered out of the boardroom dazed; some resorted to gallows humor: "Yeah, I'm a partner here. But I have nonvoting stock!" Many felt overwhelmed, imprisoned, convinced their fate rested in unsteady hands. "It was clear to everyone at this point, whether they were trading people or in investment banking, that these guys were no longer capable of effectively governing the firm," says mergers and acquisitions specialist Steve Schwarzman.

That afternoon Schwarzman went to see Shel Gordon. For months Schwarzman had been talking to people on the outside about selling the firm to gain a premium for each partner and to rescue them from what he believed was a nightmare. "Every person at Lehman Brothers in the corporate area talked to someone when it was clear the firm should have been sold or should go public," he says. "The value of security firms were at such unbelievable levels. And the business needed to have significantly more capital."

Schwarzman looked at Gordon, and saw himself: both men were disheartened. "I told Shel I thought it was pretty clear the firm was under enormous stress, and I thought it was too late to get any nonindustry purchaser of the firm," Schwarzman recalls. "But it was still possible to find an industry partner."

"Who do you suggest?" said Gordon.

"Shearson/American Express; E. F. Hutton; Paine Webber," said Schwarzman.

T HAT FRIDAY EVENING, PETER A. COHEN, SCHWARZMAN'S next-door neighbor in the Hamptons, settled in bed and decided to read a magazine before turning in. Weekends were special for Peter Cohen, his time to unwind after a busy week on Wall Street. Here he retreated to his chain saws and tools, built furniture or split wood, spent time with a wife and two children, who were, probably only next to work, the core of his life. On the eastern end of Long Island the Cohens relaxed. Peter Cohen needed that, for if there is a word that epitomizes him it is *taut*. Cohen's body is lean, hard and short; a tight cap of dark hair hugs his head; he is all business—from the neat marble-top desk to the terse responses, to the small PC monogrammed on his shirts, to the yellow pad that accompanies him wherever he sits. At Shearson/American Express, where he works, Cohen is known as a "numbers cruncher," a tough negotiator, a superb cost-cutter, a man perhaps more comfortable with numbers than with people.

Peter Cohen, the chairman and CEO of Shearson, is not an "Our Crowd" type. The son of a clothing manufacturer, he was raised in one of the "Five Towns" on the South Shore of Nassau County, not the North Shore, where German Jews built their estates; he attended public schools and Ohio State University before receiving an M.B.A. from Columbia. Cohen's office is decorated with a stark-white sculpted chain saw that looks as if it were chiseled out of salt, and with a statue, which is at eye level beside his desk, of two legs cut off at the calves and dressed in gray pinstriped trousers, black shoes and socks; the legs form a platform on which lies the remainder of the neatly folded gray suit and vest, a shirt and a tie. "My wife's view of me," says Cohen. A symbol of Cohen's willingness to cut people off at the knees, say his detractors.

In bed that night, Cohen opened the latest issue of *Fortune*. Near the end of 1983, Shearson/American Express had taken its top managers on a retreat, where it was agreed that they were interested in acquiring a blue-chip investment banking firm to complement their strength as a "wirehouse"—so named because the heart of Shearson's business was retail brokerage with individuals, and communication was mostly across telephone and teleprinter wires. When Peter Cohen's eyes focused on the Lehman story in *Fortune*, bells went off. "This is it," he said.

This was not to be a relaxing weekend. Since Peter Cohen is the CEO of Shearson, and at that time the owner of 55,340 shares of stock in the parent American Express Company—2,293 more shares than the chairman of American Express then owned—he was in a position to act. That weekend Cohen telephoned key staff people and they agreed: Lehman's strength in banking, fixed-income trading, and as a primary dealer in U.S. government securities would shore up Shearson's perceived weaknesses in those areas; it would bring the luster of Lehman's name and their client list; and it would result in a firm second only to Merrill Lynch (their chief "wirehouse" rival) in terms of total capital. With Shearson's proven ability to manage and cut costs—in the second quarter of 1984, while business all over the Street declined and Lehman's overhead ballooned—Shearson's direct operating costs were sliced by 2.3 percent, or $7.4 million from the first quarter. With that ability, Cohen and his associates agreed, a sizable chunk of the purchase price could be subsidized by lopping off people and redundant functions.

Cohen and his team did not have to speak the words "good management," but it was part of their self-concept, their conceit. They thought of Shearson, unlike Lehman, as a well-managed company. And not without reason. A January 16, 1984, in-depth analysis of Shearson by Paine Webber Mitchell Hutchins concluded: "The true measure of a firm is its ability to make money in all kinds of markets. Over the last decade Shearson has compiled one of the best records of any Wall Street firm . . . One of the most important characteristics of the company is the intense level of attention paid to managing, controlling and operating the business. At times the focus seems almost obsessive. No detail is too small, no transaction too insignificant, to escape the attention of some member of upper management. The tolerance for mistakes is also quite low. For example, brokers who cause an error which results in a loss for the firm are charged for that error on a net basis against their pay."

Management has been an essential Shearson tool because its strategy has been to grow by ingestion from a tiny firm in 1965 to a behemoth. Before it was acquired for almost $1 billion by American Express in 1981, the brokerage firm begun by Sanford (Sandy) I. Weill and a few partners had acquired ten companies, including Hayden Stone; Shearson, Hamill; Lamson Brothers; Faulkner, Dawkins & Sullivan; and Loeb Rhoades, Hornblower. With the capital of American Express, Shearson/American Express, as the merged company was called, was a mighty power.

If financial service companies were nations, American Express would rank as a superpower. It is a $10 billion-a-year powerhouse whose rivals have names like Citicorp and Merrill Lynch. American

Express officials, like planners within a vast government bureaucracy, speak of their "global policy," one that reaches into 130 countries, and whose scope is enormous. For as regulatory walls crumble and financial giants diversify, distinctions blur among brokerage, banking, insurance and retail industries. The financial services American Express provides include credit cards, traveler's checks and services, food and travel publications, insurance companies, financial planning, international banking, investment banking, money management, retail brokerage and cable television.

"Our own view is that our model should be one of a holding company able to be in any business we choose to be in," says James D. Robinson III, chairman and CEO of American Express. Twenty years from now, adds Louis V. Gerstner, Jr., then chairman of the executive committee and now president, there will be a profound "democratization of financial services." In Gerstner's vision of the immediate future, American Express cardholders will have the conveniences of one-stop financial services. In addition to current travel services, there will be American Express cash machines all over the world. Customers will be able to do their banking, financial planning and tax preparation; deal with their broker; buy insurance; invest in a money fund; write checks against the money funds—all at home, on a computer terminal.

Since size permits Wall Street giants to compete more effectively, the addition of Lehman would be another step on the long march toward a Wall Street dominated by a few financial service superpowers.

That is the framework in which Peter Cohen operated. After spending the morning on the telephone, he took a break early Saturday afternoon to drive his wife, Karen, and their son to the supermarket. At about two-thirty the Cohens in their station wagon reentered their four-acre compound, going past the copper gates, around the serpentine driveway, past the manmade pond, past the two copper-roofed glass buildings separated by a moat and connected by a bridge. "It looks like a TWA terminal," says one friend. The car came to a halt in front of the glass house.

A familiar figure stood waiting at the end of the driveway—Steve Schwarzman. Cohen's neighbor was smiling broadly.

"Peter, I've got to talk to you," Schwarzman recalls saying.

"About what?" answered Cohen, who was surprised to see him.

"I want you to buy Lehman Brothers."

"What would I ever want with a bunch of prima donnas like that," Cohen answered.

The two investment bankers did not have to exchange winks. Each knew how to play the game. They were part of a community of investment bankers, a pack, that moved in the same circles. Most were in their mid-thirties to early forties and generally were raised in upper-middle-class suburban homes. They were men of considerable financial acumen and, in their world, notoriety. The pack included Thomas Strauss, a senior partner and member of the executive committee of Salomon; Bruce Wasserstein, co-head of the mergers and acquisitions department at First Boston; Martin Gruss, who works with his father, Joseph, at Gruss & Company, a potent arbitrage and private investment firm; Kenneth Lipper, a former partner at Lehman and Salomon; Steve Robert, chairman of Oppenheimer; Jeff Kyle, president of Republic Bank; Mickey Tarnopol, head of international banking at Bear Stearns; arbitrageur Jeff Tarr of Junction Partners; Melville Strauss, a partner at the money management firm of Weiss, Peck & Greer; Richard Lefrak, of the real estate colossus that bears his family name; Rick Reiss, a partner at the money management firm of CumberLand Partners.

Although Cohen was an operations executive, a manager, he was a member of this group of go-go bankers and entrepreneurs whose names often streaked across the business pages, who put together the megabuck deals and leveraged buyouts and who had become, unlike bankers of another era, celebrities.

Among themselves, they often talked obsessively about money and deals, though never about their own deals. A few of their wives had careers or were trained for careers—Evelyn Lipper is a pediatrician and is independently wealthy,* and Karen Cohen studied architecture and was, for a time, an interior decorator. Many of these wives are active in charitable work—Ellen Schwarzman chaired the Benefit Committee for the Mount Sinai Medical Center. But most were trained to be *professional wives;* imbued with the values of the suburban country clubs in which they were reared, where their tennis and social graces were honed. Their life's goal, explains a Hamptons' friend of many of these women, "was to marry a man who completely supports you, whom you respect, and then your ambition is carried out through motivating your husband and your children." Many of these women spent their summers in the Hamptons. They entertained frequently, paying Rolls-Royce prices to cater their parties from "in" food emporiums like Dean & DeLuca's and Loaves & Fishes. "Ellen Schwarzman's flowers are like her dinners: every-

*She is the daughter of Joseph Gruss.

thing is perfect," observes a friend. "They don't just serve goat cheese. It's forty-six goat cheeses. When you walk in, you are asked, 'Would you like champagne?' " In all, this was a group of people eager to show off their perfect buffet, their perfect children, their perfect home; but always with an eye on not being too ostentatious.

Karen Cohen and Ellen Schwarzman were friends; their four children played together, and they went to the same exercise class in the Hamptons. Peter Cohen and Steve Schwarzman had another bond: they had talked many times before about a marriage between the two companies. "For a long time he would say, 'You ought to buy Lehman Brothers,' " recalls Cohen. But Cohen always responded, "Stephen, it's not something we're interested in."

There had been other overtures between the two firms, and in the past Shearson/American Express had not been interested. Salim (Sandy) Lewis, the matchmaker who helped put Shearson and American Express together in 1981, receiving a fee of $3.5 million in the process, had met with Peterson and Glucksman in 1982. "We didn't send him," says Cohen. This discussion led nowhere. Then there was a dinner in December 1982, arranged by Sherman Lewis, who ran investment banking for Shearson. The dinner was organized by Lewis and his former brother-in-law, Eric Gleacher. Cohen attended the dinner, as did Lewis, Gleacher, Peter Solomon, who was invited by Gleacher, and Herbert S. Freiman, who ran trading operations at Shearson. They went to the trouble of dining in Queens, says Gleacher, "so no one would see us." Neither Peterson nor Glucksman was told of the meeting, says Solomon, because "Shearson wasn't interested. It wasn't us saying, 'Why don't we merge.' It was us saying, 'What do you guys do? Here's what we do. If there's any interest, only two guys can talk for Lehman, Peterson and Glucksman.' "

One of the three Shearson executives who attended says Solomon and Gleacher were not so passive: "They tried to persuade us to do something. We decided not to." The timing was wrong, says the then president of American Express, Sandy Weill; they didn't want to purchase a firm like Lehman "in a boom environment" when the price would be too steep.* Price was just one factor, admits American Express chairman and CEO Robinson: "We could never figure out how to deal with the price and the superstars at a place like

---

*In June 1985, Weill, saying he was restless to once again "run and build something," tendered his resignation. He was replaced by Louis Gerstner.

Lehman. How would we avoid making people richer and then see them go elsewhere? Also, there was a worry about what role the management there would want to play. We couldn't figure out how to do it."

But with Peterson gone, with Glucksman weakened, and with Lehman careening toward losses that would dwarf those of 1973, this time Peter Cohen could figure out how to make a deal. Although he was nursing a bad cold and felt lousy all morning, suddenly Peter Cohen came alive. For the next two hours he and Schwarzman sat sipping coffee and reviewing why such a merger would be advantageous to Shearson, and what the pitfalls might be. There were several questions on Cohen's mind. Would Glucksman and Rubin be willing to step aside? Would senior people at the two firms be able to work as one? Could Lehman partners be persuaded to stay, giving up their private partnerships to become employees of a $10 billion financial services empire? Cohen remembered that when Merrill Lynch had acquired White, Weld in 1978, several status-conscious banking partners refused to join a retail house, which is what Shearson is known to be. Unlike the case with the Salomon merger with Phibro, a non-Wall Street commodities trading company, or the Bache Group's marriage to the Prudential Insurance Company of America, Shearson and Lehman departments would overlap, making a fit more difficult. Would Lehman clients stay with a combined company?

BY JOINING THE COMPANIES AND ELIMINATING DUPLICATE FUNCtions, said Schwarzman, Shearson could save $100 million; the fit made the whole stronger than the separate parts; Lehman's prestige would be showered on Shearson. "I told Peter the deal would be excellent for him personally," said Schwarzman. "It would be prestigious and newsworthy. And it would be his deal, not Sandy's."

"You don't have much time to think," Schwarzman recalls saying. "There is a board meeting Monday. The firm is chaotic and there is a real crisis of confidence. In this kind of situation the first guy in will win. You've got to act with dispatch. Which means you've got to act before the board meeting Monday." Cohen, rising from his chair, said he wanted to ponder the many questions involved and to consult with his people. He walked his neighbor to the door.

By Sunday, Cohen had reviewed these and other points on the telephone with his team and had spoken again with Schwarzman, who remembers advising Cohen to call Lew Glucksman on Monday morning. Schwarzman so distrusted Glucksman that, he says, he cautioned Cohen to be sure to mention that they had talked about a possible merger over the weekend.* That way, said Schwarzman, Glucksman would not dare summarily reject a bid from Shearson/American Express and fail to present it to the board, the way he had secretly vetoed ConAgra; and if he should dare, this time Schwarzman would be there to blow the whistle.

Before calling Glucksman on Monday morning, Cohen first placed a conference call to his two immediate superiors, chairman Jim Robinson and president Sandy Weill of American Express, Cohen's former mentor at Shearson. "I have reason to believe Lehman is going to be sold," Robinson recalls Cohen saying. "Should we take a good hard look?"

"If it's going to be sold, we should take a good hard look because it's one of the great old-line trade names," answered Robinson.

The three men knew that once before, in 1977, when Shearson was interested in acquiring a blue-chip investment house—Kuhn Loeb—Shearson moved too slowly and was bested by Lehman. So with a green light to explore a merger, Cohen hung up and dialed the chairman of Lehman Brothers Kuhn Loeb. He remembers the call this way:

"I read the present *Fortune,*" said Cohen.

"You can't always believe what you read," said Glucksman.

"I know that. But it stimulated the thought that we have a lot of complementary strengths, and maybe you'd be interested in talking."

"I'd love to meet with you if you people are serious," Glucksman recalls saying.

"We are serious," said Cohen.

They agreed to move fast, and Glucksman said he would call Cohen back after he met with his board at ten-thirty that morning.

By this time, Lehman board members had an additional reason to be anxious. The March figures were being processed, and they revealed another dismal month. All over Wall Street, business was down. But unlike Shearson, Glucksman refused to slash overhead costs, believing that the firm had to ride out the storm and be prepared to return in strength when the market perked up.

Although Glucksman would later tell *Forbes* magazine "there

---

*Cohen at first said he did not recall this advice; later he amended this: "Schwarzman told me, 'Don't tell Glucksman you told me because he hates me.' "

were no heavy losses in this firm" during his reign,* and to this day proclaims, "We had no losses. We were profitable up to the end," that is not quite the case. Lehman's books show that the equity and fixed-income trading divisions of Lehman lost $12.6 million in March before taxes and bonuses; these losses were only partially offset by the profits of the banking and money management divisions. In all, Lehman lost $5.5 million in March of 1983. From October 1, 1983, to March 31, 1984, the first six months of the fiscal year, Lehman's pre-tax, pre-bonus profits dwindled to $1.6 million (compared with post-bonus profits of $74.3 million a year earlier). Counting a $2.5 million tax credit and bonus payments, the firm's six month pre-tax profits were $733,000. This is the profit number Glucksman snookered *Forbes* with. What he also didn't share with *Forbes* were operating and trading losses in that period of about $30 million.† To appreciate the enormity of these losses, consider: Lew Glucksman almost got fired in 1973 for losing $8 million; and the 1984 trading losses exceed the $27 million the fixed-income division of Becker Paribas lost in the nine disastrous months before they were forced to sell to Merrill Lynch in August 1984. And Lehman's losses would mount in April and early May.

Lehman partners complain that these trading losses were never adequately explained. To this day Lehman traders are defensive about them. "These were not trading losses," says Dick Fuld, who was responsible for all trading at Lehman. "Maybe $5 to $10 million were trading losses. Most of it was due to no generation of income." By Fuld's novel logic, managers were not responsible for high overheads, nor should trading overhead costs or reduced revenues be counted in calculating profitability; the score should only be kept on actual trades where money was lost.

Was Fuld gambling more in 1984, perhaps in the hope of shoring up Glucksman's rule? "That was not the case," he answers. "I take it as a personal failure to lose money. Although we daily bought and sold securities, we did not take speculative long positions on fixed-income securities during that period."

The firm lost money, much as it had in 1973 when traders invested heavily in securities, gambling that interest rates would fall. Then, when interest rates rose, instead of shedding these securities, Lehman

---

Forbes, June 18, 1984.

†The banking division made $22 million and the money management division $6.8 million during these six months. Add a bonus for the partners, and the losses attributed to trading climb above $30 million.

traders held on to them too long. These losses are linked to Lehman's curious approach to what traders call marking to market, or pricing the current worth of securities in their portfolio, rather than carrying forward the value at the time of the transaction. Fuld says Lehman marked to market "every day." He is contradicted by chief financial officer Michael Schmertzler: "It had been the policy of the firm not to mark short-dated money market securities to market. This was a policy in the process of being changed." It had been Lehman policy not to mark to market Euro certificates of deposit (C.D.'s), since these were short-term instruments, payable within the year and therefore within a single accounting year. But in the early 1980's, when longer-term Eurodollar C.D.'s and similar money market instruments were developed, some stretching for up to five years, Lehman policy did not change. The firm did not mark these to market daily, as was the case with other long-term securities. By doing this, says one former Lehman partner, "it was to their advantage to buy longer-dated securities with a higher yield, which they financed with lower-cost short-term borrowings, thereby creating a current profit on the carry. So long as you didn't have to mark to market, the only risk one had was that overnight interest rates would go higher than the interest rate on the longer-dated security." In reality, one could hide enormous losses this way.

Stephen W. Bershad, who ran the London office through which many of these securities were traded, protested. "For reasons I've never fully understood," he says, "the firm had a policy where we didn't mark money market securities to market daily." Bershad says he raised the issue with various people and was "told that was the policy of the firm. I thought it didn't make sense because I didn't understand why a five-year C.D. wasn't treated for accounting purposes on the same basis as a five-year Eurobond. I, frankly, didn't make a big deal of it. I'm not an auditor."

However, Bershad remained uncomfortable and suspicious. "The firm was capable of buying up to $500 million worth of C.D.'s," he says. "If the market goes up, you can always realize your profit by selling the securities. On the other hand, if the market goes down, you don't have to recognize the loss because the securities are not marked to market. You merely continue to hold them until they are paid at face value. In Europe, our Euro certificate of deposit position got to be fairly large and no one wanted to recognize the loss. So it was just held. The question is whether that whole system was used to manufacture or control profit. Or was it just a vestige of an accounting system designed at a time when C.D.'s were ninety-day instruments and there was no need to mark to market?" The answer, Bershad thinks, comes in two parts: by not taking down the losses, the traders could avoid making themselves look bad and therefore make Glucksman look better, and also it honestly "got lost in the cracks and the accounting wasn't a major focus of interest." Bershad believes total trading losses hidden by not marking to market "could have been substantial, but because they were not marked it's impossible to know."

Inside Lehman, trading losses were no secret. And they helped produce a psychological reversal of roles. Now the bankers were carrying the traders. To this was added an insult: the money set aside for partners' bonuses was a paltry $3.3 million, only an eighth as much as the $27 million set aside the year before. Partners understood that profits were off all over the Street. But Lehman's numbers trailed the industry norm. Such trading houses as Goldman, Sachs and Salomon Brothers were generating better numbers.* Lew Glucksman was shorn of his armor. No longer was he a guaranteed money-maker. A fickle market had denuded a troubled partnership. After months of trench warfare at Lehman, partners were openly distraught.

Thus the Shearson feeler was seen as a life raft. Some partners would have preferred that the feeler had come from a nonindustry source, allowing them to preserve near total independence, as Salomon did when it consolidated with Phibro or Dean Witter when they hooked up with Sears. But now Lehman was racing the clock. Options were limited. Their hope was to induce Shearson to become a partner, one that would both infuse Lehman with fresh capital and award each partner an ample premium, while allowing the firm to remain a partnership. And although this was not discussed at the board meeting, with an established management team in place at Shearson a majority of the board assumed it meant the demise of Glucksman & Company.

"This is very serious. I think we have a buyer here," Glucksman told the board. He asked for, and received, permission to negotiate. The board was happy; Jim Boshart was not. Just a few days earlier he had been told to tell employees that Lehman was not for sale. Now

*Later it would come out that one of the giants, Prudential-Bache, reported a net loss of $113 million in 1984.

it was. Boshart raised his voice in frustration, and remembers one of his partners snapping, "Grow up!"

"If that's what growing up is," Boshart shot back, "I'd prefer to be Peter Pan."

Glucksman sympathized, but he did not side with Boshart. He felt he knew what he had to do, and he announced that he would make a breakfast date the next morning with Cohen and the four-member Lehman committee. The meeting was adjourned.

As they wandered out, many partners wondered if they could trust Lew Glucksman to put his heart into selling Lehman. As a precaution, Schwarzman met secretly that afternoon with Shel Gordon to brief him on his conversations with Cohen; and that evening, as he would most evenings for the next ten days, Peter Cohen telephoned and kept his back channel open to Steve Schwarzman. "He told me Lew handled the matter very professionally," says Schwarzman.

The next morning, Glucksman hurried across American Express Plaza, which divides Lehman's 55 Water Street headquarters from the American Express building, perched near the southern tip of Manhattan. As he rushed to breakfast he remembers vowing: "I made up my mind going to that meeting with Peter Cohen that I was going to sell the company."

The April 3 breakfast meeting was conducted at the rectangular table in James Robinson's private dining room, a small room with flowered, cloth-covered walls and a single painting of a horserace at Brighton. Attending were Robinson, Sandy Weill, Peter Cohen and members of his team, as well as Glucksman, Rubin, Gordon and Solomon, the committee from Lehman.

Eggs were served, and for the next three and a half hours, with Robinson and Weill excusing themselves from time to time, the men discussed their business philosophies, their views of the future direction of the business, what ingredients were needed to succeed.

Most of the talking in the meeting was done by Cohen and Glucksman. Each explained how he managed his firm. They talked about how the two firms might mesh. Glucksman said he hoped they might structure a deal to be fifty-fifty partners. Near the end of the meeting, remembers Shel Gordon, Peter Cohen punctured this illusion: "Let me make clear that we are not interested in any minority interest. If we are interested, it is only on the basis of a *total* deal."

"By eleven-thirty I had enough of a thumbnail sketch of their firm to know there could be a fit here," says Cohen. He turned to Glucksman and said, "Lew, we would definitely like to pursue something with you. We are prepared to act quickly if you are inclined."

"I'll call back after I talk to my partners," Glucksman responded. "How late will you be in tonight?"

"Eight P.M."

"I'll call you at seven-thirty," said Glucksman.

As he hurried back to Lehman, Glucksman was also pleased. "I liked the conversation with Peter," he says. "I realized it was the right deal for them and for us. I did not want to attempt to hold an auction in which everything could go wrong."

The Lehman board met at four that afternoon. Glucksman reviewed the breakfast meeting; the pulse of the board quickened. They were, for the first time in a long while, hopeful that a sale was near. They were heartened that Lew was acting in what they perceived as the firm's best interests, and for the first time in months they felt a sense of solidarity with Glucksman and Rubin.

Then, once again, the demons took over. "Peter Solomon will not be part of the negotiations with Shearson because of the exceptionally destructive position he has taken toward me on the outside," Glucksman recalls announcing to his startled partners. "I'm not going to let Peter Solomon be involved in my fate!" The chairman recommended that the negotiating team consist of him, Rubin, Shel Gordon, and chief financial officer Michael Schmertzler. He demanded and received an immediate vote. "The vote was to support my slate," Glucksman says, still savoring the memory.

Solomon blew up. "I've had enough of this!" he recalls shouting at the top of his lungs. "This is outrageous. This is the last meeting I'll attend." Before storming out of the boardroom, he says, "I gave Shel the high sign. What I was trying to do was to make sure there was no backsliding." Glucksman didn't notice any signal to Shel. To him, Solomon was just being his normal petulant self. "I enjoyed watching him get hysterical," Glucksman recalls. "That's the only time during this period that I enjoyed myself a lot."

That night, at seven-thirty, Glucksman called Peter Cohen and told him, "We would like to pursue something with you."

The next day, Wednesday, Glucksman was in St. Louis on business. Schmertzler sent over a packet of financial information on Lehman Brothers Kuhn Loeb. The ball was now in Shearson/American Express's court. Shearson executives began to inspect the names of the Lehman partners and began to make discreet calls, remembers Shearson vice chairman and chief operating officer Jeffrey Lane, to

others on the Street to "check out all of Lehman's key players."
Shearson was worried. If they went ahead with a merger, they
wanted to be sure they first identified those partners they wished to
keep; then they might find a contractual way to lock them in after
the merger. By the end of the week, says Lane, who had been an
M.B.A. classmate of Peter Cohen's at Columbia and who also grew
up in one of Long Island's "Five Towns," each top executive at
Shearson was assigned a list of Lehman partners to check out. "We
looked for at least three cross-references on each," he says. "It came
to a point where we knew all of the idiosyncracies of a partner, but
we wouldn't have known him if he walked in here!"

James Robinson worried about whether Lehman would lose clients after a merger, whether the two firms would fit, whether their
cultures were too diverse to blend, whether their back-office operations could be integrated. He spoke with Cohen about the contracts
Peterson and Glucksman were given beginning in 1982 to receive 1
percent each of Lehman's profits. A public firm could not honor such
an agreement. Besides, how could Shearson segregate its earnings
from Lehman's? The lawyers reported that in the event of a merger
Glucksman's 1981 contract clearly assigned this obligation to the
parent company. The nine-page agreement stipulated that in case of
a merger or sale, the contract would be "binding upon" the "successor corporation." But Peterson's severance agreement, which super-
seded this contract, was, according to Shearson's attorneys, less clear
on whether Shearson/American Express was bound to pay him 1
percent. However, litigation was in no one's interest. Would Glucksman and Peterson be willing to substitute a fixed fee? Cost was very
much on Jim Robinson's mind. He knew that in late 1982 Lehman
partners had signaled that they thought the firm was worth $800
million, which is one reason he says American Express passed on a
deal then. Now he wondered whether his view of a fair price—about
$325 million—was acceptable. Until Peter Cohen and his team could
study the Lehman books, they would not talk price.

Overnight, Cohen's team poured over Lehman's books. Cohen and
Glucksman began feeling each other out about a price at a seven
o'clock breakfast in Glucksman's chart room. Munching on bagels,
the two CEO's met alone for two hours. The tone was set by
Glucksman, who early in the meeting recalls saying, "Neither Lew
Glucksman or Bob Rubin will work for Shearson/American Express." It was no threat. In fact, they were words Cohen and his
superiors were hoping to hear. With a team in place at Shearson,

there was no management role they wished Glucksman or Rubin to perform. Cohen was grateful, and came to see in Lew Glucksman certain qualities—magnanimity, generosity—many partners at Lehman did not see.

The tone established, the two CEO's moved on to other matters. "We talked broadly about the elements that would go into a pricing," says Glucksman. They talked about the need to compensate young associates, those just below the rank of partner who owned no stock and thus would receive no premium; about how the top Lehman executives might mesh with Shearson's; about how senior executives were compensated at the respective firms; about how Shearson would manage the joint firm.

Then Glucksman's 1 percent contract came up. In addition to stepping aside as a manager, Glucksman volunteered to waive his deferred compensation agreement, which promised him 1 percent of Lehman's profits running through 1986. Glucksman says, "I have enough pride that I put above $600,000-a-year. To me it was blood money from all the people who came to work here and who we told we would not sell the business." Peter Cohen was startled, and gratified: "He had the firm's interest only, first and foremost."

The two men were joined at about nine by Rubin, Gordon and Schmertzler. They talked for another hour, reviewing what other data Schmertzler could provide Cohen. They talked about how quickly they had to move. "Glucksman suggested he would like to get together in the evening and wanted us to present to him our terms," recalls Cohen.

They parted optimistically. Glucksman sensed they would be able to make a deal and was impressed that Peter Cohen and he talked the same language, used the same shorthand to communicate. Both skipped verbal pieties, the smooth posturing of old-line bankers. Yet Glucksman knew there were obstacles ahead. He wanted about $400 million for the merger, and guessed that Shearson was thinking about a number closer to $325 million. Could they do the deal fast enough to avoid damaging leaks? How would a deal be structured? Cash? Securities? What kind of securities? Would the Lehman name appear in the new firm? And then there were the people issues. Would Dick Fuld run trading operations? Would Shel Gordon head the joint banking division? What of Henry Breck in money management? Or Glucksman's trusted right arm, Jim Boshart?

Glucksman and Cohen and their respective teams would gather that night in Cohen's wood-paneled office on the one-hundred-and-sixth floor of Two World Trade Center. The office is dominated by an immense curved marble desktop, resting on two leather-covered barrels; neat rows of phone messages parade in single file across one side of the desk; on the other is a Quotron machine. Three straight-back chrome chairs with gray cushions face the desk. Across from the desk, on the other end of the room, are two low brown leather couches separated by a marble-topped coffee table, which also rests on leather-covered barrels. Glucksman sank into one couch facing Cohen, who sat in one of his chrome chairs. Looking to his right, Glucksman eyed the eerie legs, cut off at the calves, with the gray suit resting on a two-foot-high platform.

Cohen and his team came prepared with questions, mostly of a financial nature. Both sides felt each other out about a sales price. They stood up to prepare their own sandwiches from trays delivered from a nearby delicatessen. Glucksman said they were looking for about $400 million in all—$200 million less than ConAgra said it was willing to pay only eleven months before.*

Cohen and his team then recessed, leaving the Lehman people in his office while they gathered in Jeffrey Lane's nearby office to try to arrive at a counteroffer. The Shearson executives knew Lehman was negotiating from weakness. "They saw that once the negotiations started there was no turning back," says Jeffrey Lane. "If our negotiations collapsed, they knew Lehman would blow up."

The Shearson executives returned to Peter Cohen's office. "We told them what we thought was a fair ball-park number"—about $325 million, recalls Sherman Lewis, vice chairman of investment banking for Shearson. "They didn't respond one way or the other." It was clear to the Shearson people that the Lehman people thought the price too low. Glucksman said he had scheduled a board meeting for the next morning. Cohen and Lane said they would be in Washington, D.C., in the morning and would return by twelve-thirty that afternoon.

"I'll call you at one o'clock," said Glucksman.

The Lehman board convened the next day at ten, and quickly decided that they were close to a deal, though they wanted to hold out for a price closer to $400 million. They agreed to pursue negotiations and selected Shel Gordon and Michael Schmertzler to do the negotiating. This was agreeable to Glucksman and Rubin, who, once

---

*Because part of the ConAgra purchase price would have been paid in ConAgra securities, and since these securities were of lesser investment quality than American Express's, it could be said that the ConAgra offer was worth somewhat less than $600 million.

they determined that a deal was do-able, lost heart. They never liked the idea of selling, and no longer trusted Shel Gordon, who would emerge as the Lehman figure the Shearson people gravitated toward. "Shel stood passively by while a lot of these guys hurt my reputation," says Glucksman.

Glucksman and Rubin were angry. Yet they had obligations to fulfill. So they seesawed between magnanimity and peevishness. Externally, in their negotiations with Shearson/American Express, they were models of responsibility. Internally, they rarely made an effort to heal wounds. As Glucksman settled a score with Peter Solomon, so Bob Rubin maintained a mental enemies list. He refused to attend any meeting—including negotiating sessions with Shearson —at which Solomon, Roger Altman or Steve Schwarzman were present. Solomon he accused of aggressively shopping the firm on the outside and of badmouthing Glucksman & Company all over Wall Street; he thought Altman was a double-dealer, someone who at first pretended to be their ally after Peterson left and who then turned on them; and he accused Schwarzman of being "deceitful," suspecting that he (and Solomon) were somehow involved in the presumed *Fortune* leak. Both men wanted little to do with a board they believed had betrayed both them and the independence of Lehman Brothers. Of course, their withdrawal pleased most members of the board, who felt confident that Shel Gordon was more likely to consummate a deal.

Glucksman telephoned Cohen at one o'clock. "Shearson is the right place for Lehman Brothers," Cohen recalls him saying. "We like you people. We like your philosophy. And we'd like to consummate a transaction. Shel Gordon and Michael Schmertzler have been authorized by the board to negotiate a final transaction." Glucksman told Cohen that he was off to Florida, where he had a retail sales meeting and that he would then largely bow out of the negotiations. Cohen thanked him and arranged for Gordon and Schmertzler to meet at five that afternoon in Jim Robinson's conference room.

The afternoon meeting lasted two hours, and spanned a range of subjects, including the ultimate sales price and the concept of creating a separate pool of money to reward promising associates who had hopes of one day becoming partners. At about seven, Gordon and Cohen shook hands on a tentative agreement. They parted, and Cohen telephoned John Gutfreund, asking if Salomon Brothers would serve as an adviser on a possible merger with Lehman. In any merger, both sides are usually represented by an investment banker who checks the numbers and confirms the fairness of the offering price. Choosing Salomon made sense to Cohen because the firm had been through a similar merger in 1981 and because, says Cohen, "we needed them to help in valuing Lehman's trading inventories." Clearly, Cohen's auditors had flashed a cautionary signal. An added reason was that one of Cohen's most trusted friends, Thomas Strauss, was the senior partner at Salomon, and Cohen wanted him assigned the task.

That weekend Peter Cohen's wife, Karen, and Tom Strauss's wife, Bonnie, were off to Paris on a shopping trip, attending fashion shows and art exhibits. Peter Cohen had a deal to close, one of the most momentous deals of his life, but he also had a six-year-old son and an eleven-year-old daughter to care for, meals to prepare, and an old hunting dog—"Sam," a Brittany spaniel—to walk. Cohen dispatched his daughter and a nanny to their Hamptons home for the weekend. He took his son, Andy, to the Post House in Manhattan for dinner, returning home to a ringing telephone. It was Tom Strauss. "Can't talk to you," the CEO of Shearson/American Express hurriedly exclaimed. "I've got to walk Sam. I'll call you back."

The next morning Cohen took Andy to a sporting-goods store to buy a speed punching bag for his bedroom. Then he raced uptown, dropped his son at a friend's house, where he arranged for him to spend the weekend, returned to his Park Avenue apartment to walk the dog, and sped to the Manhattan Café on First Avenue, where he was to meet Sandy Weill and Shel Gordon. Of Gordon, Weill says, "He seemed like the most senior guy there, and I wanted to get a feel from him of what he thought of the company and how we would fit." The Shearson team had spotted the personable, adroit Gordon as the prime prospect to become a senior officer in the new firm, seeing in him a natural bridge builder. Although they had not yet decided whether Gordon would be number one or number two in the combined banking department, he obviously impressed them, for the lunch lasted four and a half hours.

When Cohen arrived home the housekeeper handed him a list of telephone calls, which he spent the next two hours returning. Then he hurried to attend the Manhattan wedding of a friend's sister. There he met Michael Phillips, producer of such movie hits as *The Sting, Close Encounters of the Third Kind* and *The Flamingo Kid.* Phillips's wife was also away. "We decided to be each other's date for the evening," says Cohen. At eleven they left the wedding and went to watch their mutual friend, actor Michael Douglas, host

Saturday Night Live. "I was ready for a break," says Cohen. He arrived home at one-thirty in the morning. The housekeeper was still up, and somberly reported that his wife was not on her scheduled plane and that his dog had eaten a pencil and was vomiting. Cohen vainly tried to reach Karen in Paris, comforted his dog and went to bed.

At eight Sunday morning Cohen met Dick Fuld for breakfast at Kaplan's, a delicatessen on East 59th Street, where they discussed how the two trading operations could be integrated. On his way out, Cohen paused to place a lunch order and asked that it be delivered to his apartment by noon, when he was expecting his team to arrive. "Send paper plates, plastic forks. Send everything!" he instructed.

At ten Cohen was at River House on East 52nd Street. Joined by Robinson, who also lived there, they went to Gutfreund's duplex to discuss Salomon Brothers' initial findings and to solicit his views. "I advised them that if they could hold people, it was a good acquisition for Shearson because it brought them good investment banking and money market and trading expertise," says Gutfreund. Salomon's chief added, recalls Robinson, that he always wondered "why Lehman continued to outdraw us at the top business schools. He said Lehman had panache."

From Gutfreund's apartment Cohen headed west, back to his own home, where his team and the delicatessen order awaited. The meeting focused on people—on how to fit the two organizations together, on which Lehman partners were essential and which were not. To lock in those partners deemed critical to the continued success of the merged firm, they came up with the idea of fashioning a noncompete clause in the sales contract. Those Lehman partners judged essential would be required to sign, pledging not to join another Wall Street firm—or there would be no sale. By three o'clock, when Robinson and Weill arrived, Cohen and his team had a tentative structure to recommend: the Shearson or Lehman people who might head each department.

Suddenly, Karen Cohen swept in from Paris, laden with packages. After saying hello to everyone and spying the bountiful buffet, she beckoned to her husband, "Can I see you for a second." Karen led him into a bedroom. Trailing after her, Cohen remembers feeling pretty good. In her absence, he had juggled a number of things this weekend—one of the most momentous merger negotiations of his career, two children, a sick dog, a wedding and a meal for the Shearson/American Express team. Karen Cohen, however, was not impressed. "How can you serve your associates on *paper plates*?" she asked.

An American Express board meeting was called for the next morning to vote on the merger, but there were still issues to resolve. Cohen spent most of Monday, April 9, on the telephone, gathering information about Lehman partners. Decisions still needed to be made about what role Lehman people, particularly Shel Gordon, should play in the new firm. In arriving at these decisions, Cohen was not a totally free agent. He had the wishes, and insecurities, of his own team to contend with.

Sherman Lewis, for instance, was understandably concerned about his own responsibilities after the merger. Would he continue to run the investment banking division? Or, because banking was Lehman's strength, would Shel Gordon run the joint department? When Loeb Rhodes, Hornblower was acquired by Shearson Hayden Stone in 1979, Sherm Lewis was a good soldier, stepping down as co-CEO to run the banking division. Would he be expected to do so again? Would Lewis and Gordon get along? Cohen had encouraged Sherm Lewis to get to know Shel Gordon, and to this end the two bankers lunched for four hours on April 5. On Monday, April 9, they lunched again, and in order not to arouse curiosity they met in Weill's conference room at the American Express building. Together, they made preliminary judgments about people who would run such critical banking branches as mergers and acquisitions, divestitures and financial restructuring services. "It was apparent to me," says Lewis, "that we were going to get along well together." That afternoon Sherm Lewis visited Peter Cohen, who remembers that Lewis said, "Look, we're buying one of the major banking franchises. I think Shel should be in charge of banking."

A last minute snag developed. Before Cohen would take the deal to the American Express board he said he needed to resolve with Pete Peterson the question of his deferred 1 percent of profits. Glucksman had already ceded this contractual provision. Peterson, in several telephone conversations with Cohen, refused. Cohen and Peterson, joined by Jim Robinson, met for breakfast at the Glass Box, a coffee shop across from the U.N. Plaza. Peterson remembers that they talked mostly about client service and about his hope that Shearson would allow Steve Schwarzman to leave and to join Peterson, Jacobs. Cohen remembers that they spoke at some length about the 1 percent issue. Cohen says he informed the former Lehman chairman that although Glucksman's contract clearly required Shearson to pay him

1 percent, Shearson lawyers advised that Peterson's severance agreement was murky in the case of a merger. Peterson disputes this, saying, "There was never any question of ambiguity." Morton Janklow, who negotiated his severance agreement, says flatly, "What he was entitled to was one percent of Lehman's profits." Noting that the agreement took care to provide Peterson with a premium if Lehman were sold anytime within a two-and-a-half-year period, Janklow asks, "Do you think we would anticipate the possibility of a sale without anticipating all the possibilities a sale would bring about?"

Over coffee, Cohen hoped to shame Peterson by mentioning that Glucksman had waived this provision. He also said that since it was next to impossible to segregate Lehman earnings from Shearson earnings, surely Peterson couldn't expect to receive 1 percent of the profits of the combined firms.

"I'm not sure that I don't have a right to one percent of Shearson/Lehman profits," Cohen remembers Peterson saying.

"I can't find a lawyer to say that you don't have a claim on one percent of Lehman's profits," said Cohen. "We have to negotiate it out." Peterson agreed. However, Peterson flatly disagrees that he ever discussed a claim to a percentage of Shearson's profits: "There was never any discussion about Shearson's profits. Shearson was earning six to seven times what Lehman was earning." The question they grappled with, he says, was how to compute Lehman's profits. He recalls saying, "The last thing I want to do, *Jim,* is get involved in an accounting argument."

After much back and forth, they reached an agreement. Peterson would receive, as a substitute for the 1 percent, an additional annual payment of $300,000 for five years. Since Cohen says Lehman would not have made a profit in 1984, that is $300,000 more than Peterson would have gotten had the firm not been sold. Adding the annual $300,000 allowance for office expenses granted in his severance agreement, Shearson was now required to pay a total of $600,000 annually to Peterson for the next five years. The three men failed to resolve the question of how Shearson would honor Lehman's pledge to invest $5 million in Peterson's new venture-capital firm, but agreed to keep talking.

Before the end of the month, Peterson and Cohen had one other conversation, in which Peterson volunteered to subtract $100,000 from the $600,000 Shearson was to pay him annually. While refusing to discuss the details, Peterson says, "I voluntarily made what I think was a significant reduction. I did it so there would be good feelings all around"—among his former partners, among executives at Shear-son/American Express, and among his friends on the American Express board. A member of the American Express board put it somewhat differently: "He was afraid that it would look to his friends on the American Express board as if he were overreaching in his negotiations with us. He called Peter Cohen and said, 'Maybe it's a little too rich.' "

With that ticklish issue resolved, the American Express Company board gathered on Tuesday to consider the merger. In addition to Cohen, Robinson and several of their executives (Weill was in California and participated through a telephone hookup), the board contains some prominent public figures, including former President Gerald R. Ford, who in addition to the payments he receives for serving on the parent board also receives a $20,000 retainer for serving as a director of a subsidiary, Shearson/American Express, and another $120,000 a year to provide "management services" as a consultant; former U.S. Ambassador to Great Britain, Anne L. Armstrong; former National Urban League head Vernon E. Jordan, Jr.; and former Secretary of State Henry A. Kissinger, who joined the board soon after the merger.* For the next hour and a half the board inspected the deal, asked whether Lehman partners or clients would be lost in the merger and how much of the acquisition price could be made up by rigorous cost-cutting. Then the board enthusiastically ratified the acquisition of Lehman Brothers Kuhn Loeb.

The new banking house would be called Shearson Lehman/American Express (since changed to Shearson/Lehman Brothers); the purchase price was advertised as $360 million, of which $325 million went to the Lehman partners (with about $175 million of this sum being the premium above the book value of their stock); an additional $35 million was to be paid out as an incentive, primarily for nonpartners to stay with the new firm. In exchange, Shearson demanded that fifty-seven of the partners they wished to retain (of the seventy-two remaining at Lehman at the time of the sale) agree to sign a noncompete contract, certifying that they would not leave to join a competing firm within a ninety-mile radius of Wall Street for at least three years. The combined capital of the merged firm was officially pegged at $1.7 billion—about eight times Lehman's capital.

The Lehman board also met that morning to review the proposed

---

*Outside directors receive an annual retainer of $20,000, a $700 fee for each board meeting, and $500 for each committee meeting they attend.

sale. The terms of the deal were discussed, including Shearson's stipulation that if each of the fifty-seven partners who were asked did not sign the noncompete clause, there would be no deal. The Lehman board was not unanimous. Nor was their vote in keeping with the stereotypes of short-term "traders" and long-view "bankers." Opposition to the sale and impassioned pleas on behalf of Lehman's exalted past and majestic future were advanced by so-called "barbarians," like Richard Fuld; support for the sale came from the so-called traditionalists in investment banking, many of whom cast the same cold eye on this transaction they did on others. Fuld, who played on the Lehman baseball team, who took his first and only job at Lehman fifteen years before, cared about Lehman the way he cared about Alpha Tau Omega, the University of Colorado fraternity that elected him president. Fuld believed no price justified selling something he considered family. Although he despised many banking partners, he concluded, "I loved this place." So Fuld voted against the sale.

He was joined by his close friend James Boshart, who was both disillusioned and bitter. "This is a firm that is a hundred and thirty-four years old," Boshart remembers saying. "People are made partners of this firm as a reward for doing a good job. They didn't start the firm. My feeling is that no group of partners has the right to sell the business and deny an opportunity to nonpartners, to people who had been absolutely integral to the success of the firm the last five years . . . We are taking the brass ring away."

The third dissent came from Robert Rubin, who minced no words in accusing his partners of panicking and, above all, of a greed that filled their eyes with dollar signs and blinded them to what Lehman was, and could continue to be. The business would rebound, he said. In any merger, he warned, hundreds of Lehman employees would be summarily fired. Rubin said he was prepared, as were Fuld and Boshart, to shrink the firm in order to preserve its independence. To many of his fellow board members, Rubin was acting like Rubin— negative, passive, resistant to change. Rubin, however, thought he was the noble sentimentalist, not the cynic.

Those favoring the sale spoke of the advantages, including a fresh infusion of capital, that Shearson/American Express would bring. They spoke of being a full-service firm, of competing toe to toe with the giants. Little emphasis was placed on the premium the partners would pocket, or the partners' genuine anxiety about bankruptcy. And, out of politeness or exhaustion, little was said in this room of the political as opposed to economic reasons for the sale. "Our decision to sell was actually not motivated by economic considerations," says Peter Solomon, overstating his case. "Our problem was a political problem. We had a political situation that could not be resolved, and that's why we were sold."

Except for Lew Glucksman, everyone—including Bill Welsh—spoke. The majority of the board clearly favored the sale. Then it was Lew Glucksman's turn. He felt miserable, ambivalent. He did not really want to sell, yet he believed there was no other way to assuage the board. He knew that power at the firm had passed to the board. And, he says, "I recognized there was no role for me in the sale to Shearson. This was hardly my choice." So Glucksman swallowed hard and said he was impressed with Shearson/American Express as an organization and as a group of people. He said he was fearful for the future of Lehman as an independent partnership and felt this was the less undesirable solution. Reluctantly, Lew Glucksman cast his vote with the majority.

"We were all terribly relieved," says François de Saint Phalle. "It was like waking up from a nightmare."

I N ALL, THE NEGOTIATIONS LASTED SEVEN DAYS, FROM THE initial session on April 3 to the board meeting on April 10. After a hundred and thirty-four years as a private partnership, Lehman Brothers was to become the eighteenth Wall Street firm to merge with Shearson/American Express.

The sale of Lehman was splashed across the front pages. It made the networks, the news weeklies, the business publications. It was big news, and Glucksman and Rubin felt humiliated, felt they were cast as the heavies, as if they were responsible for murdering a venerable firm. For Pete Peterson, on the other hand, the sale appeared to be a vindication. In the Candy Kitchen in Bridgehampton, where he went each Saturday and Sunday morning at about seven to read the papers, have tea and a dry bran muffin, and to mingle with the other business executives, editors, TV producers, journalists, writers, publicists and farmers who congregate there, he clucked knowingly about the sale. Absent his restraining hand, Peterson noted, Lew Glucksman and his gang had destroyed a firm he had spent ten years building. In the newspapers, Peterson resurfaced in a lofty, magisterial role. He was pleased to say, the press reported, that he had agreed to serve as an unpaid consultant to Shearson/American Express. "They asked me if I would help them with organizational structure and investment banking," Peterson told the *Times*. "I felt a strong moral obligation to help during a temporary period."

Peterson's posture infuriated Shearson executives, who were still smarting from their strained negotiations with the former Lehman chairman. "Peterson was not a consultant, except in Peterson's mind," snapped chief operating officer Jeffrey Lane. One other senior Shearson executive exclaimed, "He's really a number! That son-of-a-bitch! He was a self-appointed consultant. That caused a lot of grief here. People at Lehman were wondering what we were doing. It was awfully difficult to call the press and say, 'No, he's not an unpaid consultant!' " But the virulent reaction the name Peterson invoked among Shearson executives was out of proportion to the alleged "crime." Partly, it was a backlash against Peterson's insistence on being paid for his 1 percent of the profits, in contrast to Glucksman's beneficent waiver of this contractual provision. Partly, it was Peterson's insistence that Shearson honor another clause in his severance agreement calling for a $5 million investment in Peterson, Jacobs & Company. Partly, it was because Peterson was talking to his friend Jim Robinson, not to the Shearson people. When he met with Robinson and Cohen for breakfast on April 9, for example, Peterson would address his friend "Jim," ignoring Peter Cohen. And partly, it was the condescending contempt Shearson executives felt Peterson displayed toward them, mere officers in a "wirehouse." No doubt these frustrations aroused bitterness at the word "consultant." In a formal sense, Shearson was right: Peterson was not a consultant. But in an informal sense, he was. "He agreed to help us," says Sandy Weill of American Express. Peterson did meet with Lehman bankers to discuss strategy, did talk to and try to soothe Lehman clients, did consult with his colleague and neighbor, James Robinson.

There were other obstacles to be overcome before the merger would become final on May 11. On the day of the announcement, Peter Cohen came to address the Lehman partners at five in the afternoon. They crowded together in the boardroom. It was Cohen's intention to answer questions, but after enumerating the advantages of the merger, Cohen waited in vain for questions. "They were shell-shocked," he explains, by news of the sale. Something else shocked them. Partners recall* Cohen boasting "I want you to know we have a great organization. I made $1.2 million last year, and seventeen people at Shearson made more than me!"** This was not comforting to Lehman partners. "We all rolled our eyes," recalls Henry Breck, "because after taxes we all made more than him." And, adds a partner, "We were our own boss."

At Lehman, relief at being rescued from Glucksman & Company was mixed with apprehension, which radiated throughout the organization. Many of the associates, those just below the partner level, were distressed that they would not have the opportunity to become partners. "There was deep resentment on the part of nonpartners at what was done," says former vice president Steven Rattner.† "The feeling was that partners took their money and left us very little. They sold the firm when they felt a need to cash out." At one meeting, an associate recalls, a nonpartner shouted at banking partner William A. Shutzer, "You guys have denied me a career at Lehman!" Another associate, who asked not to be quoted, complained that only the senior associates would tap the $35 million set aside in the purchase price for associates. "All those not here for three or four years are not eligible. In investment banking there are 290 associates at Lehman. They only provided money for one-third of them."

Secretaries were also distressed. "We're all depressed," said one. "The salaries at Shearson are lower. They don't pay bonuses to secretaries. They leave it to your boss to decide whether to give you a bonus out of his own pocket. Here my bonus was $3,000, $4,000 a year. The benefits are not as good. You have to contribute to your own life insurance and hospitalization. Lehman used to give you that." Knowing Shearson's reputation for cost-cutting, insecurity was rampant at Lehman.

There were obstacles to be overcome before some partners would sign the noncompete clause. On Saturday, April 14, Cohen and members of his team met all day with Shel Gordon, Bob Rubin and Dick Fuld to discuss the final list of partners who would be asked to sign,

*Cohen says that Robinson, not he, made this point.

**In 1983, Cohen's salary was $336,539 and his bonus $925,000. If the worth of the appreciation of his American Express stock was included, the worth of his 1983 earnings would dwarf those of one Lehman partner.

†Vice presidents were senior associates.

tying themselves to the new firm for three years. By the end of the day the list was ready, and the contracts were scheduled to be signed on April 17 and 18. But there were hurried last-minute negotiations with partners. Henry Breck and a few partners in the money management division, who enjoyed special profit-sharing arrangements at Lehman, wanted to be sure these arrangements carried over. (They did.) Negotiations with at least two banking partners threatened to break down. Alan Finkelson, who had reached an agreement with Lew Glucksman when he joined Lehman the previous summer to receive at least $750,000 in compensation and to go up to 2,000 shares of stock, would not sign without an agreement to honor these provisions. When this lawyer ultimately signed, he insisted on scrawling on the bottom of his contract that it was his understanding that he would continue to receive at least $750,000 annually. (Cohen later agreed.) Steve Schwarzman had another problem. He wanted out. He wanted to join his friend Pete Peterson at Peterson, Jacobs, and he discussed this with his neighbor Peter Cohen, who initially assured him they would "work something out." Schwarzman took this as a pledge, and when word of this leaked, a tempest arose. If Schwarzman could depart, why not another partner? To permit one to escape negated the purpose of the noncompete contract, which was to tie up Lehman's talent. Cohen had no room to maneuver. He told his neighbor there would be no sale if he did not sign. And Schwarzman, deeply disappointed, relented and was the last partner to sign. The announcement that "all the partners of Lehman Brothers requested to do so had signed employment contracts" was made on April 19.

There was also the matter of losses to contend with. There was a stipulation in the tentative agreement with Shearson that Lehman would meet a net worth test. That is to say, if Lehman's book value dropped below $145.1 million, which was the value of Lehman's equity as of March 31, 1984, Shearson could adjust the purchase price downward dollar for dollar. However, since Lehman losses were mounting, Bob Rubin says they agreed to lower Lehman's net worth test to $133 million. But even this number started to look shaky. "During the three to four weeks of the merger," admits Dick Fuld, "there was a tremendous amount I did not focus on in that period. There were losses." In April, interest rates rose precipitously. "If Glucksman and Fuld were minding the store and saw that our losses were getting bigger and bigger," observes one partner, "instead of sitting on them, they would have sold the securities. Their mind was not on the business."

According to internal Lehman documents, the firm lost $37 million in April—and since banking and money management were together generating profits of about $10 million, this meant that losses credited to trading approached $47 million in April. There were further losses in the first two weeks of May.

According to Shearson documents, a Coopers & Lybrand audit of the Lehman Brothers Kuhn Loeb Holding Company revealed that by May 4—in just a month—the book value of Lehman had plunged from $145.1 million to $124.5 million. And it would drop still further by May 11, the day the sale was finalized. According to a footnote in American Express's 1984 annual report, their aggregate total cost for the acquisition, including fees, was $380 million. The footnote to their consolidated financial statements goes on to say: "The excess of the total acquisition cost over the fair value of net assets acquired was approximately $272 million and is being amortized using the straight-line method over 35 years." Subtract one number from the other and the conclusion is this: Lehman's book value on May 11, 1984, had plunged to $108 million.

Peter Cohen rejects this number, insisting that the true figure is "closer to $118 million," though he will not provide an exact number. Chief operating officer Lane says the $108 million figure is accurate "from a bookkeeping basis," explaining: "From January 1 to May 11, 1984, Lehman had operating and nonoperating losses of $59 million." Lane says that these losses were not just in trading but included banking and branch office revenues that were off. They include, says Lane, reserves that Shearson set aside for severance payments, for legal settlements, and for bonuses. None would have been Lehman expenses, but they were legitimate expenses of a merger. In the course of a publicly announced merger, explains one Lehman banking partner, work often slows during negotiations; revenues unavoidably taper off; and those brokers bidding for shares traded by Lehman bid less, rightly figuring that Lehman is dealing from weakness.

Accepting Peter Cohen's roughly $118 million figure for Lehman's official net worth, this means that from March 31 to May 11 Lehman's book value plummeted by $27 million, which represents a pre-tax loss of about $54 million—$74 million if one strictly follows the bookkeepers. To gauge the enormity of these losses using Cohen's best-case calculations, consider: Lehman's pre-tax profits fell from about $110 million between October 1982 and May 1983 to pre-tax losses of about $54 million in a comparable period a year later—a negative swing of about $164 million. Coupled with the exodus of partners, it means that in the ten months preceding the merger, Lehman's book value plummeted by almost $57 million, or by about one-third.

Glucksman and Rubin say that some of the losses existed only on paper. They complain about the overly conservative way Salomon Brothers marked or valued their fixed-income and money management positions. And Rubin says he was never worried about meeting the net worth test. "Even if Salomon Brothers marked things differently, we said there was a whole list of other things. It was no problem," he says. Those "other things" included an employee pension fund overfunded by $5.5 million, after-tax; tax reserves of about $5 million after-tax; an investment account, ranging from venture capital to European investments, that was undervalued by about $2 million after-tax; and real estate reserves worth about $2 million after-tax. In all, Lehman had about $15 million worth of after-tax assets not included in its publicly stated net worth. The reason, says Rubin, was the "conservative" way they did their accounting. Rather than lower the official $360 million merger price, which would have been publicly embarrassing to Shearson and perhaps fatal to Lehman if they resisted, Shearson amended the contract and abolished the net worth test. They knew they had a cushion. To be a stickler on the net worth test, Cohen reasoned, might lose them the "good will" they needed from Lehman partners to make the merger work.

Peter Cohen and Bob Rubin say that Shearson volunteered not to reduce the net worth test. Cohen also says that his audit of Lehman's books produced "no surprises." Not so, says one Lehman partner who was close to the negotiations. "We could have taken our tax reserves and offset a certain amount of our losses by saying these reserves were no longer necessary," he says. "We went to Shearson and said that if they wouldn't lower the net worth test, we'd make up the difference by using our tax reserves to boost our net worth. Also, we'd take in our revenues now. The problem is that if we accelerated revenues and the tax reserves were gone, Lehman would cover its losses and Shearson would lose. Their response was: Don't do that. We'd rather show the losses and we'll take all those goodies for ourselves. That was what the negotiations were about."

When Lehman partners learned of this transaction, many groused. Were Glucksman and Rubin hiding these reserves to offset trading losses, and thus preserve their power? Did they even know of these reserves? Perhaps these assets would have hiked the sale price of Lehman Brothers, resulting in a larger payout to partners. Some partners saw incompetence, others deceit. "They were screwing their own partners," observes a former partner. "By hiding these reserves, they could use them anytime they wanted to reverse losses. They were hoping the market would turn around. If not, they could use these reserves to offset losses."

There were no surprises, insists Glucksman. Despite the evidence found in Lehman's own internal gray books and Peter Cohen's testimony, to this day Glucksman insists, "This company would have shown a profit for the period ending July 31, 1984." Bob Rubin says, "We didn't overlook anything. The overfunded pension can't be taken into your income except over ten years." Therefore the true one-year after-tax value of, say, the overfunded pension fund was only $500,000.

When the smoke settled, several previously undisclosed facts emerged. Lehman suffered losses that were never fully revealed to its partners. These hidden losses compelled Shearson to drop its net worth test. Lehman had assets whose full value may not have been included in calculating its stated $360 million sales price. Instead, these assets fattened Shearson's net worth, not Lehman's. And, as one banking partner wryly observes of Glucksman & Company, "They were remarkably conservative in valuing Lehman's nonmarketable assets and remarkably lax in valuing Lehman's securities."

This controversy was related to one other that erupted around the time the merger was finalized in May 1984. It centered on the distribution of Lehman's April gray books. A May 16 interoffice memorandum from the Lehman treasurer summarizes the firm's April performance: "Gross income for the month of April was $10,161,000. After deducting expenses of $47,181,000, the loss before taxes and OIC [officers incentive compensation] was $37,020,000. No officers incentive compensation was provided this month. After a net credit for federal, state and local income taxes of $20,099,000, the net loss was $16,921,000."

As soon as the gray books and this memo were distributed to all partners and principals, they were hurriedly retrieved. Messengers were sent to each partner's office to get them. Michael Schmertzler scooped up Bill Welsh's copy himself. "The books are wrong. Let me have it back," Welsh recalls him saying. Some partners never saw them at all. When he returned from an uptown meeting, François de Saint Phalle discovered that his gray book had been snatched from his desk.

The order for the recall appears to have been suggested by Peter Cohen. Conceding that he was upset, Cohen says, "There was no reason to start publishing financial information subject to a great deal of misinformation. That gray book did not accurately reflect what went on." Lew Glucksman says the numbers were inaccurate because the transfer of assets to Shearson made the losses appear worse than they were. "The firm never lost $37 million," he says. "There was a write-down but not a write-up. It was to their advantage in terms of the sale to have a write-down." In other words, Lehman's treasurer wrote down all of the trading losses Salomon Brothers reported, without taking into account Glucksman's disagreement over how Lehman's securities were to be valued and without writing up the undervalued Lehman assets.

Whatever Glucksman's explanation, many partners were irate, their ears closed to explanations. This one final act in the Lehman melodrama prompted partners to hyperbolically compare the actions of the messengers with those of Nazi storm troopers. Glucksman & Company, others said, were engaged in a Watergate-type coverup. It seemed to be part of a pattern. As partners weren't told of Alan Finkelson's deal, or ConAgra's offer, or the secret bonus arrangement with three "senior bankers," so they were not told of hidden losses that helped drive the value of their common stock down by $169.42 per share.*

It was a fitting close to a troubled partnership.

T A MUSEUM OF NATURAL HISTORY BENEFIT SOON AFTER the sale, the wife of a partner asked Ellen Schwarzman, the daughter of a wealthy Ohio manufacturer, "How do you feel?"

"Rich," she joked.

*According to the May 16, 1984, treasurer's memorandum.

Her husband Stephen, thirty-seven,* who owned 2,000 shares, pocketed $6.1 million from the transaction. But he was miserable, and in mid-1985 Schwarzman negotiated a financial arrangement with Shearson officials that permitted him to join Peterson in the formation of the Blackstone Group, a new private investment banking firm.

For a relatively modest investment of their own capital—de Saint Phalle says he put up about $150,000 to own about $4 million in shares, before the premium—partners walked away with a princely sum. Because there were two classes of stock—common and preferred—and senior partners owned more preferred stock, each partner was paid differently. And because partners also participated in private investments that were liquidated, many partners received more money from the sale than the price paid by Shearson/American Express. Here, from authoritative Lehman sources, is a scorecard on how certain partners made out on the sale:

Richard Bingham, forty-eight, a board member and chief of the San Francisco corporate finance office, who owned a bit more preferred stock than Schwarzman, who had less seniority, netted $6.5 million for his 2,000 shares.† After the merger, the redheaded former Kuhn Loeb banker who stayed clear of internal Lehman squabbling and plots continued to stay clear of New York office politics by remaining in San Francisco, where he runs the West Coast corporate finance office of the combined firms.

James Boshart, thirty-nine, also owned 2,000 shares. Because he held fewer preferred shares, he realized $6.2 million. Boshart was one of two of the partners who signed a noncompete clause and then decided to leave soon after the merger. With Jeffrey Lane filling the chief administrative slot, Boshart would be forced to accept a lesser role. In the end, this likable former basketball star was as estranged from many of his partners, as was Bob Rubin. He purchased a house in Colorado and went skiing with his three children. True to his nickname, "the Boy Scout," Boshart preferred staying home for three years—which he was still doing in the summer of 1985—to working alongside his special demons, Solomon, Schwarzman and Altman.

Quiet William Welsh, fifty-three, who was popular among his partners, received $7.7 million for his 2,000 shares. Just months after signing the noncompete clause, and after failing to reclaim his old

---

*All ages in this chapter are as of April 1984.

†Throughout this section the number of shares refers to common stock. The proceeds from the sale given for each partner includes the value of his preferred stock as well.

job as head of New York retail sales operations, Welsh decided to retire to study foreign languages and travel around the world. In the winter of 1985, he sent postcards from Bora Bora to his former colleagues.

Managers who ranked above Bingham, Boshart and Welsh, but just below the top rung, owned 2,250 shares. Glucksman's ally Henry Breck, forty-seven, the former C.I.A. official and longtime banker who became head of the money management division over Peterson's opposition, pocketed $8.2 million for his 2,250 shares. After the merger Breck continued to run Lemco, but was asked to report to Francis Froenkel, a Shearson employee who runs its managed assets division. In May 1985, Breck was relieved of his responsibilities as head of Lemco.

François de Saint Phalle, thirty-seven, received $7.4 million for his 2,250 shares. In the merged firm the man partners referred to as "the pro," after sharing responsibility with a Shearson executive for the capital markets group, now runs this operation alone and is invited to travel to China with Peter Cohen.

Roger Altman, thirty-seven, who had been a Peterson protégé and then ingratiated himself with Glucksman, also served on both the board and operating committees. Because he left Lehman to serve in government, his 2,230 shares were worth less. Altman collected $6.6 million. After the merger and after his candidate for president lost, Altman lobbied for and was a leading candidate to become New York's Deputy Mayor of Economic Development. But Mayor Edward Koch chose someone else. Altman now works in the banking department of the new firm. But he has less time to call on his valued contacts since, in the fall of 1985, Altman began teaching two days a week at the Yale School of Organization and Management.

William Morris—"the cynic"—one of three "senior bankers" who had complained about the 1983 bonuses and shares and was hushed with a generous boost in his bonus and the retention of his 2,500 shares, received $9.5 million. In March 1985, Morris decided to work only part-time and became a senior adviser to Shearson/Lehman Brothers.

Harvey Krueger, fifty-five, the former president of Kuhn Loeb, kindly "Uncle Harvey," who got along with everyone but Bob Rubin, pocketed $9.1 million. This "senior banker" continues to service his stable of banking clients for the merged firm. He now has the wealth to devote even more time to his favorite Jewish charity, and in June 1985, Krueger became chairman of the board of governors of Hebrew University in Jerusalem.

Peter Solomon—"the brat"—received $7.8 million for his 2,400 shares. (He and Krueger had donated 100 shares to charity in 1983.) The man who dared offend Glucksman landed on his feet just weeks after the merger when he was put in charge of the mergers and acquisitions department.

Solomon, forty-five, owed his appointment to his sometimes secret ally, Shel Gordon. The soft-spoken Gordon, who supervised banking and quarterbacked the behind the scenes maneuvering to sell the firm, netted $7.8 million on his 2,750 shares. Gordon, forty-eight, also emerged as the Lehman official with the highest rank in the new firm. In addition to being put in charge of all banking activities, he was appointed a senior vice chairman of Shearson/Lehman Brothers, given a place on the board of directors and on the planning group, which runs the merged firm.

Richard S. Fuld Jr., thirty-eight, who supervised all trading operations at Lehman, netted $7.6 million for his 2,750 shares. He, too, was made a senior vice chairman, a board member, and placed on the planning group of the merged firm. He now runs commercial paper, government, mortgage and money market securities. Fuld currently ranks number two, behind Shearson's Herbert S. Freiman, who supervises all trading activities.

Lew Glucksman's 4,500 shares netted him $15.6 million. Glucksman became a consultant to American Express, signing a four-and-a-half-year noncompete clause that gave him an annual salary for which, says Jeffrey Lane, "he can watch ships but can't go to work for Morgan Stanley." In the months immediately after the merger, Glucksman was named an executive vice president in charge of an expanded financial insurance group, including the troubled Fireman's Fund Insurance Corporation. The former chairman of Lehman now reported to an American Express executive vice president.

Robert Rubin's 2,750 shares included more preferred stock, so he pocketed $10.3 million. Rubin, fifty-two, also signed the same noncompete contract as Glucksman, and had more time to watch ships. In March 1985, Rubin let it be known that he planned to resign, and opened a one-man financial consultancy with an office overlooking Lehman's former One William Street building. That same month, Glucksman also resigned, saying he had moved to the Jersey shore and planned to open his own financial consulting firm—Glucksman & Company—in Princeton, New Jersey, where he will be closer to his fishing boat. One of his clients is American Express.

Pete Peterson got about $6 million from the sale on top of the $7 million he had received when he cashed out in the summer of 1983.

In exchange for his 1 percent of profits agreement, Peterson agreed to a cash settlement of $200,000 a year for the remainder of his five-and-a-half-year severance contract. Add to this sum the $650,000 he (as well as Glucksman) received in the fall of 1983 for his 1 percent of profits, the $13 million collected for his Lehman shares and the premium, the $1.5 million bonus he received in 1983,* the more than $1.5 million in supplemental retirement benefits (office allowance) for five and a half years, and the sum that Peterson walked away with was about $18 million—$23 million if one counts the $5 million Shearson ultimately agreed to invest in Peterson, Jacobs.

Those junior partners or young associates, who had accumulated little or no equity, did less well. Robert B. Millard, who was made a partner in September 1983 and who ran risk arbitrage at Lehman, didn't have enough time invested. The sale, Millard admits, "came a little early for me"—he made only $900,000 on his 500 shares of stock, plus an unspecified amount that Shearson threw in from the approximately $50 million ultimately set aside for younger partners and associates. Those associates on the brink of becoming partners had no stock to cash in; they lost, forever, the promised brass ring held out to them when they were recruited—that they could become a partner at Lehman Brothers.

At least one new partner made a surprising windfall—former brigadier general and Heisman Trophy winner Pete Dawkins, forty-six. Just seven months after he joined Lehman to direct the public finance department and was given 500 shares of Lehman stock, Dawkins found himself more than $1 million richer. He also found himself number two in the public finance division, reporting to a Shearson executive. Dawkins said he spent his time "looking after the relationship component of the business." After a rough initial period, in May 1985 Dawkins landed on his feet. He was promoted to a top job in the banking division, where he was placed in charge of business development. Another new partner recruited by Glucksman, Alan Finkelson, decided in mid-1985 to return to the practice of law, and was welcomed back as a partner at Cravath. Chief financial officer Michael Schmertzler, who was part of Lehman's negotiating team, also decided to leave and join Morgan Stanley. He claimed that since he was joining them as a banking partner, such

---

*In fairness, Peterson was at Lehman through 1983 and was entitled to a bonus.

a move did not violate the noncompete clause because he would be performing a totally different function than the one he performed at Lehman. Fearful of setting a precedent, Shearson has taken Schmertzler to court, blocking, at least for a time, his move to Morgan Stanley.

There was one other surprise—in April 1985, Shel Gordon said that he was fatigued with the administrative, or people, side of the banking job and wanted to step aside. The decision was "his choice, not ours," says Peter Cohen. He admits that Shel was "uncomfortable making tough decisions" and that Shearson executives prodded him to "make a decision," but nevertheless he says that Gordon was welcome to remain in charge of banking. Some Lehman partners groused that Gordon, typically, did not want to antagonize anyone, so decisions backed up. That Gordon would decide to step down was not a first. He had given up a big job in 1972 as president of a subsidiary of the Philadelphia Life Insurance Company to join the faculty at the Wharton Graduate School. This time, Gordon would stay with the parent company, accepting what he calls a more "challenging" position as head of the Shearson/Lehman Brothers investment committee. He will now guide the merged company's performance in merchant banking. "I've spent the last ten years of my life managing people," said Gordon. "My real love is as an investor. I told someone I'm going to repot the plants."

To step into Gordon's shoes in banking, Shearson's management chose Peter Solomon, who also remained head of the M. & A. department. Instead of directing the banking division alone, as Gordon did, Solomon is now listed as co-director with Shearson's Sherm Lewis. Nevertheless, fearless Peter Solomon, the outspoken self-described "voice in the wilderness," who felt he had never received the title and recognition he deserved, had emerged as the great survivor. Did Solomon see irony in this twist of events? "I've always been underrated," Solomon answers. "I was the last person taken off the waiting list in my entering class at Harvard. And I was the first in my class to be nominated a Harvard overseer. That's the story of my life."

J UST DAYS AFTER THE MERGER A WOMAN ENTERED ROGER Altman's office carrying a variety of colored stickers. Scanning the assortment of paintings, furniture and pictures in the neatly appointed office Altman shared with François de Saint Phalle, the woman interrupted his conversation to ask: "Could you tell me which paintings and furniture belong to you personally and which belong to Lehman?" Startled, Altman showed her his personal belongings. The woman quickly affixed yellow stickers to each piece of corporate property and then hurried off to the next office.

Color-coded stickers were but one of many changes introduced by Wall Street's newest supermarket. Within weeks memoranda addressed "To: All Employees" and sent "From: Communications" were placed on each desk. The subject: "Telephone Deletions." In alphabetical order there followed row after row of names, with extension numbers. In all, about seven hundred employees were laid off from both firms. Total savings, says Shearson's Jeffrey Lane, amounted to $75 million.

Parker Prout, Lehman's director of personnel, was one of those excised, as were fifteen of the thirty-three people in his department. Prout, interviewed on his last day at work and operating from behind a bare desk in an office barren of books, paper or paintings, said he understood. But he thought a way of life, as well as books and people, was on the way out. "Investment banking houses like Lehman reeked of a kind of luxury," he said. "See the forty-third floor. Impressing clients was part of the firm's history. The partners' dining room is particularly opulent. That filters down into the culture of the firm. The offices are done in a lovely wood finish. Typical of what used to be old partnerships. Partners felt independent. On the other hand, the retail houses are very highly structured and highly managed and conscious of cost control. At Shearson, their human resources [personnel] departments' desks are battleship gray, their floors are covered with linoleum, their phones are black. At Shearson, expenses are on everyone's lips."

Ralph Schlosstein, a bright Lehman vice president who was probably close to becoming a partner at the time of the transaction, dissects the different cultures this way: "Both Shearson and Lehman are in the same business in many respects. But Shearson's business is driven by the sellers of financial products. The key people there are retail brokers and institutional sales people. Investment banking in their organization existed to create a product. Look at their organization: the distributors and the sellers of financial products are in many ways the key people. So they don't position securities they couldn't sell. At Lehman, people grew up with a focus primarily on the corporate client. A lot of the distribution and trading system of Lehman was built to serve our corporate finance clients. So at Lehman, until relatively recently, you had an organization dominated by corporate finance."

As in any merger, there were transitional pains, which Shearson tried to be sensitive to. Deciding that Lehman "good will" was worth something, Shearson lowered, then waived, the net worth test, sticking to their original purchase price of $360 million. They were careful to place Lehman partners in key management positions in the new firm. As Lehman Brothers signaled Kuhn Loeb that it would have a voice in the merged company by appointing its president, Harvey Krueger, to head the banking department, so Shearson sent a reassuring signal to Lehman partners by elevating Sheldon Gordon to direct the joint banking department. They comforted traders by giving Dick Fuld major responsibility for trading operations. Reflecting his senior status and talents, as well as his alliance with Shel Gordon, Peter Solomon was granted the promotion and recognition denied him, and seemed finally at peace.

Nevertheless, from the point of view of Lehman employees, the days after the merger were full of anxiety. There were adjustments to a new management culture. Secretaries complained that employee benefits were not as ample at Shearson as at Lehman. "You've got to fill out a form for everything you do," complained one exasperated secretary. "I know this is sheer snobbery, but the class of people is different. You're dealing with a lot of polyester here. The morale is very low." Artie Weigner, who started at Lehman in 1933 as a runner and retired after the merger, says, "Shearson taking over Lehman Brothers is like McDonald's taking over the '21.'" William S. Proops, director of Lehman's dining facilities, toured his sumptuous dining rooms and wondered aloud whether Shearson would continue those special and expensive flourishes that have distinguished many private banking houses. Proops was trained at the École Hôtellerie in Lausanne, Switzerland, and at the Cordon Bleu in Paris. To him, the Lehman ambience—the Pétrus and Haut-Brion cradled in the wine cellar, the sterling silver cigarette boxes and salt-and-pepper shakers, the fresh flowers, the Impressionist paintings, the tuxedoed waiters—honored the entrepreneurs who dined there and perfumed Lehman with an air of elite *first class*. Proops worried that Shearson managers would focus on the expense, not on the purpose of the expense. In the first year and a half after the merger, those fears proved groundless. But new uncertainties arose because Lehman's offices were to be moved in October 1985 to a new American Express complex.

Many talented younger associates—like Steven Rattner—decided to leave partly because they felt the new firm would stifle the entrepreneurial spirit. "I just don't think Lehman Brothers will be the place to practice the kind of investment banking a lot of us came to practice," says Rattner, who is thirty-three years-old. "Though Lehman Brothers tried to be a full-service firm, it was like seventy-seven firms run by seventy-seven partners. It was entrepreneurial. The real expertise was selling your brains. I just didn't think Shearson would be able to foster that kind of activity." Rattner went to Morgan Stanley, where he is a vice president in charge of their efforts in the communications industry, and where he can still aspire to become a partner.

Anxious to staunch a potential outflow of talented associates, Shearson sweetened the $35 million pot of money set aside for them. Without making a public announcement, the 10-Q form they filed with the Securities & Exchange Commission for the quarter ending June 30, 1984, stated that the "aggregate cost of the acquisition" was "approximately $380 million"—not $360 million. Asked about this discrepancy, Peter Cohen said that a piece of this $20 million went to Salomon Brothers and to the lawyers and accountants who worked on the merger—perhaps $5 million in all. The remaining $15 million or so he said was set aside to reward associates. This plan has suffered a setback, for less than a year later Cohen said they expect to spend far less than the extra $15 million on associates. Clearly, the bleeding of associates was not arrested.

From the Lehman partners' point of view, the early reviews of the merger were mixed. François de Saint Phalle admits Lehman "has lost some of its investment banking base." In the year following the marriage, Lehman lost some of its blue-chip clients. The American Broadcasting Company, a longtime client, did not select Shearson/ Lehman when it chose an investment banker to engineer its merger with Capital Cities Communications, Inc. Others who took their merger business elsewhere include Chase Manhattan, the Continental Group and Uniroyal. On the other hand, de Saint Phalle says, "We have new products to offer corporations that the old Lehman didn't have." Despite slippage in banking, Shel Gordon says he sees nothing but opportunities: "There are things that will make investment banking firms of the future dominant. One is the depth and quality of their distribution system. The second is capital. The third is the investment banking franchise and its history. Only four or five firms have this third factor—Goldman, Morgan Stanley, First Boston, Lehman, and Lazard in some ways. It's a way of thinking of business as an investment banker—the ability to put yourself in the shoes of a CEO who is thinking strategically, not how to structure the next transaction. Very few firms have that. I would argue that no one else has those three things in place the way Shearson/Lehman Brothers does."

But Gordon concedes that what looks good on paper might not translate into practice. As the death of the House of Lehman helped demonstrate, inchoate personal feelings, ambitions, anxieties often play pivotal roles. Puffing on a large cigar he brought back from the Lehman dining room, Gordon says, "I was just talking to a major client at lunch. The client's main concern, and the reassurance he wanted, was that we would not just become a mass distribution firm and that we will keep the quality of our relationship and quality of service." That elusive word—*quality*—is implicit in the words of the chairman of a blue-chip company that has relied on Lehman for many years: "I don't want to talk to Sears & Roebuck about my business. I always knew my investment bankers felt a stake in my company. My embarrassment would be theirs. There was a tie. Now I worry we will lose that tie."

This concern is echoed by some partners. They are not embarrassed to say they are elitist, fearing that size squelches talent, that an entrepreneurial attitude will be the first victim of the merger. "Big institutions cater to unexceptional people," says one Lehman partner who signed the noncompete contract. "Imagine Ivan Boesky, the great arbitrageur, working at a big commercial bank!" After the noncompete clause lapses, this partner predicts: "The journeymen Shearson will keep. The talented people will redistribute." In two years, Lehman lost the acknowledged banking talents of Pete Peterson, Bob Rubin, Lew Glucksman, Eric Gleacher, Yves-André Istel, Steve Schwarzman, William Morris, Henry Breck, Alan Finkelson, George Wiegers and Steven Fenster, who decided to extend a sabbatical and to continue on the faculty at the Harvard Business School.* Will prospective clients focus on the talent that has left or the pool

---

*In the fall of 1985, Fenster resigned from Lehman to become a consultant to a former client, Chase Manhattan Bank.

of talent that remains, including low-profile partners like Frederick Frank, the banking division's single largest revenue producer? In the wake of the merger, will the new firm lose Lehman's special cachet? "There was a great distinction in being a partner at Lehman Brothers," partner Henry Breck said soon after the merger. "It gave you pride. You were known as a smart, tough guy who lived by his intelligence and integrity. What a passport to carry. There wasn't a person in the world I couldn't call."

From the point of view of top Shearson executives, the merger made a lot of sense. As Schwarzman had suggested to Cohen in their first meeting, Shearson's proven ability to pare costs would permit them to save, over five years, half the cost of the purchase price. Shearson also had transferred to their books a number of Lehman hard assets worth between $108 and $118 million, not including the overfunded pension and tax reserves, and real estate. In addition, Shearson received a tax refund of $95 million on past federal taxes paid by Lehman. Soon after the sale, Shearson also sold one of Lehman's assets—Lehman's lease at 55 Water Street—for $25 million pre-tax. The merged firm, it was announced, would eventually move into the new downtown Manhattan American Express complex. In all, these cost savings and assets add up to more than $400 million, exceeding the purchase price. And this sum does not include the income-generating value of such Lehman businesses as commercial paper, investment banking or investment management. From a cost point of view, the merger made great sense for Shearson/American Express, for the future income-generating value of Lehman's business was acquired for free.

From a customer point of view it made great sense, says Jeffrey Lane: "We're a wholesaler and a retailer. Why shouldn't you use us as your banker." Shearson/American Express was able to purchase what it could not easily build, observes former president Sandy Weill. "It's good for us. It puts us in a very important position in investment banking and some trading areas it would have taken us ten years to build."

Peter Cohen remains bullish. "The whole firm had a good last six months," he says. "Look at our results versus the other public firms. We have outperformed this industry." In the first two full quarters since the firms were married in May 1984 (July through December), Shearson/Lehman Brothers' net after-tax profits were $62 million in the second and third quarters of 1984, compared to $74 million in a

comparable 1983 period, when the market was humming.* Glucksman's trading operations, in particular, rebounded strongly, again
generating the lion's share of Lehman's profits. "We have been
profitable in trading in every month since the merger," says Jeffrey
Lane. In the January through March quarter of 1985, surging trading
and money management business helped drive up Shearson's net
profits by 25 percent, to $31 million.

The other quantitative way to measure the performance of Shear-
son/Lehman Brothers is with the various rankings issued by those
who keep score. Here the scorecard, as compiled by the Securities
Data Company, a financial data service, is decidedly mixed. In some
areas—like underwriting taxable new issues or initial public offers of
common stock, where full credit is given each underwriter—the
ranking of the merged firm was about the same as it would have been
had the dollar totals of the two firms been combined in 1983. In some
key areas the news was gloomy. In mergers and acquisition activity,
between January 1983 and May 1984, the date of the merger, Lehman
did seventy-nine deals and Shearson twenty-two. From May 1984 to
April 1, 1985, the merged firm did sixty deals—a sharp drop. Moreover, the firm completed only a handful of deals over $100 million.
Since M. & A. was considered a jewel in the Lehman crown, that is
not good initial news for Shearson/Lehman Brothers.

On the other hand, some scores kept by Securities Data paint a
brighter picture of the marriage. In 1983, Lehman ranked fifteenth
and Shearson fourteenth in issuing new tax-exempt municipals,
where full credit is given to each manager. Taken together, their
combined dollar totals would have ranked them fourth. At the end
of 1984, the combined firm had moved up to third. On taxable new
issues underwritten and where the full credit goes to the lead manager, in 1983 Lehman ranked seventh and Shearson eleventh. By the
end of 1984, the married firm ranked sixth. In the smaller Eurobond
market, in 1983 Lehman managed three Eurobond issues totaling
$375 million, ranking them thirty-second; Shearson/American Ex-
press ranked fifty-eighth. By 1984, although the indicators were new,
Shearson/Lehman Brothers moved up to rank sixteenth, managing
eleven issues worth $1.3 billion. And in initial public offerings of
common stock, where full credit is given to the lead manager, in 1983
Shearson ranked seventh and Lehman twelfth. Taken together, their
dollar volume would have placed them fourth. By the end of 1984,
the merged firm ranked third.

*Shearson's fiscal year, unlike Lehman's, coincided with the calendar year.

"The merger is going very well," Cohen said in December 1984. "Better at this point than a lot of us thought it would. The transition was easier. The one great challenge has been to take two different cultures and to have a new culture emerge. We're on our way to doing it."

Perhaps. But just a few weeks earlier, in late November, Cohen had an experience that might give him pause. Accompanied by Jim Robinson, Cohen came to the meeting room on the forty-second floor of Lehman—the same room in which Peterson announced that he was leaving. Invited to attend were the Lehman partners. Cohen and Robinson wished to discuss how the merger was going, to review compensation and bonus plans and to field questions. In his clipped, efficient way, Cohen began the meeting by announcing that he had five items to cover on his agenda, including the matter of Lew Glucksman, who was then actively involved with American Express. Word had filtered back to some partners that Glucksman was well thought of at American Express, and there was some concern that he would return. Cohen did not get to the Glucksman item on his agenda, talking first and at some length about compensation. Bankers were worried about their bonuses, which would be paid that winter. But some were more worried about Glucksman.

"Let's get on to Glucksman!" Peter Solomon interrupted.

"Lots of rumors are being spread about Lew Glucksman," Cohen recalls saying. "He's not coming back to this company. He's behaved honorably throughout the negotiations and done an honorable job. Let's look forward."

Jim Robinson then took the floor to echo Cohen. He explained, according to several Lehman partners, "what Glucksman was doing, and made it sound like they had rehabilitated Lew Glucksman."

At this point Harvey Krueger rose to speak. "It is totally out of place in this group to discuss Lew Glucksman, or the 'rehabilitation' of Lew Glucksman," he recalls saying. "If he were to come back, I would be proud to work for him. He made a lot of people in this room wealthier than they thought they'd ever be."

WAS THIS MEETING A HARBINGER OF DIVISIONS THAT WILL PERSIST, or the dying gasp of the past? The jury is still out on that question, as it is out on many others. Can the two cultures really blend? Will Shearson be able to impose its rigorous management structure without suffocating Lehman talent? Can they work as a team? Will giants like Shearson/Lehman Brothers be able to recruit first-rate people? Will they be able to convey to corporate clients a sense of individualized, customized service? Robert E. Rubin, a general partner and a member of the management committee at Goldman, Sachs, asks a larger question: "Wall Street has been a highly entrepreneurial arena. Lots of venture dollars are organized here. Leveraged buyouts come out of Wall Street. The merger wave, without regard to the question of whether it is a good thing for society, comes out of Wall Street. Can that entrepreneurial spirit remain alive in units as large as American Express? If not, can Wall Street remain a highly entrepreneurial world? And, if it doesn't, does it make a difference? Will this source of energy diminish?"

Wall Street and others can debate these questions for years to come. What is clear, however, is that the steady concentration of wealth in fewer and fewer corporate hands on Wall Street—like the corporate concentration of wealth in farming, in Hollywood, in computers, in the media, in financial services, in the automotive and consumer package goods industries—marches on.

T HE FALL OF THE HOUSE OF LEHMAN OPENS A WINDOW onto the turbulent changes taking place on Wall Street, and within capitalism. Looking through that window, different people seize on different explanations to describe what they see.

One school sees the sale of Lehman as inevitable, brought about primarily by capital needs and institutional forces beyond the control of Pete Peterson, Lew Glucksman or any mere mortal. Individuals may have made mistakes that hastened what happened to Lehman by a year—or five—but to this way of thinking, the sale was inevitable because private partnerships that try to compete with financial superpowers are doomed.

"Five years from now there wouldn't have been a Lehman Brothers," Peter Cohen said eight weeks after the merger. "Lehman was running out of capital." Economic necessity dictated the merger. In Cohen's view, Shearson/American Express was both a savior of Lehman Brothers and a promoter of greater economic democracy. Financial superpowers like Shearson/American Express may concentrate wealth, but they do so in a more democratic fashion than the amassed wealth of an earlier era, he says. "We're part of a big public company. The wealth created by the Harrimans, Morgans and Rockefellers was individual wealth. You don't have that going on on Wall Street today. This is a huge country with a huge amount of capital. If our capital ten years from now is $4 billion, it will still only be a small part of a large arena."

Former Lehman partner Steven Fenster believes that what happened is much more an institutional story than a human one: "It was inevitable that a private firm like ours would become part of a larger firm within two to three years." The rush of economic events and capital pressures, he says, have altered America, and not just Wall Street. "If you look all around America, you will find almost no privately owned industries, other than lawyers and doctors, who benefit from regulation. When I came to Lehman we had showcase capital. But it really wasn't used in the business." Two decades ago, markets were stable, interests costs and inflation low, the overhead of firms was small, fees were steady, competition gentlemanly, and government regulations paced approval for underwritings; companies were rarely menaced by hostile takeovers, there was "no such thing as positioning a private placement," no risky trading of bonds in secondary markets, and certificates of deposit were just beginning. To shrink Lehman, as Bob Rubin and others argued, would have been perilous, says Fenster. Many more employees would then have been laid off. The cost of abandoning Lehman's branch office network, its already contracted leases, its new and elaborate communications system, the severance payments required, would have been prohibitively steep. Clients would no doubt have fled, fearing they would no longer receive full service. And, Fenster concluded, "What happens if you shrink and you're wrong? If the boutique failed, you would have damaged your franchise and lost the safety net of a sale."

Asked about the fate of those Lehman associates just below the partner level, Shearson's vice chairman and chief operating officer,

Jeffrey B. Lane, said, "We've tried to deal with them by asking, 'Is the era of private bankers over?' If it is, they have to face up to this Brave New World. I think it is over. Lehman has to cause the other private investment bankers to view themselves objectively. There's always a role for the small boutiques. The problem is the firm that is neither fish nor fowl." Neither small nor big enough. "We're a wholesaler and a retailer. Why shouldn't you use us as your banker?" Lane believes that those investment banks just below the top rung of financial supermarkets—perhaps even including the premier private partnership of Goldman, Sachs—are dinosaurs.

The analogy to a supermarket is apt, because what has been happening on Wall Street over the past decade bears a remarkable resemblance to changes at the checkout counter. As Piggly Wiggly stores helped chase the corner grocer out of business earlier in this century, so banking partnerships on Wall Street which offered broader banking services to customers forced other firms out of business. Or compelled them to merge. As supermarket chains eventually drove Piggy Wiggly stores out of business, so banking houses with more capital, less costs per transaction, lower fees and a wider scope of financial services, including burgeoning trading products, chased smaller firms to the sidelines.

Today, this argument goes, another change is taking place at the checkout counter and in banking. The no-frills warehouse store and the so-called "superstore," which offers nonfood as well as food items, threaten supermarkets because they offer even lower prices and more display space and automated one-stop shopping. Similarly, Wall Street's "superstores"—Merrill Lynch, Salomon Brothers, Equitable (which swallowed Donaldson, Lufkin & Jenrette in 1984), Prudential/Bache, Sears/Dean Witter and Shearson/Lehman Brothers—pose a threat to smaller investment banks.

In the past five years, almost one out of every five retail supermarkets has closed. In the same period, while the number of securities firms is little changed, the concentration of wealth within investment banking has undergone a fairly dramatic change. According to the Securities Industry Association, in 1979 the top ten securities firms claimed 45.8 percent of all industry capital and 48.7 percent of all revenues; by mid-1984, the top ten firms monopolized 54.7 percent of all security industry capital and 57 percent of all revenues. The next fifteen largest securities firms claimed but 16.6 percent of all capital and 17.4 percent of revenues. When the sale of Lehman was announced, speculation sprinted throughout Wall Street that other private firms would soon follow—perhaps Morgan Stanley. Or Bear,

Stearns. Or Kidder, Peabody. Or L. F. Rothschild. Maybe even the "crown jewel," Goldman, Sachs.

Indeed, soon after the sale of Lehman a senior partner at Goldman, Sachs said his partners' nerves were frayed. "We are absolutely off the record, right?"* he said. "Some people here think our $700 million is enough capital to run the firm. Some people feel those who question whether it is enough capital are really using a code word for: Let's sell."

The code words and the moods shift with the fortunes of investment banking. Back around 1981, after a sluggish period on Wall Street, a cluster of firms was swallowed by the giants—Shearson by American Express, Bache by Prudential, Dean Witter by Sears, Salomon by Phibro. Yet when Wall Street was soaring—between 1981 and 1983—no major investment banks merged. When business slid in 1984, Lehman merged with Shearson/American Express, A. G. Becker with Merrill Lynch, Donaldson, Lufkin & Jenrette with Equitable. In an effort to replenish its capital base and join the ranks of the top ten securities companies, in mid-1985 Bear, Stearns & Company announced that it would go public after sixty-two years as a private partnership. And after rejecting a merger offer, L. F. Rothschild, Unterberg, Towbin announced that it, too, would soon convert from a partnership to a public corporation. Each is following the First Boston pattern in which a percentage of shares are sold to the public and the remainder are retained by the partners. Those who subscribe to the fatalistic *(It's Inevitable)* school of thought believe that if business is bad, private partnerships will die; if it's good, they might survive, particularly if they don't try to compete with the financial superstores.

If this consolidation is fated, then it follows that individuals are not to blame; larger institutional forces, the crush of history, the economic and political environment, are to blame. And, surely, among these forces must be counted the social and economic environment of America in the 1980's. A freer market economy has been in the ascendancy for the past decade, energized by a variety of catalysts, including the presidency of Ronald Reagan. Whatever excesses arguably exist on Wall Street—the scramble for mergers, leveraged buyouts, fat fees, arbitrage speculation, junk bonds or greenmail†—the Securities & Exchange Commission wants to regulate by relying on market forces, not on its policing power. This

---

*By "off the record," he meant that he did not wish to be quoted by name.

†A company that is a target for a takeover pays a bounty to the predator to encourage him to take his advances elsewhere.

restraint springs from several factors, including the political mood of the nation and a belief that government prescriptions are sometimes worse than the disease they are meant to cure.

Times have changed. In the 1960's, the emphasis of American society was on social freedom; today greater emphasis is placed on economic freedom. Among Americans in general it has always been respectable to be a millionaire, certainly to strive to become a millionaire. What may be different today is the preoccupation even many on the left have with money. Wall Street is *in;* the Great Society is *out. The New York Review of Books* now publishes the economic wisdom of Peter G. Peterson and Felix Rohatyn. Around the globe, from China's Communist rulers to Socialist President François Mitterand of France, the profit motive is in the ascendancy. The grim economic experience of most centralized Communist regimes has helped convince intellectuals that social freedom is not possible without economic freedom.

Of course, moods—and election results—change. But today, says Jeffrey Lane, forty-two, the force of history imperils most private investment banks. Size will permit powerful financial service empires to provide the cheapest and most varied services to consumers. "I think we will see an era of superpowers in institutional international competition," says Lane. "The wall between banking, insurance and brokerage will completely crumble. And competition will be international. The large players will be Citibank, Sears, American Express, maybe American Can or Security Pacific, BankAmerica, A.T. & T. and I.B.M., large German and French banks and Japanese trading houses."

The inevitable march of history is one interpretation of the events surrounding the sale of Lehman. Through the same window, others glimpse something else. They see human more than institutional culprits. To this way of thinking, what happened at Lehman is a tale of political intrigue unrivaled in Washington, of incompetence unmatched in the civil service, a sordid tale of vanity, avarice, cowardice, lust for power, and a polluted Lehman culture. These human ingredients—not a capital shortage, not impersonal market forces, not deregulated banking, not competition from financial superpowers—are what ultimately crushed an illustrious institution.

John C. Whitehead, on whose desk sat a sign with the single word —"Excellence"—and who retired at the end of 1984 as co-chairman of Goldman, Sachs, which he joined in 1947, insists Goldman will never follow Lehman's lead.* A strong corporate culture, he believes, compels Goldman partners to think first of the firm, rather than themselves. "I think Lehman went under in part because the culture there was not conducive to teamwork," he says. "Ever since Bobbie Lehman's death they've been a group of bright, able individualists who all happen to work in the same office but feel a principal responsibility to themselves, not the firm. Bobbie Lehman held that group together by his prominence." Whitehead blames Glucksman for booting out Peterson, whom he admires, and for making short-sighted decisions. He blames Lehman partners for being greedy—"They should have retained more of their earnings." Instead, he says, they diverted earnings from the firm in the form of swollen bonuses and dividends to themselves.

WHITEHEAD IS A TRADITIONAL CONSERVATIVE, A GOD-FEARING Republican who is anchored to a core set of convictions and who is appalled by what he considers the frenzied, speculative atmosphere that has invaded investment banking. Like others on Wall Street, he believes capital limitations are just one of many limits individuals, firms and governments cope with daily: "Everybody here knows we have restraints on capital. Capital should be a restraint. It helps you make selections. You have to make choices. We can't do both leveraged buyouts and arbitrage—or we can only do a little of each." Although Goldman, Sachs has over $700 million in capital, it has made certain choices, deciding, for instance, not to offer money management services. First Boston rebounded as a firm not because it advertised full services but, in part, because it excelled in at least one arena—mergers and acquisitions. Now it excels in others, including underwriting. Drexel Burnham's phenomenal growth was fueled by junk bonds. Smaller investment banks such as Lazard Frères or Allen & Company continue to thrive. According to one Lazard partner, "Of every dollar we receive at this firm, seventy cents is pre-tax profit. At firms like First Boston, the profit margin is only 8 or 10 percent."

There is a larger human context that might be invoked. The backdrop to what happened at Lehman was the unstable climate in which we live—a transactional, deal-oriented psychology on Wall Street and elsewhere. Television programs are abruptly canceled by poor

*In April 1985, Whitehead was nominated by President Reagan to become Deputy Secretary of State.

ratings, team owners like George Steinbrenner suddenly sack managers, star athletes sack local teams for the lure of free agency, boards sack CEO's after a couple of weak quarters, fickle consumers clamor to follow this year's instant fashion or celebrity fad. A sense of standards, of tradition—like the refusal of San Francisco to discard slow-moving cable cars or *The New Yorker* magazine's refusal to jazz up its graphics—often seems odd, quaint, inefficient. This larger human context can be invoked by those who claim that Lehman was a victim of forces beyond the control of individuals.

But this argument also supports a view that places blame on submissive Lehman partners. "The thing that brought Glucksman down," observes Peterson's attorney, Morton Janklow, "was not avarice, not lust for power, not personal insensitivity or cruelty—though they should have. What brought him down was losing money. He was like Jim Aubrey. Everyone hated Aubrey at CBS. Yet he was only brought down when the ratings declined."

Thus the failure of Lehman Brothers can be traced to the failure of Lew Glucksman to be a statesman-leader, can be traced to the collapse of comity and civility among a group of partners more interested in themselves than the firm, can be traced to a corporate culture poisoned by too much individualism; it is a story of greed for money, power or glory. Even before Glucksman assumed power, as Peterson has said, a majority of the partners probably favored selling the firm. As Peterson didn't say—but his wife did—the former chairman also hoped to sell before he reached sixty.

What happened at Lehman is a reminder that human relationships matter as much as the bottom line, if not more. "I don't think there is a larger story here," says Henry Breck. "You have the story of a social contract with people that broke down. Essentially, you had a group of bickering people who resolved their differences by selling. This is not Vietnam or Watergate. It's a personal story." That seems to have been the story of David Tendler of Phibro and John Gutfreund of Salomon Brothers. Their working partnership did not disintegrate in 1984 because their merger was failing or because the firm was losing money. Gutfreund, unlike Glucksman, waged an open battle for board support to remove Tendler as co-CEO, and did so for the most ancient of reasons: power. Power, and a need for greater fulfillment, prompted Sandy Weill to resign as number two at American Express. He said he wanted to run his own show again. An equally personal, if uglier, battle took place at Apple Computer. When business soured in 1985, so did the brotherly relationship between its two top executives, co-founder Steven Jobs and the president he recruited from PepsiCo, John Scully. Their business differences led to lapsed communications, which led to estrangement, then mistrust, and finally to Jobs' resignation.

Looking at what happened at Lehman in this human context, one sees that some behavior simply may not have been rational, even if practiced by tough-minded, profit-oriented businessmen. It wasn't "rational," observes Pete Peterson, for Glucksman to keep ConAgra's offer from the board, to give himself more stock, to appoint Bob Rubin president. "Why not consolidate your position first, particularly with the investment bankers? Why make these moves when the firm was losing money? It's not rational. Even Machiavelli wouldn't do it that way." Nor was it "smart" for Peterson to treat Glucksman and many of his partners in the frostily aloof way he did.

What happened at Lehman can also be seen as a microcosm of what is happening in the world of finance. The transactional world of trading is replicated in the transactional world of mergers and acquisitions, where deals are made at a dizzying pace. In 1984, there were 2,543 mergers and acquisitions, reports W. T. Grimm & Company of Chicago. These transactions set a dollar record—$122.2 billion, up from $73.1 billion in 1983. According to the April 30, 1984, *Fortune*, "A record-breaking sum, about $398 billion, was spent by U.S. corporations in the last decade on mergers and acquisitions. In all, some 23,000 deals were sealed, including 82 in which Fortune 500 companies were swallowed up." Billion-dollar-plus deals are now commonplace, as are million-dollar-plus M. & A. fees. The blockbuster $13.4 billion merger of the Gulf Oil Corporation and the Standard Oil Company of California in March 1984, for example, resulted in a record $63 million in fees—about half of which went to Salomon Brothers and the remainder to Morgan Stanley and Merrill Lynch.* First Boston netted $10 million for putting together, in just four hectic days of negotiations, the Getty Oil merger with Texaco.

The transactional, speculative nature of financing extends to other widespread practices. Greenmail—which literally means black*mail*ing companies with *green* money—is now a common occurrence. To repulse a hostile takeover by Sir James Goldsmith, who had captured 8.6 percent of its stock, the St. Regis Corporation enticed Goldsmith to sell his stock back—for a $50.5 million profit. To escape the

*New York *Times,* September 30, 1984.

clutches of Saul P. Steinberg, Walt Disney Productions paid him $297.3 million for the 11 percent ownership he secured a short time before for $265.6 million—a cool $32 million profit; Disney also agreed to pay $28 million to cover Steinberg's "out of pocket" expenses. Rupert K. Murdoch backed away from his plan to take over Warner Communications—after Warner agreed to purchase his 7 percent stock ownership for a $40 million premium, plus $8 million in legal expenses.

In such a climate, companies often find their attention diverted to short-term, defensive stances. They are advised to swallow "poison pills," making it prohibitively expensive for another company to acquire them. They are advised to exercise the "crown-jewel option," selling off a lucrative subsidiary—as Carter/Hawley Hale threatened to sell Waldenbooks to block a takeover by The Limited.* They undertake a "leveraged buyout," in which managers purchase their own company by pledging corporate assets as collateral for loans that the company—not the managers—must repay. They design "golden parachutes," in which managers who lose control can bail out of the company with lucrative severance agreements.

The public now reads of high-finance megadeals and corporate warfare as we read of the off-air frolicking of the stars of TV's *Dynasty.* Will T. Boone Pickens conquer mighty Gulf Oil? What are the Bass brothers *really* up to? Will Bill and Mary find a white knight to save Bendix? Will a "poison pill" or "Pac-Man" defense succeed in staving off an unfriendly takeover?

The romance of corporate combat sometimes cloaks a more subtle clash between short- and long-range interests. A preoccupation with short-term results—focusing on current rather than long-term shareholders, selling less secure junk bonds, peddling assets to boost earnings, gobbling up smaller companies to inflate revenues, reducing long-term capital investments in order to stretch fourth-quarter earnings—is not unique to the world of finance. Federal deficits are partly the result of a political preoccupation with immediate gratification (votes), as is the soaring out-of-wedlock birth rate (sex). Norman Lear's long-running smash comedy, *All in the Family,* opened to depressed ratings, but television executives were more patient a decade or so ago, and after sixteen weeks Archie Bunker and family climbed from the ratings cellar. In 1984, Lear had a new comedy show—*a.k.a. PABLO.* It was canceled after only six shows.

*They eventually sold Waldenbooks to K-Mart.

The change in business is mirrored in the changes going on in investment banking. As Wall Street strayed from merchant banking, in which firms invested their own resources in companies they believed in, and from traditional banking services, where bankers spoke proprietarily of "my client," today investment banking is increasingly a transactional, service business. Investment bankers became more like lawyers—if the client could afford the fee, they rarely said *no,* for everyone deserved representation. What one does *professionally* is often segregated from what one thinks *personally.*

When asked, "What fees wouldn't you accept?," many Lehman partners responded that they wouldn't do business with "the mafia," or they wouldn't do business where there was a conflict between two clients, or with a bad credit risk. But when pressed for further examples, they usually reacted as if they had not thought before about the question, as if saying *no* was something that government and young women were supposed to do.

"Investment banks respond to clients' interests," says Roger Altman, who admits to having ambivalent feelings as a citizen—as does investment banker Felix Rohatyn or prominent merger and acquisitions attorney Martin Lipton—about some of the things he does professionally. "Investment banks follow clients. The same as accountants or lawyers," he says. "It wasn't the investment bankers who told the oil companies to get in the mergers game." But once they were in the game, Altman says, he was "all for putting additional resources into the mergers area. My job then and now is to help earn the largest amount possible for the shareholders. Since large profits continue to be earned in the merger area, I've supported it all the way. That's our business."

This reasoning bothers conservative men like John Whitehead, who believe investment banks should sometimes lead as well as follow. "We are a service business," he says. "Sometimes—as Goldman does in our refusal to underwrite nonvoting stock or to participate in hostile takeovers—there are some times we take a stand in the public interest." The assumption investment bankers and their business partners often share is that a free market behaves rationally. This may come as news to anyone familiar with the sharp swings of the stock market. Because of the excesses of the true believers in supply-side economics and the unalloyed virtues of a free market, today conservatives as well as those on the left debunk this article of faith. "Market theorists love to rhapsodize about the wisdom of markets," Republican Senator Pete V. Dominici, the conservative

chairman of the Budget Committee, wrote in the *Wall Street Journal.* *
"But part of this wisdom consists of dealing harshly with fools who believe that the good times are without end."

Investment bankers commonly perform as the economy's magicians, as wise intermediaries who match ideas and wealth, users and savers of capital; they provide lifelines for embryonic companies; they devise creative products that pump desperately needed capital into, say, starved housing, as they have done with Fannie Mae's and mortgage interest-rate swaps. But, increasingly, many investment bankers justify *everything* they do.

"All this frenzy may be good for investment bankers now," banker Felix Rohatyn has said, "but it's not good for the country or investment bankers in the long run. We seem to be living in a 1920's jazz age atmosphere."

At Lehman, as on much of Wall Street, the operating ethic is *fees* —fees to cover expanding overheads, fees to boost profits and stock value and bonuses. "The fees paid today are outrageous," says Herbert Allen, Jr., of Allen & Company, who collects his share of fees. "They are not in relation to the product delivered. If Gulf Oil merges with Standard Oil and the two chief executives agree and then call in Lehman and Allen & Company, the investment banks didn't originate the deal, and they only do a week of work. Yet they get $20 million for the deal. It's nonsense! What would happen if they called investment banking firms for competing bids? The fee would be 50 to 90 percent less. It's a terrible system. Investment bankers are like ambulance-chasing lawyers who sue on every deal on the basis of getting fees. It's a bribe. Directors of many corporations are derelict in their responsibility and are paying investment bankers huge fees for long reports which only serve as protective padding for their own rear ends."

Attorney Martin Lipton disagrees with Allen, somewhat. "I am making a fortune," says this intelligent, personable man. "I think it's wrong and I'm urging changes. I'm not doing something wrong or illegal. There are lots of things in this area that we refuse to do." Asked if he felt hypocritical because he benefits from a system he deplores, Lipton answered: "I'm in a position like anyone who works in an area and sees abuses and says they should be changed. You have to draw a distinction: in areas of uncertainty one doesn't substitute

Wall Street Journal, May 14, 1985.

one's judgment for another's. We're not dealing with moral judgments. We're dealing with economic beliefs. I've never been comfortable enough in my economic beliefs to push them on other people
who disagree with me. A lot of people feel that takeovers ought to
run riot. That the problem today is too much regulation and restric-
tions. You can almost say I'm in the middle."

While it is often observed that deregulation has weakened client
ties to investment banks, it is also true that a preoccupation with fees
can weaken the loyalties of bankers to their clients. Since they are
not producing a standard product, often they produce what Robert
B. Reich, professor of business and public policy at Harvard University has christened "paper entrepreneuralism." For the investment
banks, the M. & A. activity, the "poison pill" and "Pac-Man" ma-
neuvers, the greenmail and leveraged buyouts, the risk arbitrage
speculation on whether T. Boone Pickens will win or lose—all mean
money. Everything becomes a transaction, like the sale of Lehman.

ONE DOES NOT HAVE TO ROMANTICIZE THE ROBBER BARONS OF
the last century to recognize the rootlessness, the frequent absence
of a sense of tradition in today's high-overhead, transactional world
of Wall Street. One also doesn't have to choose sides, either blaming
fate or human culprits for the fall of the House of Lehman. "The test
of a first-rate intelligence is the ability to hold two opposed ideas in
the mind at the same time, and still retain the ability to function,"
F. Scott Fitzgerald wrote in *The Crack-Up*.

No doubt, what happened at Lehman owes something to both
personal and institutional factors, to excess greed and insufficient
capital, to fear of Glucksman and fear of bankruptcy, to a mosaic of
reasons. Whatever one's perspective, it is hard not to see that the plug
has been pulled on an important piece of corporate history. With the
passing of Lehman, Wall Street's oldest continuing partnership has
disappeared. A link stretching back one hundred and thirty-four
years has been severed, as have commitments to Lehman employees
who invested their lives in a private partnership, or the seven hundred or so employees who were laid off by the merged firm. Of
greater moment, the death of Lehman signals the passing of a way
of life—of a handshake as solid as a contract, of mutual loyalty

between client and banker, of fierce but respectful competition, of a belief in something larger than self—in this case, *The Firm*.

D OES IT MATTER THAT LEHMAN BROTHERS NO LONGER EX- ists as a private institution? It mattered to partner Ronald L. Gallatin, then thirty-eight, who joined the firm in 1972 and became a partner in 1978. While the majority of his partners on the board felt relief that Lehman, and their own capital, were res- cued, Gallatin says he cried all night the day the merger was an- nounced. "Something very dear to me, that was part of my life, wasn't there anymore," he says. Although Gallatin stresses that he is today happy with the results of the merger and with the Shearson people, he says, "No sum of money could ever replace the sense of pride we had at being partners at Lehman. During its some one hundred and thirty-four years of existence, our firm has been known for developing creative financial techniques and has given incompa- rable financial and professional opportunities to its employees. We were able to raise equity and debt for companies through methods that we created. Without these methods these companies would never have grown as they did. By raising equity for companies, Lehman created a firm economic base that became the linchpin for economic growth in this country."

Since Shearson/Lehman Brothers will continue to raise capital for companies, one can legitimately say that Gallatin's view is a senti- mental one. The business of Wall Street is raising and making money. The new firm, like the old, will no doubt succeed in both. But those inchoate values—pride, sentimentality, tradition, a sense that one was running one's own company and could fly as far as one desired —may be lost.

Lost, as well, is a memory. "This is a firm that survived the Civil War between the North and the South, and could not survive the civil war between Peterson and Glucksman," says former Lehman partner Michael Thomas. "Memories are 50 percent of life. What will kill this country in the end is shortness of memory. A consensus of memory is important. I think of people like Peterson and Glucksman as custodians."

Former partner Herman Kahn, seventy-six, who went to work at Lehman as a $15-a-week office boy in 1928, became a partner in 1950 and retired as an active partner in 1970, lives off the memories. He retains a romanticized view of a business that has produced its share of scoundrels: "To me, investment banking was a noble undertaking, whereby capital was used for social purposes as well as personal gain. When I started in this business of investment banking, you had an investment banker like you had a family doctor."

Kahn was sitting in a small office at 660 Madison Avenue— Lehman's uptown offices. He wore a high collar and sat behind an orderly desk. He was joined by another former partner, Paul Manheim, seventy-nine, who had also gone to work at Lehman Brothers in 1928. Both were among the few old-timers still alive, and they clung to their memories. Ignoring the feuds, the partners who didn't speak, the snobbery and what would today be considered insider trading, Manheim says, "In our day it was a club. We were all friends. To them"—recent Lehman partners—"it was like joining Metropolitan Life." To both men, the sale of Lehman was a sacrilege, "a tragedy." "I wept," says Kahn. "My home was destroyed. My church burned down. My grandfather's grave was desecrated . . . Bobbie is spinning in his grave."

The same word—"tragedy"—is invoked by another Lehman partner, Stephen Schwarzman, who is half their age and a man of recognized talent and charm. Asked why it was a tragedy, Schwarzman looked up from his lounge chair on the brick deck of the pool at his weekend house in the Hamptons and gave a very different answer. He did not first say that the sale of Lehman was a tragedy because of broken traditions, or laid off employees, or empty promises or the end of another private partnership.

The first words Schwarzman thought to say were: "This is a tragedy because the business was not sold at the optimal time. Hence, an optimal price was not realized."

AFTERWORD

THE COMIC JAY LENO TELLS A STORY ABOUT THE TIME HE PER-formed in rural Alabama and told his bagel joke. It happens to be one of his favorite jokes, yet no one laughed. Leno was morose — until a bell went off in his head: *Suppose they don't know what a bagel is?*

"How many of you know what a bagel is?" he asked, peering out at his audience.

Silence.

A lone hand went up, and a burly man explained, "A *bea-gel* is a huntin' dog!"

Something like that happened on Wall Street in May of 1986, when investment banker Dennis Levine pleaded guilty to insider trading. Although no stranger to bagels, not until Levine's notoricty did many denizens of the financial community seem to know what insider trading was. They assumed it was a form of thievery practiced by a few rotten apples. Rarely was it asserted that the barrel may be rotten.

Then came the revelations about Ivan Boesky. On November 14, 1986, the SEC announced that Wall Street's most celebrated and successful arbitrageur had pleaded guilty to illegal insider trading. To atone for his crimes, Boesky agreed to pay a $100 million penalty, accepted a lifetime banishment from the American securities industry, and pleaded guilty to a single felony count carrying a potential prison term of up to five years.

The Boesky bombshell has been likened to Watergate, and the

analogy is apt. For the securities industry, like the Nixon administration, began by denying the rot existed. When the Levine news broke, Wall Street reacted much as members of the Nixon administration did, insisting: *We are not crooks.* Leaders of the financial community protested that the sins of a few should not be visited on the many. Dennis Levine merely demonstrated, they insisted, that any business is afflicted with a few worms. At worst, they said, Wall Street had a Yuppie problem, a few callow youths who lacked the standards of their elders. "I firmly believe it's an aberration, and it's happening at the fringe," said Shearson Lehman's CEO, Peter Cohen, in July 1986.

Cohen was, I fear, cushioned from the truth. As in the case with Washington lobbyists like Michael Deaver, or with the way campaigns are financed by those who do business with government, or with the municipal corruption scandals unraveling in New York or Chicago, there was abundant evidence on Wall Street of lax ethical standards. An inspection of the Levine case would have suggested that while he was a thief, the culture or ethos of Wall Street bore at least a measure of blame. During the time he worked at three investment banks, for instance, Levine was alleged in 54 instances to have relied on insider information to buy stock in companies about to be acquired or to make other deals. In more than half of these transactions, neither Levine nor his employers were insiders. The implication should have been unavoidable: Levine was relying for his tips on a network of spies. His tips came from a web of people who perhaps did not think it unusual (or wrong) to peddle such information. Despite the indictments of investment bankers at three separate firms and a distinguished takeover attorney, some of whom pocketed no money but merely traded information to show off and impress superiors, the Levine case was dismissed as an aberration.

But as happened with Watergate, the evidence accumulated. Why did the stock prices of so many companies about to be acquired suddenly jerk up prior to a takeover? In the five days prior to their merger with General Electric, for example, RCA's stock price climbed from $48.75 to $63.50 a share, with ten million shares traded. Similar run-ups preceded other business marriages. Clearly, more than hunches or a handful of miscreants were involved.

Still, Wall Street's elders bridled at suggestions that maybe there were many more culprits, that maybe an ethos was also culpable. They didn't make a connection between the deal-making culture that would sell Lehman Brothers as casually as another pork belly, and a breakdown in values. They didn't comprehend that greed unbridled by tradition or caution or government restraints might induce hubris. Wall Street was enjoying another great year — its sixth in a row. Why dwell on the dark clouds when the world of finance, like Reagan's America, was standing tall in the sunshine? Wall Street was not unlike the White House after the Watergate break-in. Flush with success, harumphing that no attention should be paid to a "third-rate burglary."

Enter Boesky, who pleaded guilty to a first-rate burglary. According to the federal government, Boesky's insider trading network had as many capos as the Gambino crime family. As I write this in December of 1986, law enforcement authorities have wallpapered Wall Street with subpoenas. And those who issued reassurances last spring that the Levine case was an aberration were now silent, shaken, or scrambling to find a defense lawyer.

One of those shaken was Richard West, dean of New York University's Graduate School of Business. "I may have been a little naive," he admits. "Last spring I said that Dennis Levine was the exception, that corruption was not pervasive. As more shoes drop, I now think it is pervasive."

No longer does it seem reckless to suggest that the symptoms of the disease have been apparent for some time. It is often said that Wall Street is dominated by financial conservatives, people who soberly count their pennies, sternly temper their passions, cautiously embark on new ventures, think long-term and are vexed if debts pile up. Untrue. Wall Street, as the Lehman saga should suggest, is a community of surprising promiscuity.

Most Wall Street partnerships—like the venerable Lehman Brothers—went the way of the dinosaur at least in part because their partners lacked patience and were greedy for the fast buck. The stock market careens up and down like a roller coaster partly because it is dominated by large institutional investors who speculate on the short-term profitability of stocks rather than invest in long-term values. This fundamental impatience is reflected in the transactional climate that now grips the Street—*Make a deal. Get an edge. Buy. Sell.*

The old Wall Street, of course, had its share of scoundrels and knaves. But it concentrated more on granting conservative financial advice to corporate America and to raising capital. It did not become so enmeshed in doing "deals." It is instructive that in 1980 the 20 largest firms that dominate investment banking collected $10.9 billion in revenues. Just five years later, reports the Securities Industry

Association, their revenues almost trebled, to $28.8 billion.

What Dean West refers to as a "speculative fever phenomenon" is mirrored in the geometric growth of trading, mergers and acquisitions, divestitures, leveraged buyouts, greenmail, and a blizzard of "new products." Many of these transactions have benefited the client, and the economy. All have benefited the investment banker, permitting them to close another "deal," to collect another fee. No investment bank better exemplifies this trend than Drexel Burnham Lambert, Wall Street's newest giant. Drexel's innovative use of "junk bonds"—high yield but more speculative and, therefore, riskier securities that often look to the takeover target's cash flow to retire the debt—has helped fuel the takeover frenzy that permits smaller sharks like Carl Icahn to gulp TWA. In recent years, Drexel has issued about $120 billion of "junk bonds" to finance hostile takeovers.

To chase Drexel's near monopoly on this speculative form of financing, investment banks now clamor to invent ways to compete. To lure Sir James Goldsmith as a client, and to snare a potential fee of upwards of $200 million, Merrill Lynch & Co. was willing to bet the company, promising to use its own capital to offer $1.9 billion in financing if Sir James made a takeover bid for the Goodyear Tire & Rubber Co. (Alas, Sir James decided not to pursue the deal, his disappointment massaged when Goodyear agreed to buy his stock, throwing in a greenmail bonus of $93 million, plus his legal and banking fees, for backing out.) Lacking Drexel's vast network to sell junk bonds, both Shearson Lehman and the First Boston Corporation have pledged their own capital to offer clients billion-dollar-plus bridge loans. At year end, Salomon Bros. went through a wrenching corporate debate about whether, in order to remain number one, they didn't have to relax their standards and plunge into the junk bond business.

This ferment merely underlines the importance of mergers and acquisitions, a prime source of profitability for Wall Street firms. In the takeover game, the natural allies of the corporate raiders and the M&A specialists were the arbitrageurs, people like Ivan Boesky. Since the arbs often bet on whether a firm would be taken over, and therefore whether its stock would rise or fall, and since they have enormous pools of capital at their disposal and can become powerful allies in a takeover battle, there is a temptation to jump into bed together. With the arbs on their side, the corporate raiders need put up less capital to win a battle. With good information, the arbs make millions.

The amounts of money being made on Wall Street in recent years, and the need to meet swelling overheads—expenses among the 20 top investment banks rose from $9.5 billion to $26 billion between 1980 and 1985—placed new pressures on the players. Each transaction made it possible to keep pace with escalating overheads. Each "deal" brought its gladiators a lucite plaque to display like a trophy, a fee running into the many millions, and lavish bonuses. It became commonplace to earn $2 million a year on the Street. Warriors kept score by how many deals they did, how big their annual bonuses were. Investment bankers became, observed Felix Rohatyn, like "rock stars."

Envy was in the air. "These scandals are the direct product of the takeover frenzy," says one prominent Wall Street player. "Wherever you have the kind of activity that a takeover frenzy produces, you begin to attract hungrier people. It becomes like a Gresham's Law: Bad people flock to easy money."

But more than envy or bad people were at work. Greed became acceptable on Wall Street and in America. In this new Gilded Age, guilt was out. Wealth was in. Pete Peterson and his partners marveled at the $70 million William Simon made on one deal. They looked for "deals" that would make them even richer, propel them to number one. As if entering a church, everyone was awed that Michael Milken, the driving force behind Drexel's "junk bond" success, made an estimated $30 million annually. At Lehman, as elsewhere, the fiercest arguments were often not about business strategy but bonuses. Business schools reported that alarming numbers of their recruits were shunning the call of corporate America, with its relatively modest starting salaries and long apprenticeships, preferring the quick rewards of investment banking. To compete with investment banking, which now siphons lawyers from the best law schools, starting salaries at premier law firms soared. Hoping to stem defections, Citicorp doubled its annual compensation for traders from $350,000 to $700,000.

Several conclusions leap out, at least to me. On Wall Street, as in any large organization, values usually trickle down, not up. The notion, common soon after Levine was apprehended, that he and his cohorts were infected with a virulent form of greed divorced from the environment in which they worked, is false. Of course, to blame the environment is not to excuse Levine or Boesky. They are responsible for their acts. And, of course, most bankers are honest and many perform feats to keep the engine of capitalism humming. But remember that corporations are hierarchical, not democratic. Values flow downward, and are imposed by those who set salary scales. Dennis Levine, like others, was rewarded for his success in getting information, for "gaining an edge," as they say on the Street. Dennis spent hours on the phone trading information. Partners marveled at how much this 32-year-old knew. They thanked Dennis for tips that led to new clients or profitable investments. They shoveled huge bonuses his way. Perhaps they did not know what Dennis was doing because they did not want to know. Or perhaps swapping information had become so commonplace, and gaining an "edge" so crucial, that the ethical line blurred.

Which leads to a second conclusion: The problem on Wall Street is one of conformity as well as corruption. The peer pressure on the Street, like the peer pressure in the ghetto, has become twisted. In the ghetto, peer pressures coax teenagers to believe that being "bad" is good, that it is "cool" to drop out of school, to snort coke or have babies. On Wall Street, peer pressures compel bankers to close "deals," to shove aside competitors to lure fees, to think more of "winning" than of the do's and don'ts of how the game is played. Wall Street is at war. And like in any war, unspeakable and unsavory behavior is excused.

The ends excuse the means. Score is kept by how many deals each warrior brings in, how much money is made. Conservative virtues—wisdom, caution, frugality—are not prized. Long-term loyalties—to the firm, to clients, to stocks—are often deemed inefficient. In such a climate, the most outrageous acts can be deemed normal because they are common.

On Wall Street, The *deal* is no longer a means to an end. And investment bankers, caught up in their exhausting 16-hour days, in the vortex of pressures from deadlines to voracious overheads to bonuses, in their mindless quest to keep up with the Joneses, often come to think of themselves as lawyers do. Seeing themselves as part of a service business, investment bankers, like lawyers, make few moral judgments. Their excuse is that everyone has a right to representation. They don't decide whether something is right or wrong. Their job is to make a deal.

I was stunned, in reporting this book, at how little thought most Lehman partners gave to the do's and don'ts. At the end of a series of interviews with each, I usually asked this question at the final session:

What wouldn't you do? To what piece of business, to what deal, would you say *No*?

What stunned me was how little thought ordinarily went into the answer. It was like watching the Tin Man in the *Wizard of Oz* think. You could almost hear the rusty parts of their brain clank. After a lengthy silence, the partner would invariably say something like: "I wouldn't do business with the Mafia!" Or: "I wouldn't do business with a bad credit risk!" It became obvious that in these go-go years, these smart men had not thought much about limits, about saying no. Their greed, their frenetic competitiveness, their abandonment of tradition, is part of the Wall Street culture that spawns a Dennis Levine or Ivan Boesky.

Lehman, like their competitors, had leapt into the world of "speculative capitalism," as Henry Kaufman, a managing director at Salomon Bros., calls it. In a rare public dissent, Kaufman disagreed with his firm's lurch into the junk bond business, telling the New York *Times*: "We cannot escape the fact that we have some financial responsibility. We are not just in the business of pushing companies around."

On the day he confessed, Ivan Boesky issued a public statement expressing his own fears and hopes: "My life will be forever changed, but I hope that something positive will ultimately come out of this situation. I know that in the wake of today's events, many will call for reform."

What reforms the suddenly contrite Boesky would call for remain unclear at this writing. The most therapeutic reform might be to see that Boesky—and the many accomplices whose names will surely explode in future headlines—serves a stiff jail sentence. That grim prospect might send a stronger signal to Wall Street than any legislation Congress could pass. Perhaps it would prompt the talented people who populate the financial community to pause, to think and reflect.

Maybe then they would see that the crime on Wall Street is not just securities fraud. Nor are the culprits just named Boesky or Levine. The larger crime is unrestrained greed. Wall Street is a place where intelligence is too rarely tempered by wisdom, where patience is a lowly virtue. That is Wall Street's rotting barrel problem. To ignore it is to conform to H.L. Mencken's portrait of Calvin Coolidge: "He would have responded to bad times precisely as he responded to good ones—that is, by pulling down the blinds, stretching his legs upon his desk, and snoozing away the lazy afternoons."

INDEX

Abraham & Company, 43
Abraham & Straus, 104
A.G. Becker, 45–46, 233
Alfred Sloan Foundation, 98
Allanos, Mathum, 40
Allen, Herbert, Jr., 142, 240
Altman, Roger C., 17, 22–24, 65, 83, 127,
    188, 239
  bonus shares, 130–131
  on capital adequacy, 144
  Lehman Board membership, 148
  payout to, 219
  personal history of, 71–72
  on sale of company, 169
American Express Company
  Board, on merger, 206, 208
  buyout offer from, 154–155
  Cohen's stock in, 188–189
  financial services of, 190
  See also Shearson/American Express
Apple Computer, 236
Arbitrageurs, 142, 191, 233
Arcari, Mario M., 151
Arkison, Robert, 79
Associates, 212
  merger and, 221, 231–232

Ball, George, 10, 34, 39, 43, 48, 50, 56
  as intermediary, 89–98, 101–107
Banca Commerciale Italiana (BCI), 43
  Lehman shares, 106, 179
Banking Act (1933), 30
Banking industry
  changes in, 234–242
  commercial paper, 14, 28, 44–47, 116,
    133
  deregulation and, 139
  full-service, 33, 234
  image of bankers, 53, 226, 235
  international, 140
  investment. See Investment banking
  "new products", 24, 43–44
  profit from, 128, 234
  relationships in, 80, 236
  special bracket firms, 70
  supermarket analogy, 232
  traders and, 11–12, 52, 118, 148, 234
Bass brothers, 184
Bear, Stearns & Company, 191, 233
Bell & Howell, 35, 37, 40
Bernbach, William, 10
Bershad, Stephen, 61, 179, 196
Bidding wars, 53

Bingham, Richard, 66, 131, 156
  Board nomination of, 149
  departure of, 160
  Gordon and, 172–173
  payout to, 218
  on sale of company, 169
Bi-Partisan Budget Appeal, 68, 73–74
Birmingham, Stephen, 29
Blumenthal, Michael, 72
Board of Directors, 25, 34, 65
  audit committee, 105
  capital committee, 173, 177, 182
  compensation committee, 165
  executive committee, 55, 57, 62–63,
    65, 127
  Glucksman and, 112, 148–152, 156,
    171–176
  governance issues, 108
  internal battles of, 183
  membership issues, 42, 65, 148–149
  Monday luncheons of, 150, 153
  operating committee and, 147
  Peterson resignation and, 101–111
  salaries of, 127
  on sale of company, 173–176
  secrecy regulation, 175
  sellout negotiations by, 173–176,
    202–203, 209–210
Boesky, Ivan, 226
Bonds
  Eurobonds, 228
  junk, 233
  market collapse, 48
  tax-exempt, 44, 228
Bonuses, to partners, 62–65, 126–131
  CEO power and, 127
  compensation committee and, 165
  Glucksman's policy, 128
  quarterly plan for, 135
  secrecy of, 217
  Shearson offer and, 214
Boshart, James S., III, 13, 18–19, 26, 28,
    60, 66, 87, 107, 127
  Board membership of, 148
  bonus to, 130
  CEO conflict and, 88–89
  d'Urso and, 80
  as intermediary, 69, 74, 86, 93, 96
  payout to, 218

  Peterson and, 69, 110
  Rubin and, 151
  on sellout, 170, 175, 198–199, 209
  stock decisions, 132
Braggiotti, Enrico, 80, 101
  concerns of, 116–117
  on Glucksman, 111, 125
  on Peterson, 113
Breck, Henry, 24, 78–79, 83–84
  Board membership of, 148
  on capital adequacy, 144
  departure of, 226
  as Lemco head, 120
  payout to, 219
  on sellout, 168, 181
Brown, Robert, 18
Buchanan, Peter T., 74
Bundy, McGeorge, 98
Business Week, 50, 141, 183
Buyouts
  crown jewel option, 238
  leveraged, 8, 233, 238
  See also Mergers, and acquisitions
Byers, Jeffrey, 35

Cabot, Paul C., 124
Capital
  banking markets, 139–140
  capital adequacy, 139, 142–144, 226,
    230–231
  Prudential loan, 145
  restraints on, 235
Capital committee, 182
Capital gains tax, 129
Capitalism, changes in, 230–231
Carter, John B., 5, 7
Carter Administration, 72, 103
CEO. See Chief Executive Officer
Certificates of deposit, 196
Charities, of bankers, 129, 191
Chief Executive Officer (CEO)
  bonuses and, 127
  ownership by, 132
  power of, 114
  salaries of, 127–128
Children's Television Workshop, 15, 84
Churning, 67
Clay, Lucius D., 33–34, 39, 48
Cleary, Gottlieb, Steen & Hamilton, 91

Clients, loyalty to, 124–125, 239
Cohen, Karen, 190–192, 204–205
Cohen, Peter, 188
    acquisition plans of, 189
    Fuld and, 205
    Glucksman and, 198, 200–201
    Lehman partners and, 211–212
    on merger, 227, 229, 231
    role in negotiations, 191–206
Commercial paper, 14, 28, 44
Commercial Paper, Inc., 46–47, 54, 116,
    133
ConAgra offer, 153–157, 163, 202
    Board and, 181
    Glucksman's veto of, 194
    second offer from, 177–178
    secrecy of, 217, 237
Cone, Terry M., 15
Connally, John, 38–39, 59, 73
Continental Group, 88, 180–181, 225
Cooney, Joan Ganz (Mrs. Peter Peterson),
    15, 26, 59, 74, 77
    corporate board role of, 84
    on Glucksman, 77, 84, 90, 94
    on Peterson's termination, 96–97
Cost-reduction committee, 66
Council on Foreign Relations, 14
Crown jewel option, 238
Cullman, Joseph, 125

Davies, Paul, 33, 39, 48
Davis, Martin, 179, 182
Dawkins, Peter M., 119, 126, 132, 146,
    payout to, 221
Dean Witter Reynolds, 138
De-clienting, 11
Deficit, federal. See Bi-Partisan Budget
    Appeal
Deregulation, 139
de Saint Phalle, François, 9, 23, 65, 118,
    127
    bonus to, 130–131
    as head of syndicate department, 73
    payout to, 219
    on Peterson, 112
    on sellout, 169, 181
Diller, Barry, 128
Drexel Burnham, 235
Duncan, Melba J., 20, 82, 85

D'Urso, Mario, 79–80, 115, 122

E.F. Hutton, 187
Ehrman, Frederick L., 32–34, 39, 47–48,
    51, 91
Employee equity division, 118
Equitable Life Assurance Society, 3, 5,
    182, 232
Eurobonds, 228
Euromoney Magazine, 61
Executive committee, 55, 57, 62–63, 65,
    127
Extraordinary Popular Delusions and the
    Madness of Crowds (Mackay), 12

Fenster, Steven R., 83, 137, 143–144
    departure of, 226
    on merger, 231
Ferris, Paul, 140n
Financial World, 54
Financier: The Biography of Andre Meyer
    (Reich), 125
Financing. See Banking industry
Finkelson, Allen, 119, 126, 217
    departure of, 226
    payout to, 221
First Boston Corporation, 108, 136, 152
    capitalization patterns of, 233
    M. & A. division, 191, 235
    reputation of, 184
Fisher, Richard B., 74
Fixed income division, 118
Forbes, 194
Fortune, 121, 183–186, 194, 203
Frank, Frederick, 227
Freiman, Herbert S., 192
Fried, Arthur, 79
Friedman, Alvin E., 57
Fuld, Richard S., 54, 62, 65, 101, 111, 113,
    118, 127–128
    bonus to, 130
    capital issue and, 173
    Cohen and, 205
    communications problems of, 158–159
    payout to, 220
    on sellout, 209
    on trading, 158, 195

Gal, Joseph J., 41

Gallatin, Ronald L., 242
Gang of Four, 56
Garten, Jeffrey, 140
General Cigar Company, 29
General Electric, 182
Gentlemen of Fortune: The World's Merchant and Investment Bankers (Ferris), 140
Gerstner, Louis V., Jr., 190
Glanville, James, 33, 54–59
  McMoran deal and, 56–57
Gleacher, Eric, 24, 47, 119, 192
  bonuses of, 130
  ConAgra and, 156–157
  Glucksman and, 111–112
  Peterson on, 153
  resignation of, 136, 226
Glucksman, Inez (Mrs. Lewis L. Glucksman), 15, 46, 124
Glucksman, Lewis L., 4, 9
  at American Express, 229
  Board and, 81, 100, 115–120, 171–176
  as CEO, 59, 70, 73, 75, 116, 118, 171
  Cohen's meetings with, 198–201
  commercial paper and, 14
  contract of, 200
  cost-cutting by, 66, 123
  divorce of, 124
  emotional nature of, 13, 16, 51–52, 125, 161
  five-point program, 134
  Fortune leak and, 185
  Glanville and, 55–56, 58
  Gordon and, 71
  life-style of, 51, 123–124
  management strategy, 26, 60, 78–79, 117–120, 125–126, 132, 164
  partners and, 105–106, 133, 198
  personal characteristics, 15, 69
  personal history, 10–13, 33, 45–46, 82
  Peterson and, 5, 7, 12, 16, 21–22, 40, 48–49, 68–69, 85–86, 90–91, 95, 100
  promotion of, 59–60, 75–76
  recruitments by, 126
  Rubin and, 20, 64
  sale of company and, 171, 182, 210, 220, 236
  Shearson and, 198–199, 229

Solomon and, 199
  trading and, 11–13, 17, 46
Glynn, Lenny, 86, 126
Goldman, Marcus, 28, 44
Goldman, Sachs & Company, 28–29, 46–47, 70, 74, 108, 120, 124, 230
  possible sale of, 233
Goldsmith, Sir James, 237
Goodman, Jerome, 99
Goodman, Sally, 99
Gordon, Sheldon, 9, 23, 65, 71, 106, 113, 117, 127, 146
  Board's respect for, 166, 173
  Lewis and, 206
  resignation of, 222
  sellout and, 172, 187, 203–204, 206
  Solomon and, 174
Graham, Katharine, 38, 50
"Gray books", 137, 165, 178
  recall of, 216
Greed
  accusations of, 138–139
  bonuses and, 132–133
  Boshart on, 175
  Glucksman on, 138
  profit motive and, 234
  sellout and, 167
Greenmail, 233, 237
Gutfreund, John H., 40, 114, 137, 236
  merger and, 203, 205
  salary of, 127
Gutman, Monroe, 33

Hajim, Edmund A., 25, 65, 77, 101, 120
  departure of, 78–79, 122
  Peterson and, 105
Harper, Charles M., 154, 157, 177
Harriman, Averell, 83
Hellman, Warren, 30, 34, 39–42, 49, 84, 125
Hendrickson, Robert M., 9
Herbert, Hilary A., 28
Hertz, John, 32–33
Hill, J. Tomilson, III, 7, 9
Hitchcock, Tommy, Jr., 35
Holbrooke, Richard C., 81, 161
Hood, James W., 18, 82, 100, 110, 118
  Fortune article and, 183
  on Rubin, 152

ITT, 141–142
In Search of Excellence, 115
Institutional Investor, 86, 125–126, 183
Interest rates, rise in, 182, 213
Investment banking, 30, 33, 42, 44, 233
 banking community, 191–192, 223–224
 capital markets and, 139–140
 changes in, 239–240
 global interests of, 140
 superpowers, 231
 takeovers by, 53
Iacocca, Lee, 124
Istel, Yves-André, 25, 47, 57n, 63, 88,
 101
 bonus to, 130
 departure of, 135–136, 236
 personal history, 105

Jacobs, Eli, 25, 76, 95, 97, 102
Janklow, Morton L., 95, 98, 108n, 155
 on Glucksman, 98–99, 236
 Mishkin negotiations, 98–99
Jews, history on Wall St, 10, 28, 56
Johnson, Lyndon, 92

Kahn, E. J., Jr., 124
Kahn, Herman, 33–34, 48, 243
Kaplan, Allan, 51
Kaplan, Gilbert, 125
Kennedy, Edwin, 33
Kissinger, Henry, 38, 50, 80, 83–84
Koch, Edward, 72
Krueger, Harvey, 25, 52, 57–58, 63, 65,
 68, 101, 103–104, 109, 127
 on bonus schedules, 128
 Glucksman and, 113, 125
 Hajim and, 79
 payout to, 219
 reputation of, 105
 on sellout, 167
Kuhn Loeb merger, 20, 43, 52, 80,
 103–104
Kyle, Jeff, 191

Lane, Jeffrey, 202, 211, 227, 232
Lazard Frères, 40, 56, 58
Lear, Norman, 238
Lefrak, Richard, 191
Lehman, Emanuel, 27, 29

Lehman, Henry, 27
Lehman, Mayer, 27–28
Lehman, Philip, 29
Lehman, Robert (Bobbie), 31–32, 48, 80
 Glucksman and, 44, 46
 personality of, 33–34
Lehman Brothers, 3–4. *See also* specific
 divisions, partners by name
 annual report of, 100, 110. *See also*
  Gray books
 audit of, 214
 banking department, 52
 "Big Power Play at Lehman, The", 126
 Board. *See* Board of Directors
 capital needs, 136–137, 142–144, 159
 clients of. *See* specific clients by name
 commercial paper, 46–47, 54, 116, 133
 compensation at, 114. *See also*
  Bonus(es)
 competitors of, 41, 108, 141
 ConAgra and. *See* ConAgra offer
 executive committee, 55, 57, 62–63,
  65, 127
 foreign offices of, 140, 179
 gray books. *See* Gray books
 history of, 27–34
 individualism in, 134
 Kuhn Loeb merger, 20, 23, 52, 103
 lawsuits against, 67
 Lemco, 77–78, 120, 181, 189
 London office, 179
 losses of, 34, 160, 194–197, 214–216,
  225, 236
 management changes in, 78–79,
  117–120,
 mergers, and acquisitions, 43, 127, 130,
  160, 225, 228
 money management at, 77–78
 offers for, 153–157, 177–180
 offices of, 54, 179
 organizational culture, 33, 233–234
 partners in. *See* Partners, Lehman
 pension plans, 64
 sale of, 17, 107, 150, 154, 165–166, 173,
  183–186, 191–210
 share distributions, 62–64
 Shearson merger, 191–222
 trading divisions, 48, 62, 160
 troika, in banking, 72, 104, 118

value of, 214–215
Leveraged buyouts, 8
Levy, Gustave, 44, 46
Levy, John M., 99
Lewis, Salim (Sandy), 155, 192
Lewis, Sherman, 192, 206
L.F. Rothschild, 46, 233
Lipper, Evelyn, 191
Lipper, Kenneth, 33–34, 41, 50, 123, 172, 191
Lipton, Martin, 53, 112, 239–240
Litton Industries, 32
Loeb, Solomon, 29
Loeb Rhodes, Hornblower, 206
Loews Corporation, 178
Loomis, William, 55

M. & A. *See* Mergers, and acquisitions
Mackay, Charles, 12
Mai, Vincent, 65, 118
Mazur, Paul, 33
McMoran Oil & Gas Company, 56–57
McNamara, Robert, 38, 98, 143
Mergers, and acquisitions, 43, 206, 225
    capital adequacy and, 144
    causes of, 231
    entrepreneurs and, 230
    expenses of, 214–215
    fees in, 240
    history of, 233, 237
    of investment banks, 141
    at Lehman, 43, 127, 130, 160, 225, 191–222, 228
    specialists in, 53, 111–112
    takeovers, 53, 184, 238, 240
Merrill Lynch, 108, 189, 232
Meyer, Andre, 31, 125
Millard, Robert B., 221
Mishkin Edwin B., 91
    Janklow and, 98–99
Mondale, Walter, 72
Money market account, 44
Morgan Stanley, 74, 108, 136
Morris, William, 23, 58, 63, 72, 86, 100–101, 104, 109, 113, 127
    on bonuses, 128
    on capital adequacy, 144
    departure of, 226
    hatred of Peterson, 104

payout to, 219
on sellout, 168

Nakasone, Yasuhiro, 14, 81
National Enquirer, 36
Newsweek, 72, 126, 149
New York Athletic Club, 10
New Yorker, The, 124
New York Review of Books, The, 234
New York Stock Exchange, 34, 140
New York *Times,* 108n, 186
Niven, Jamie, 35
Nixon, Richard M., 14, 109
    Peterson and, 37, 39

Offensend, David, 18
Operating committee, 65, 117, 127, 130
O.P.M. Leasing Services, 67–68
Our Crowd (Birmingham), 29, 176
Over-the-counter trading, 87

Paine Webber, 187
Paine Webber Mitchell Hutchins, 189
Paley, William, 35, 50, 80
Partners, Lehman, 18–19, 30–33, 47.
See also specific partners by name
    bonuses to, 126–127, 130
    capital concerns, 122, 142–146
    Cohen with, 211–212
    ConAgra offer and, 173
    defection of, 135–136
    departure of, 122, 160
    Glucksman and, 105, 125–126
    greed among, 138–139
    individualism of, 134
    junior, 212, 221, 231–232
    loyalties of, 104–105, 112–114
    M. & A. division, 131
    noncompete clause, 209, 212
    nonpartners and, 212
    panic among, 137, 161, 180
    passivity of, 115
    payout to, 160, 164, 181–182, 214–221
    Peterson and, 22, 104–106, 110–111
    sellout and, 61–62, 155, 167–170
    Shearson merger and, 205–208, 225
    troika of, 72, 104, 118
    wives of, 191–192
    women as, 110

Pension plans, 64
Percy, Charles, 37
Percy, Loraine, 37
Peterson, Joan (Mrs Peter G. Peterson).
    See Joan Ganz Cooney
Peterson, Peter G.
    annual income of, 97
    Board and, 25
    Board memberships of, 50
    bonus reduction of, 64
    Boshart and, 19
    co-CEO decision, 48–49, 59–60, 121
    ConAgra and, 155
    early years at Lehman, 40–42
    farewell party, 161–163
    Fortune article and, 184
    Glanville and, 55–56, 58
    Gleacher and, 153
    Glucksman and, 3–9, 21–22, 26,
        50–51, 78–80, 86–87
    image of, 67–68, 109
    life-style of, 50, 69, 83–84, 121–122
    management strategies, 6, 17, 40–43,
        52, 60, 66, 74, 90
    marital problems, 58–59
    medical problems, 58, 83
    on New York, 15
    O.P.M. lawsuit, 67–69
    partners and, 22, 104–106, 110–111
    pension of, 64
    personal characteristics, 14, 21, 70
    personal history, 23, 26–27, 35–38
    public activities of, 81
    resignation speech, 101–102
    as Secretary of Commerce, 38
    on sellout, 206–207, 210–211, 236
    severance agreement, 92, 94, 96–98,
        107, 113, 184, 200, 207, 221
    on trading, 54
    transition plans of, 61, 75, 90, 92
    wives of, 15, 37, 39. See also by name
Peterson, Jacobs & Company, 107
Peterson, Sally Hornbogen (Mrs. Peter G.
    Peterson), 37, 58, 85
Petropoulos, George, 35
Petropoulos, Peter See Peterson, Peter G.
Philadelphia Life Insurance Company, 71
Phibro/Salomon, 114, 137–138, 178, 233
Phillips, Michael, 204

Pickens, T. Boone, 184, 238
Political action committee (PAC), 119
Pope, Generoso, 36
Press coverage, 183–186
    Lehman sale, 210
    Peterson ouster, 115–116, 121–122
Pritzker, Jay, 179
Profit motive, 234
Proops, William S., 224
Prout, Parker, 223
Prudential/Bache, 232–233
Prudential Insurance Corporation, 179,
    182

Rattner, Steven, 122–123, 146, 212, 225
    resignation of, 225
Reagan Administration, 73, 233
Reich, Cary, 125
Reich, Robert B., 241
Reiss, Rick, 191
Rifkind, Simon, 58
Robert, Steve, 191
Robinson, James D., III, 190, 192–194,
    198, 200, 229
Rockefeller, David, 17
Rohatyn, Felix, 22, 31, 234, 239
    on banking, 239–240
Roosevelt, Franklin Delano, 148
Rose, Billy, 34
Rosenthal, Mitchell, 59
Rubin, Robert S., 19, 20, 23, 26–27, 43,
    49, 52, 55, 64, 68, 78, 101, 113, 127
    on capital adequacy, 145
    as chief operating officer, 118
    ConAgra offer and, 153–154
    enemies of, 203
    Glucksman and, 90–91
    on mergers, 151, 209, 230
    promotion of, 116, 147–152
    resignation of, 226
    Solomon and, 106

Sacks, David G., 57
Sage, Andrew G.C., II, 32–33, 39
Salary, structures, 127
Salinger, Inez. See Glucksman, Inez
Salomon Brothers, 33, 40, 108, 232
    as Lehman adviser, 203, 205
    losses of, 48

merger of, 236
parent company of, 114
Sawyer, Diane, 161
Schiff, Dorothy, 29
Schiff, Jacob, 29
Schlesinger, James R., 50
Schlosstein, Ralph L., 14, 223
Schmertzler, Michael, 79, 120, 196
  gray books and, 216
  on losses, 181
  as sellout negotiator, 203
Schultz, George, 37
Schwarzman, Ellen, 191–192, 217
Schwarzman, Stephen, 18, 66, 83, 88, 115
  bonus to, 131
  Cohen and, 191–194
  departure of, 206, 213, 226
  Glucksman and, 194
  mergers committee and, 160
  payout to, 217–218
  Peterson and, 162–163
  on sellout, 187, 243
Sculley, John 127
Sears, Roebuck & Company, 29, 138
SEC. See Securities and Exchange
  Commission
Securities & Exchange Commission
  (SEC), 225
  regulation by, 233
  Rule 415, 139
Securities Data Company, 228
Securities Industries Association, 165, 232
Segars, Hugh R., 27
Severance agreements, 214. See also by
  partner's name
Shares, in Lehman Brothers, 106–107
  distribution of, 62–64, 115
  value of, 142, 217
  withdrawal of, 122
Shearson/American Express, 4
  acquisitions by, 188, 192
  history of, 189
  Lehman losses and, 213
  management of, 230
  net worth test by, 215–216, 224
  offer to Lehman by, 208–210
  Paine Webber analysis, 189
  Peterson and, 211
  Schwarzman proposal to, 187

Shearson Hayden Stone, 206
Shearson/Lehman Brothers
  investment committee, 222
  layoffs by, 233
  loss of clients by, 225
  positions at, 222
  ranking of, 228
  resignations at, 226
  sale of building by, 227
  as superstore, 232–233
Shearson Loeb Rhodes, 138
Shoemaker, Alvin V., 74
Shutzer, William A., 212
Silber, William L., 158
Simon, William E., 8
Simpson Thatcher, 32
Smith, Adam. See Goodman, Jerome
Solomon, Peter, 25, 63, 77, 101–102,
  119–120, 127, 192
  on bonuses, 128–129
  on capital committee, 174
  Glucksman and, 149–150
  on greed, 133
  on Hajim, 79
  history of, 103–104
  payout to, 219
  personality of, 10, 81, 103–109, 115
  Peterson and, 83
  on press release, 108–109
  Rubin and, 150
  on sellout, 167
  at Shearson/Lehman, 222
Steinberg, Saul P., 238
Strauss, Melville, 191
Strauss, Thomas, 191, 204
Studebaker, 29
Superstores, 232
Syndicate department, 72
Szold, Harold J., 33

Takeovers, 240
  bidding wars, 53
  greenmail, 238
  rumors of, 184
Tarnopol, Mickey, 191
Tarr, Jeff, 191
Tendler, David, 114
Thomas, Joseph A., 32, 41
Thomas, Michael, 19, 126

Tillich, Paul, 102
Time, 121–122
Times, New York, 108, 186
Tisch brothers, 178
Touche Ross, 156, 178
Trading
  arbitrageurs, 142, 191, 233
  banking and, 12, 52–53, 118, 159, 162
  Fuld study, 158
  image of, 53–54
  importance of, 17
  interest rates and, 177
  Lehman traders, 62, 82, 114, 195–197
  mergers and acquisitions, 237
  over-the-counter, 87
  rise of, 46
  strategies in, 11
Traum, Jerome, 155
Troika, in banking, 72, 104, 118

Underwriters, ranking of, 228

Venture capital, 107
Von Bismarck, Andreis, 35

Wagner, Francis, 67n

Wall Street
  changes on, 230, 235–236, 239–241
  history of Jews on, 27–30
  losses on, 182
  "superstores", 232
Wall Street Journal, 186, 240
Walters, Barbara, 121
Wasserstein, Bruce, 191
Weigner, Arthur, 87, 224
Weill, Sanford (Sandy) I., 189, 192, 194,
  198, 204
Weinberg, John L., 70, 74
Weinberg, Sidney J., 124
Weisl, Edwin, Sr., 32
Welsh, William E., 83, 100–101, 105–106,
  114, 120, 131, 136
  payout to, 218
  on sellout, 169–170
Whitehead, John C., 20, 70, 74, 239
  on Lehman failure, 234–235
  on Peterson, 120–121
Wiegers, George A., 13, 82–83
  departure of, 226
Williams, Monci Jo, 183
Women
  as Lehman partners, 110
  as professional wives, 191–192